An American Place

Enjoy —
Larry Joghue

An American Place

CELEBRATING THE
FLAVORS OF AMERICA

LARRY FORGIONE

PHOTOGRAPHS BY DANA GALLAGHER

WILLIAM MORROW AND COMPANY, INC.
NEW YORK

It is the policy of William Morrow and Company, Inc., and its imprints and affiliates,
recognizing the importance of preserving what has been written, to print the books
we publish on acid-free paper, and we exert our best efforts to that end.

Library of Congress Cataloging-in-Publication Data

Forgione, Larry.
    An American place/Larry Forgione.
        p. cm.
    Includes index.
    1. Cookery, American.   I. Title.
    ISBN: 0-688-08716-7
TX715.F699 1995
641.5973—dc20   94-42810
                                                       CIP

Printed in the United States of America

    2   3   4   5   6   7   8   9   10

BOOK DESIGN BY JOEL AVIROM & JASON SNYDER

To my grandmothers,
Granny Lu and Grandma Stella,
for the honesty in their cooking

and to

James Beard,
the father of American cooking,
friend and mentor

Acknowledgments

THIS BOOK WAS MANY years in the making. Considerable time and thought went into the final recipes here. It seemed at times as if we would never finish.

There are so many people to thank for *An American Place*'s finally getting to print, and many who have influenced me over the years.

Let me first thank the person who stuck by this project over the years and without whom this book would never have been completed: Mary Goodbody. As my personal editor, she sat through many hours of interviews, questions, answers, recipes, and made sense out of my thoughts and ideas and put them into words.

My gratitude to Richard D'Orazi, my chef, who has been with me for over fifteen years and always helped keep all of us at An American Place focused from day to day, year after year.

To Ann Bramson, my editor at William Morrow and Company, who always believed in this book and whose patience I admire.

To Eugene Winick, my literary agent, who has been invaluable in keeping us all on track.

To Stevie Pierson for all her efforts in reorganizing my thoughts and helping put them into words.

To our photographer, Dana Gallagher, and her crew for capturing in the photographs the feelings of this book.

To my general managers, Kevin Dwyer and Beverly Hanapole, who keep things running smoothly at both restaurants.

To those who have gone through the kitchens at An American Place and contributed their culinary talents: Melissa Kelly, Shari O'Brien, Craig Rutman, Tony Nogales, and John MacPherson.

To Norris Wilson, who has been my food steward for over fifteen years. And to all of my staff for doing their best day to day. They represent the essence of our restaurants. A special thanks to my partners, Michael Weinstein and everyone at Ark Restaurants, for their support of all my projects.

Over the recent years of the evolution of cooking in America, I have been fortunate enough to call many of my talented and creative colleagues my friends. I thank them all for their inspiration, constant support, and dedication to our common goal.

My heartfelt thanks to Michel Bourdin for taking me "under his wing" and showing me the joys of cooking.

I would also like to thank all the farmers, foragers, cottage industrialists, cheesemakers, fishermen, and ranchers who have worked as hard as any chef to improve the quality of the food products that are so readily available in America today.

To Justin Rashid, my partner at American Spoon Foods, for always being there for a challenge and a discovery.

To Mr. Czack and all those at the Culinary Institute of America, who helped me form during those important years.

I would like to thank my parents, Michael and Frances, for always being there for me and for their encouragement when I needed it the most.

Most important of all, however, I especially want to thank my wife, Julie, and our children, Marc, Bryan, Cara, and Sean, for their love, support, understanding, and patience over all these years. From the bottom of my heart, *thank you.*

The recipes in this book are meant to show the harmony and marvelous bounty of America in a style that has been the cornerstone of An American Place. Enjoy!

Contents

An
American
Place

Introduction

AMERICAN FOOD IS MY PASSION—that is, real American food. What's real about my American food is that it has all the fresh, ripe flavor that I remember from childhood. Back then, we were more closely linked to our food sources: The person who grew the food sold it directly to the person who cooked the food who in turn brought it to the table all warm and delicious. There's no denying that fresh always tastes better. My goal over the past twenty years has been to reclaim and reestablish those essential American flavors lost to us in the rush for newer and quicker.

American cuisine is amazingly diverse. It's exhilarating in its variety of native ingredients, and—when made with the freshest, choicest, most flavorful meats, fish, and produce—can easily hold its own with the very best. When I'm stirring a robust chowder filled with scallops harvested only hours before from Long Island's Peconic Bay; when the fragrant aroma of a pork roast with peppered apples fills my kitchen; when, after a great deal of experimenting, I figure out how to make Chicken à la King and infuse it with all the flavor it must have had when it became an American favorite sixty years ago; when I'm frosting an old-fashioned Chocolate Devil's Food Cake, I know I've returned American food to its most original and satisfying flavors. The recipes in this book are all American recipes, from classic to new, from simple to complex; each one, in some way, incorporating the rich legacy of our culinary past into an innovative contemporary cuisine.

Ironically, I discovered my professional awareness of American food for the first time when I was in London in the mid-1970s, studying classic European cuisine under chef Michel Bourdin at the famed Connaught Hotel. I was at the Connaught for almost three years and, day after day, I was exposed to ingredients that were a revelation to me: everything farm-fresh, just-caught, newly harvested, hand-picked, and home-grown. Though I had studied at the Culinary Institute of America, the idea of cooking American food in America never even occurred to me—and it certainly would have struck the staff at the

Connaught as a bit odd, since they couldn't envision a cuisine without foie gras or truffles as an integral part of its underpinnings.

Yet I began to think about how Americans *did* eat and how we cooked. I began, for the first time, to think about possibilities—to realize that America's natural resources were extraordinarily rich and to think that with proper care and attention we should be able to cultivate produce good enough to rival the earthy chanterelles, exquisite morels, and ripened strawberries that I had come to appreciate in Europe.

But nothing gave me a greater sense of urgency about reviving American foods at their best than my first taste of a legendary *poularde de Bresse* in the Connaught kitchen. It wasn't just that each bite tasted so intensely, miraculously flavorful—the real shock was that the *poularde de Bresse*, for all of its fancy nomenclature and lineage, reminded me exactly of the ordinary but spectacularly flavorful chickens my grandmother raised on her farm on Long Island. This realization, in turn, reminded me of all the fresh foods I had grown up with and taken for granted, but which since then seemed to have disappeared. Where were the rich, ripe cheeses, seasonal field greens, local melons, native game birds, fresh lake fish, farm eggs, heirloom apples and potatoes, later summer berries, and autumn squash varieties?

I returned from London in 1977 and in 1979 became chef at Brooklyn's The River Café, where I showcased American specialties. I remembered what American food had once been and I became determined to make it all it could be again. With a firm conviction that in order to start cooking the kind of American food I envisioned—honest food, nothing contrived, food that tasted and *felt* good—I knew the first thing I would need was the very best ingredients.

I started working with farmers, producers, foragers, fishermen, mycologists, and hunters to bring the best possible products to the table. A good example of my pursuit of the finest and best-tasting product possible is chicken. I felt that the commercially available bird was more fatty than flavorful. I was sure there had to be a way to improve the taste. I met Paul Kaiser, a former microbiologist and weekend egg farmer in Warwick, New York, who agreed to raise chickens for me the way my Grandma Stella did when I was a child. I insisted that the chickens not be cooped up all day but allowed to roam. This would make them healthier and tastier. To describe these chickens, I coined the phrase "free range," and soon Paul was selling free-range chickens to all the top restaurants in New York.

For the wonderful earthy mushrooms that cannot be farmed, I researched and found mycologists and foragers who picked not only wild mushrooms but all sorts of wild edible greens and lettuces from the fields and woods of Long Island, upstate New York, Michigan, and California.

Perhaps one of the most rewarding relationships was with a young forager, Justin Rashid, who was to become my partner in a company dedicated to the finest ingredients our country has to offer, American Spoon Foods. Justin started by supplying me with morels, wild hickory, and butternuts: He met with Native American trappers who sold us wild game; he helped me talk farmers into raising specialty produce; and in my travels to his state of Michigan, he introduced me to Mr. Olsen in Traverse City. Mr. Olsen had the largest herd of native buffalo east of the Mississippi. He agreed to supply me with fresh meat and I therefore had the distinction of reintroducing buffalo to New York City for the first time in fifty years. But it was Justin's introducing me to Michigan's wondrous fruit belt that caused us, in partnership, to build the small kitchen that was to produce the best preserves in America—the old-fashioned way. That is how American Spoon Foods got started in 1981 and continues to operate today, offering the finest and best-tasting products we can produce.

Today, we sell sixty thousand cases of jams and preserves a year to all fifty states and six different countries. We experimented with sweetness and created what we call "spoon fruits," jams that capture the essence of sweet summer fruits without using any sugar at all. They're made from a variety of different fruits—ripe red Montmorency cherries, black raspberries, heritage red raspberries, plump Michigan blueberries—kept as pure as they started out, sweetened only with concentrated fruit juices. Our jellies are made from wild fruits that have simply been crushed, heated, and pressed—without adding any water. The varieties we produce are as colorful and bold as an early American sampler: wild chokeberry-apple jelly, tart cherry cranberry conserve, oven-baked apple butter spiced with cinnamon. For all of these jellies and jams, we pay local growers extra to leave the fruit on the tree or vine to ripen naturally—nothing is picked before it has reached its peak.

After I'd spent a few years searching for the best of America, something wonderful happened: Local suppliers started to call me up and say, "I've got some great local bass," or "I've got a whole bushel basket of tiny chanterelles pears I thought you might be interested in." A small farm devoted to producing goat cheeses was started in New York State, old-fashioned cured Smithfield hams were once again in vogue, a family in Michigan started growing antique potatoes and selling fully ripened miniature vegetables. The supply grew as the demand grew, and people started to cook more and eat better.

This explosion of interest in fresher, better indigenous ingredients spawned more farmers' markets, and fresh regional ingredients began to be as readily available to home cooks as they were to restaurant chefs. Supermarkets started to stock extraordinary varieties of foods—Bibb lettuce and mesclun sat next to iceberg, wild rice was as accessible as white rice, fresh salmon was in the fish section along with frozen flounder. Mail-order food companies opened up another new source for cooks.

But, as odd as it may sound, the one thing that really changed *my* life as a professional cook was overnight delivery. It opened up possibilities that had never existed before. I could get a bushel of just-picked baby white asparagus from Michigan, sparkling fresh shrimp flown straight in from Key West, baskets of wild blueberries flown nonstop from the shores of Lake Superior. Geographic boundaries and time constrictions ceased to exist. Local went national. And what was ripe in Georgia or fresh-caught in Cape Cod on a Tuesday afternoon could be on my menu in New York City Wednesday night.

By 1983, I had my own restaurant, An American Place, in New York City, featuring the best of every region of America. I created the menus and recipes for this restaurant by remembering my past and immersing myself in historic American cookery. My classic culinary education also came into play, as did my good fortune to have been one of the disciples of the father of American cooking, James Beard.

It was Jim, in fact, who suggested the name An American Place for my restaurant.

James Beard, with his encyclopedic knowledge of American cookery, taught me so much about the past and helped me understand the principles and philosophy behind our culinary legacy. Only he could spend an hour and a half talking intelligently about the nuances of apple pandowdy or the difference between a bisque and a chowder. But, as seriously as Jim took the subject, he would hear about a recipe and say to me, "Well, that sounds like fun," knowing that more than anything, food should be both a pleasure to cook and a joy to eat. Which is, of course, the main goal of this book. Everything I've learned and loved and created and couldn't wait to share has found its way into these recipes.

Since I firmly believe that not only should food just taste good, it should also feel good, there's comfort food like sublime New England Cod cakes with Tartar Sauce, and the creamiest of golden hashed brown potatoes. There's food that will remind you of the kind of homey favorites your mom cooked (or you wished she had): a thick, pureed vegetable soup, roast chicken, Apple Pandowdy, Spiced Ginger Ice Cream.

But there is also food that won't remind you of anything you've ever tasted before, recipes that I hope will surprise you, delight you, inspire you, and show you what today's outstanding American ingredients, used imaginatively, can produce: rich Roasted Corn and Beef Soup, a peppery Cress Salad with Baby White Asparagus and Wild Hickory Nut Vinaigrette, an elegant Lobster and Fennel in Cabbage Leaves with Basil Oil, silky Soft Pumpkin-Corn Pudding, Scalloped Ginger Sunchokes, Roast Goose with Plum Glaze, Pork with Peppered Apples and Onions.

With an eye for taking what's best from the past and making it fit today's tastes, there are main courses like Sautéed Breast of Chicken with Bacon, Mushrooms, and Wilted Spinach and Salmon with Cracked Wheat Crust, which offer complex and vibrant tastes but are light, healthful, and simple to cook. There's a classic American oyster bisque reinvigorated with fresh ginger. There's Banana Betty, a zesty rum-laced update of Apple Brown Betty. There are recipes for special occasions and many more that acknowledge the fact that we live busy lives: dishes such as Heartland Chowder, Sautéed Shrimp with Watercress and Grits Cakes, Grilled Mahi-Mahi with Pineapple-Chile Barbecue Sauce, Spicy Honey-Glazed Grouper with Fig, Chile Duck Pilaf, and Grilled Spring Lamb with Rhubarb and Dandelion that will bring you delicious and impressive results without having to spend hours in the kitchen.

There are recipes that belong to what I call the "Bring Them Back Alive" school of American heritage, dishes like Waldorf Salad, which must have started out as something special in the 1920s, but evolved into a sweet, goopy mess of a salad, filled with stringy chunks of celery and stale walnuts, overdressed with commercial mayonnaise. Old-Fashioned Caesar Salad, Baked Lobster Savannah, Fried Ipswich Clams, Philly Cheesesteak, and Fruit Ambrosia are others in this category of once- glorious dishes that I wanted to return to their former greatness. I hope that you will think of them differently after you've tried them in their new incarnations.

There are also some rare and wondrous dishes for which the wisdom was knowing when to leave well enough alone: Albemarle Sound Pine Bark Fish Stew, General Robert E. Lee's Favorite Soup, Blue Crab and Corn Pudding, Country Ham and Sweet Potato Salad with Honey Vinaigrette, New England Cod Cakes with Tartar Sauce, Quince and Raspberry Tart. Old-Fashioned Strawberry Shortcake on page 267 is just the way this dessert started out years ago: the best unsweetened whipped cream, the ripest berries, and a home-baked biscuit. This particular recipe, in all its simplicity and perfection, comes from James Beard's mother. When I made it for Jim at the restaurant, he paid me the ultimate compliment: "There can be no dessert better, only fancier."

I hope that whatever you make gives you great satisfaction and boundless pleasure and leaves you feeling that you have discovered American food in ways you never imagined. After twenty years I'm still experimenting, still learning, and, best of all, still excited about the never-ending process.

Soups and Chowders

THE SOUPS I LOVE MOST are just about meals in themselves—rich, hearty, and especially welcome at a time when we don't have all day to spend in the kitchen. You'll find that Grandma's Chicken Escarole Soup, Heartland Chowder, New England Cheddar Cheese Soup, and Long Island Country Corn Soup need only some warm, crusty bread and a green salad to be a substantial Sunday supper. I like to brush slices of peasant bread with butter and grill them to serve with the soup. To make almost any of these soups into what is essentially more of a stew, just add more of the main ingredient: Double the amount of clams in the chowder, for example, or add more duck to the Hearty Duck Soup with Wild Rice, more crabmeat to the two She-Crab Soup recipes (one a simplified version of the original), and more chanterelles to the Creamy Leek and Chanterelle Soup.

There are some traditional recipes I've added new twists to: oyster bisque with a hint of ginger, fish chowder made with smoked fish, clam chowder unexpectedly spiced with Italian sausage. And there are some historic recipes that haven't changed much since the 1800s, like General Robert E. Lee's Favorite Soup and Albemarle Sound Pine Bark Fish Stew.

What will never change is the ultimate satisfaction of eating soup, a food that slows you down, warms you up, and reminds you that there is no place like home. Of all that's good about American cooking, soups and chowders are in a class by themselves.

LONG ISLAND COUNTRY CORN SOUP

SERVES 6 TO 8

½ pound (about 1¼ cups) dried hominy (corn samp), picked over and rinsed

1 pound dried navy beans, picked over and rinsed

10 cups water

1 meaty ham bone or 2 cups roughly chopped country ham

1 tablespoon fresh thyme leaves

½ teaspoon minced garlic

½ pound smoked sausage, such as kielbasa, in one piece

1 small onion, diced

1½ cups fresh corn kernels (from approximately 4 ears)

Salt and freshly ground black pepper

¼ cup plus 2 tablespoons chopped flat-leaf parsley

SAMP IS A DERIVATIVE of the Narragansett word for corn—the Narragansetts being the Native Americans who populated Long Island and Connecticut. It's identical to Southern hominy and Spanish pisole. Each is made by treating corn kernels with wood ash so that the outside of the kernel bursts open, leaving a soft, dumpling-like cushion of starch. Hominy is sold in many supermarkets and specialty shops; pisole is available in Spanish markets.

Jim Beard used to talk about samp and although I had never seen it, I was always intrigued by his description. I felt I had made a real discovery when I walked into a farm stand on eastern Long Island one day and saw a sack on a shelf labeled "samp." The farmer said he cooked it with broth, smoked sausage, and vegetables. I took his suggestion and came up with this hearty soup. At the end, I add fresh corn, which complements the samp and gives the soup a burst of fresh corn flavor.

Put the hominy and beans in a large bowl and add enough cold water to cover. Let soak for at least 8 hours, or overnight.

Drain the hominy and beans and put them in a large saucepan. Add the water, the ham bone, if using, the thyme, and garlic and bring to a boil over high heat. Lower the heat and simmer, partially covered, for 2 hours, or until the beans are tender.

Add the sausage, onion, and corn and simmer for 20 minutes more. Season with salt and pepper.

Remove the ham bone, if using, and the sausage from the soup. Pull the meat from the ham bone and dice. Cut the sausage into small pieces. Return the ham and sausage to the soup. If you did not use a ham bone, add the country ham to the soup. Ladle the soup into bowls, and sprinkle with the parsley.

SENATE BEAN SOUP

■■

SERVES 6 TO 8

1½ pounds dried navy beans, picked over and rinsed

10 cups Chicken Stock (page 33) or canned broth or water

1 meaty ham bone or 2 cups roughly chopped country ham

1 small onion, diced

1 rib celery, diced

1 large potato, peeled and diced

½ teaspoon minced garlic

Salt and freshly ground black pepper

¼ cup plus 2 tablespoons chopped flat-leaf parsley

THIS IS MY INTERPRETATION of a soup served in the dining room of the U.S. Senate. While researching the recipe, I was given a version that contains only beans, onions, ham, and corn; others added potatoes and other vegetables. I have not been able to document precisely who introduced the soup to the Senate—one story is that it was a great favorite of Senator Henry Cabot Lodge, who requested that the Capitol chefs recreate the soup for him when he was away from home; the other is that a senator from Michigan came up with the idea for the soup as a way to promote dried navy beans, a major crop in his home state. In either case, the soup has been served in the Senate dining room for close to one hundred years and is a non-partisan favorite!

Put the beans, in a large bowl and add enough cold water to cover. Let soak for at least 8 hours, or overnight.

Drain the beans and put them in a large saucepan. Add the stock and the ham bone, if using, and bring to a boil. Reduce the heat and simmer, partially covered, for 1½ to 2 hours, or until the beans are tender.

Add the onion, celery, potato, and garlic and simmer for 30 minutes more. Season with salt and pepper.

Remove the ham bone, if using, from the soup. Pull the meat from the bone and chop it into small pieces. Return the ham to the soup. Or, if using country ham, add it to the soup. Sprinkle with the parsley and serve.

VARIATION

Hearty White Bean Soup

Add 2 tomatoes, peeled, seeded, and diced, to the soup with the other vegetables. Remove about one third of the soup puree and add back to the soup as a thickener.

PUREE OF ANY VEGETABLE SOUP

■■■

SERVES 6 TO 8

2 tablespoons unsalted butter

1 small onion, sliced

1 potato, peeled and sliced

½ teaspoon minced garlic

3 cups chopped vegetables, such as
broccoli, zucchini, peas, cabbage, or
cauliflower (if using a vegetable with
seeds, such as zucchini or other
squash, cut in half and scrape out
the seeds)

4 cups Chicken Stock (page 33) or canned
broth or water, or more if necessary

Salt and freshly ground black pepper

Optional Garnish

2 cups diced vegetables (the same
vegetables used in the soup), blanched
in boiling salted water until al dente

WHENEVER WE SERVE a pureed vegetable soup, the waiters are constantly asked if there is cream in it. But just pureeing the vegetables gives the soup a nice, creamy consistency without added calories and fat. You can use almost any vegetable here.

Melt the butter in a large saucepan over low heat. Add the onions, potato, and garlic and cook, stirring, until the onions are translucent, making sure they do not brown. Add the chopped vegetables and cook for 2 to 3 minutes more. Add the stock or water and bring to a boil. Reduce the heat and simmer for 8 to 10 minutes, or until the potatoes are tender.

Transfer the soup to a food processor or blender and process until smooth. (If using a blender, you may have to puree the soup in batches.) Return the pureed soup to the pan and rewarm. Season with salt and pepper. If the soup seems too thick, add a little hot stock or water. Serve garnished with the cooked diced vegetables if desired.

VARIATION

Cream of Any Vegetable Soup

If you want extra richness, try this version of the soup.

Serves 8

Cook the vegetables in the stock or water as directed above; when the potatoes are tender, strain the vegetables, reserving the cooking liquid, and put them in a food processor or blender. Add just enough of the cooking liquid to facilitate pureeing, and blend or process until smooth.

Bring 2 cups of heavy cream to a boil in a medium saucepan. Lower the heat to a simmer, and stir in the vegetable puree, adding more of the reserved cooking liquid if necessary to adjust the thickness to your liking. Season with salt and pepper. Strain through a fine sieve and serve.

CREAMY WHITE ONION SOUP
WITH BLACK PEPPER

■■■■■■■■■■■■■■■■■■■■■■■■■■■■■■■■■■■■■■■

1 tablespoon unsalted butter

3 pounds white onions (about 8 large
    onions), thinly sliced

1 tablespoon freshly ground black pepper,
    plus extra for serving

¼ cup white wine

6 cups Chicken Stock (page 33) or
    canned broth

2 cups heavy cream

3 tablespoons cornstarch

Salt

THIS RECIPE CALLS FOR white onions rather than the more familiar yellow onions. White onions have papery-thin white skin and are a little sweeter and less acidic than yellow ones. If sweet onions such as Vidalias, Walla Wallas, Mauis, or Texas Sweets are available, use them.

Melt the butter in a large saucepan over medium heat. Add two thirds of the onions and the pepper and reduce the heat to low. Cook for 2 to 3 minutes, stirring frequently, until the onions are translucent. Making sure they do not brown. Add the wine, raise the heat, and simmer for 1 to 2 minutes. Add the chicken stock and bring to a boil, skimming off any foam that rises to the surface. Reduce the heat and simmer for 10 to 15 minutes until reduced by one third.

Transfer the soup to a food processor or blender and puree until smooth. (If using a blender, you will have to puree the soup in several batches.)

Mix 2 tablespoons of the cream with the cornstarch to make a smooth paste.

Pour the remaining cream into the saucepan and bring to a boil. Stir in the pureed soup and return to a simmer. Stir in the cornstarch mixture, add the remaining onions, and season to taste with salt. Simmer for 4 to 5 minutes, until the onions are just tender. Serve with freshly ground black pepper sprinkled on top.

CREAMY LEEK AND CHANTERELLE SOUP

ᴏᴏᴏᴏᴏᴏᴏᴏᴏᴏᴏᴏᴏᴏᴏᴏᴏᴏᴏᴏᴏᴏᴏᴏᴏᴏᴏᴏᴏᴏᴏᴏᴏ

SERVES 6 TO 8

6 leeks, white parts only

1 tablespoon unsalted butter

1 tablespoon minced shallots

¾ pound chanterelle mushrooms,
    trimmed, cleaned, and sliced

6 cups Chicken Stock (page 33) or
    canned broth

2 cups heavy cream

3 tablespoons cornstarch

Salt and freshly ground black pepper

THIS SOUP IS WONDERFUL WITH ALMOST ANY MUSHROOMS. Don't hesitate to substitute morels, shiitakes, portobellos—whatever.

Split the leeks lengthwise and discard any tough outer pieces. Rinse thoroughly to remove all dirt and grit, and thinly slice.

Heat the butter in a large saucepan over medium heat until foamy. Add the shallots, three quarters of the leeks, and three quarters of the chanterelles, and cook, stirring, for 4 to 5 minutes, until softened.

Add the chicken stock and bring to a boil. Lower the heat and simmer for 10 to 15 minutes, until the liquid is reduced by one third.

Transfer the soup to a food processor or blender and puree until smooth. (If using a blender, you will have to puree the soup in several batches.)

Mix 2 tablespoons of the cream with the cornstarch to make a smooth paste.

Pour the remaining cream into the saucepan and bring to a boil. Stir in the pureed soup and return to a simmer. Stir in the cornstarch mixture and season to taste with salt and pepper. Add the remaining leeks and chanterelles and heat for 2 to 3 minutes; do not boil. Serve.

CAROLINA LIMA BEAN SOUP

■ ■

SERVES 6 TO 8

1 pound dried baby lima beans, or 2
    pounds shucked fresh or frozen beans
    (see opposite)

1 tablespoon unsalted butter

1 onion, finely diced

1 carrot, peeled and finely diced

1 rib celery, finely diced

1 tablespoon minced garlic

1 meaty ham bone

8 cups Chicken Stock (page 33) or
    canned broth or water

Salt and freshly ground black pepper

I CAME UP WITH THIS SOUP after reading an old cookbook from the Carolinas. Similar to split pea soup in consistency and heartiness, it can be made with fresh, frozen, or dried limas. Fresh or frozen limas do not need to be soaked, as dry beans do, but fresh beans should be blanched and the tough casings removed and discarded. Approximately five pounds of fresh bean pods yield a pound of shelled beans.

If using dried lima beans, put them in a large pot, cover with cold water, and let soak for 8 to 10 hours, or overnight. Drain and rinse thoroughly.

Melt the butter in a large heavy saucepan over medium heat. Add the onion, carrot, celery, and garlic and cook, stirring, for 3 to 4 minutes, until tender.

Add the soaked lima beans, ham bone, and stock or water and bring to a boil. Lower the heat and simmer, for 45 to 60 minutes, skimming off any foam that rises to the surface, until the beans are tender. If using fresh or frozen beans, add them after 40 to 45 minutes and cook for 10 to 12 minutes longer, until tender.

Remove the soup from the heat, remove the ham bone, and set it aside to cool slightly. Ladle about one third of the soup and beans into a food processor or blender and puree. Return the puree to the pan and stir to blend.

Pull the meat off the ham bone and chop it. Add it to the soup and season with salt and pepper. Reheat and serve.

NEW ENGLAND CHEDDAR CHEESE SOUP

SERVES 6 TO 8

½ tablespoon unsalted butter

2 onions, diced

2 potatoes, peeled and sliced

1 tablespoon minced garlic

6 cups Chicken Stock (page 33) or canned broth

2 cups heavy cream

¼ teaspoon dry mustard

1½ cups grated sharp Cheddar cheese

Dash of Tabasco

Dash of Worcestershire sauce

Salt and freshly ground black pepper

¼ cup chopped fresh chives

THIS POTATO-BASED SOUP is perfect for cold autumn days when you want something filling. Because it's made with Cheddar cheese, it reminds me of New England, where some of the finest Cheddars in the country are produced. It's essential to use a high-quality Cheddar for flavor, rather than processed cheese, although the high fat content may cause the soup to curdle if it is not treated gently. Smoked cheddar is a good choice, if you like its flavor. Grate the cheese and then stir it into the soup at the very end of cooking so that it melts and does not "cook." Pureed potato is the ideal medium to absorb the oils from the cheese and distribute its intense flavor throughout the soup.

Melt the butter in a large saucepan over low heat. Add the onions, potatoes, and garlic and cook, stirring, until the onions are translucent, making sure they do not brown. Add the chicken stock and bring to a boil over medium heat. Reduce the heat and simmer for 12 to 15 minutes, or until the potatoes are tender.

Transfer the soup to a food processor or blender and process until smooth. (If using a blender, you may have to puree the soup in batches.)

Pour the cream into the saucepan, stir in the mustard, and bring to a boil. Reduce the heat and simmer for 3 to 4 minutes. Add the pureed soup and simmer for about 4 minutes more. Slowly add the grated cheese, stirring to melt it. Season with the Tabasco, Worcestershire sauce, and salt and pepper. Sprinkle with the chives, and serve.

GENERAL ROBERT E. LEE'S FAVORITE SOUP

■■

SERVES 6 TO 8

2 tablespoons vegetable oil

2 tablespoons unsalted butter

1 small onion, sliced

1 carrot, peeled and sliced

1 rib celery, sliced

1 clove garlic, minced

¾ cup cream sherry

20 ripe plum tomatoes, halved and seeded

6 cups Chicken Stock (page 33) or canned broth or water

1 cup tomato puree

Salt and freshly ground black pepper

Garnish

¾ cup fresh corn kernels (from approximately 2 ears)

⅓ cup diced onion or thinly sliced scallions

⅓ cup diced carrot

⅓ cup diced pale-green inner ribs celery

2 small tomatoes, peeled, seeded, and coarsely diced

¾ cup diced zucchini

⅓ cup cream sherry

I THINK THERE'S SOMETHING SPECIAL about a recipe that's imbued with history and flavor. This soup is a good example. I saw a similar recipe in an old community cookbook published around 1920. Evidently, General Lee liked a tomato-based garden vegetable soup so much he often requested it when he traveled. The sherry reveals this as an old Southern recipe. When I first made the soup, I used dry sherry, as I am sure they did in the nineteenth century. However, I eventually switched to cream sherry, because it has a richer, less alcoholic flavor.

Heat the oil and butter in a large saucepan over medium heat. Add the onion, carrot, celery, and garlic and cook for 10 minutes, or until the vegetables have softened, stirring often so that the vegetables do not brown.

Add the sherry and simmer for 2 to 3 minutes. Add the tomatoes and cook, stirring constantly, for 5 minutes. Add the chicken stock or water and the tomato puree, raise the heat, and bring to a boil. Lower the heat and simmer for 15 to 20 minutes, until reduced by one third.

Pass the soup through a food mill or puree in a food processor or blender. (If using a blender, you may have to puree the soup in several batches.) Return the soup to the pan and add the corn, onions or scallions, carrots, and celery. Bring to a simmer and cook for 5 to 7 minutes. Add the diced tomatoes, zucchini, and sherry, and simmer for 1 minute longer. Serve.

ALBEMARLE SOUND PINE BARK
FISH STEW

■■

SERVES 6 TO 8

4 slices bacon, chopped

2 jalapeño peppers, seeded and
finely diced

1 large onion, diced

1 teaspoon minced garlic

2 potatoes, peeled and diced

2 tomatoes, peeled, seeded, and diced

2 tablespoons chopped fresh marjoram

6 cups Fish Stock (page 34) or
Chicken Stock (page 33) or canned
broth

1½ pounds firm-fleshed fish fillets,
such as rockfish, sea bass, or
grouper, diced

Salt and freshly ground black pepper

¼ cup chopped flat-leaf parsley

CENTURIES AGO, THE COLONISTS used the bark and roots of young pine trees to make a sustaining broth in the wintertime when food was scarce. Undoubtedly they learned to do this from the Indians, who steeped tree roots and bark to make cures for various ailments. There is no tree bark in this soup, but the combination of sweet marjoram and bacon produces a sweet, smoky flavor that many people swear is pine. The marjoram is the key to the flavor of the soup; be sure it's fresh.

I looked at several old recipes, particularly one in *Evan Jones's American Food*, before devising this version.

Sauté the bacon in a large saucepan over low heat for 1 to 2 minutes. Add the jalapeños, onions, garlic, potatoes, and tomatoes and cook, stirring for 2 to 3 minutes. Add the marjoram and stock, raise the heat, and bring to a simmer. Simmer for 5 to 6 minutes, or until the potatoes are tender.

Stir in the fish and simmer for 4 to 5 minutes longer. Season with salt and pepper, sprinkle with the parsley, and serve.

SMOKED FISH CHOWDER

■■■■■■■■■■■■■■■■■■■■■■■■■■■■■■■■■■■■■■

1 tablespoon unsalted butter

2 onions, sliced

1 teaspoon minced garlic

2 cups smoked fish trimmings or ¾ pound
    smoked fish, such as salmon,
    whitefish, and/or sturgeon, cut
    into chunks

2 cups dry white wine

4 cups Fish Stock (page 34) or Chicken
    Stock (page 33) or canned broth

4 cups heavy cream

3 tablespoons cornstarch

Pinch of cayenne pepper

Salt and freshly ground black pepper

Garnish

1 onion, finely diced

2 potatoes, peeled and finely diced

1½ cups diced smoked fish, such as
    salmon, whitefish, and/or sturgeon

¼ cup chopped flat-leaf parsley

WE MAKE THIS SOUP to use the trimmings we have from the various smoked fish used at the restaurant.

Melt the butter in a large saucepan over medium low heat. Add the onions and garlic and cook, stirring, for 2 to 3 minutes, making sure the onions do not brown. Add the smoked fish, wine, and stock and bring to a boil. Reduce the heat and simmer, skimming any fat or foam from the surface, until the liquid is reduced by two thirds (you should have about 2 cups liquid).

Mix 2 tablespoons of the cream with the cornstarch to make a smooth paste.

Pour the remaining cream into the soup and bring to a simmer. Stir in the cornstarch paste and simmer for 5 to 6 minutes. Season with the cayenne and salt and pepper, and remove from the heat.

Put the diced onion and potato garnish in a large saucepan. Strain the soup through a fine strainer into the pan. Bring to a simmer and cook for 5 to 6 minutes, or until the potatoes are tender. Stir in the diced smoked fish and parsley, and serve.

LOBSTER AND CORN CHOWDER

SERVES 6

2 cooked 1-pound lobsters (see page 81)

2 tablespoons cornstarch

6 cups light cream

4 tablespoons unsalted butter

1½ cups fresh corn kernels (from approximately 3 ears)

2 large potatoes, peeled and diced

1 medium onion, finely diced

Pinch of cayenne pepper

Salt and freshly ground black pepper

LOBSTERS IN AMERICA used to be so abundant that they would crawl right out of the ocean onto the beach. But when the colonists first arrived, no one ate them, and, in fact, the Indians ground them up for fertilizer! In an old diary from colonial times I came across a writer musing about how brave the first man to eat a lobster must have been. (And how lucky!)

This wonderful recipe is classic New England. However, a lot of traditional recipes for lobster stew or chowder instruct you to cook the lobster meat with the vegetables and discard the shells. Instead, if you are buying and cooking fresh lobsters, or even if you have asked the fishmonger to cook the lobster for you, save the shells. Put the shells in the pot with the cream and milk and let simmer for a while, then strain, and you will have something that tastes twenty times better than if you used just the lobster meat alone.

Remove the lobster meat from the shells and cut it into 1-inch pieces. Set aside. Put the shells and bodies in a large saucepan.

Stir the cornstarch into the cream until smooth, and add to the saucepan. Bring to a boil over high heat, lower the heat, and simmer for 6 to 8 minutes.

Meanwhile, melt the butter in a large saucepan over low heat. Add the corn, potatoes, and onions and cook, stirring, for 2 to 3 minutes.

Strain the hot cream and add it to the vegetables. Simmer for 2 to 3 minutes, or until the potatoes are tender. Add the reserved lobster meat and season with the cayenne and salt and pepper. Simmer for 1 minute more. Ladle the chowder into bowls and serve.

SHE-CRAB SOUP NUMBER 1

■■■

SERVES 6 TO 8

1 onion, sliced

1 carrot, peeled and sliced

2 ribs celery, sliced

1 bay leaf

10 cups Chicken Stock (page 33) or canned
    broth or water *or* a combination

Salt

6 female hard-shell crabs, washed well
    under running water

2 tablespoons unsalted butter

½ teaspoon mace

½ teaspoon allspice

½ teaspoon cayenne pepper

¼ cup dry sherry

2 cups heavy cream

3 tablespoons cornstarch

2 tablespoons grated lemon zest

Freshly ground black pepper

2 tablespoons chopped flat-leaf parsley

WHEN I THINK of she-crab soup, I think of Charleston, South Carolina, which is famous for the soup. This version is the "real" thing, made with she-crabs and their roe. The roe acts as a thickening agent for the soup, and it adds a really sweet flavor as well.

She-crabs have rounded bibs, male crabs have pointed bibs. You can see the bib when you turn the crabs over. Fish markets that clean a lot of crabs will often save the roe for you if you ask; then, you can make the soup with either male or female crabs and simply add the roe.

Put the onion, carrot, celery, bay leaf, stock or water, and a pinch of salt in a large pot and bring to a boil. Add the crabs and return the liquid to a boil, then lower the heat and gently simmer for 10 to 12 minutes, until cooked through. Remove the crabs with tongs or a slotted spoon and set aside to cool.

Bring the stock back to a slow boil and boil until reduced by half. (You should have 5 cups of liquid.) Strain and set aside.

Meanwhile, remove the crab meat from the shells and scrape out the orange roe. Refrigerate the meat and roe and reserve the shells.

Melt the butter in a large saucepan. Add the crab shells and sauté for 3 to 4 minutes. Add the mace, allspice, and cayenne and cook, stirring, for 1 to 2 minutes. Add the sherry and cook for 1 minute. Add the reduced stock and bring to a boil. Lower the heat and simmer for about 10 minutes, skimming off any fat or foam from the surface.

Mix 2 tablespoons of the cream with the cornstarch to make a smooth paste.

Stir the remaining cream into the soup and bring to a boil, then stir in the cornstarch paste. Lower the heat and simmer for 3 to 4 minutes. Strain the soup through a fine strainer into a saucepan.

Pour about 1 cup of the strained soup into a blender, add the reserved crab roe, and puree. Add the puree to the soup along with the reserved crabmeat and the lemon zest. Season with salt and pepper, and reheat. Garnish with parsley and serve.

SHE-CRAB SOUP NUMBER 2

■■■■■■■■■■■■■■■■■■■■■■■■■■■■■■■■■■■■■■■

SERVES 6 TO 8

1 tablespoon unsalted butter

2 tablespoons finely chopped onion

2 pounds lump crabmeat, with roe if possible, picked over for shells and cartilage

½ teaspoon mace

½ teaspoon allspice

½ teaspoon cayenne pepper

¼ cup dry sherry

6 cups heavy cream

3 tablespoons cornstarch

2 cups milk

2 tablespoons grated lemon zest

2 tablespoons chopped flat-leaf parsley

Salt and freshly ground black pepper

THIS VERSION OF CRAB SOUP is easier to make than the one on page 21 because you do not need the roe and can buy crabmeat already picked. Although it does not have quite the same depth of flavor as the first version, it is still very good. You can use either fresh crabmeat or pasteurized; if you come across fresh crabmeat with a lot of orange flecks in the meat, buy it: The orange pieces are the roe.

Melt the butter in a large saucepan over medium-low heat. Add the onion and cook, stirring, for 1 to 2 minutes. Add the crabmeat, mace, allspice, and cayenne and cook, stirring, for 1 to 2 minutes. Add the sherry and cook for 1 minute.

Mix 2 tablespoons of the cream with the cornstarch to make a smooth paste.

Pour the remaining cream into the saucepan, and the milk, and bring to a simmer. Stir in the cornstarch paste and simmer for 3 to 4 minutes. Add the lemon zest and parsley, season with salt and pepper, and serve.

BAY SCALLOP CHOWDER

■■■

SERVES 6 TO 8

1¼ pounds bay scallops, tough side
    muscles removed

4 cups Chicken Stock (page 33) or
    canned broth

1 tablespoon unsalted butter

1 onion, diced

2 large potatoes, peeled and diced

2 cups heavy cream

3 tablespoons cornstarch

1 cup fresh corn kernels (from
    approximately 3 ears)

Salt and freshly ground black pepper

2 tablespoons chopped flat-leaf parsley

I LIKE TO MAKE THIS CHOWDER when the sweet scallops from Long Island's Peconic Bay are available. Like Nantucket Bay, Peconic Bay—formed by the two forking fingers of Long Island—produces some of the best-tasting scallops in the world. Good bay scallops have an incredible sweetness you do not find in sea scallops. During the brief time when I can get Peconic Bay scallops that's *all* I want to eat.

This is a simple, straightforward recipe, with nothing in it to mask the flavor. Shrimp, mussels, and lobster are all also good in this chowder.

Put the scallops and any juices in a large bowl. Add the chicken stock and stir gently, then strain the liquid into a bowl. Set the scallops aside.

Heat the butter in a large saucepan until foamy. Add the onions and potatoes and cook gently over medium-low heat for 2 to 3 minutes, until the onions are translucent. Add the stock mixture, raise the heat, and bring to a boil. Lower the heat and skim off any foam that has risen to the surface.

Mix 2 tablespoons of the cream with the cornstarch to make a smooth paste.

Add the remaining cream to the soup and bring to a simmer. Stir in the cornstarch mixture, raise the heat, and bring to a boil. Lower the heat and simmer for 4 to 5 minutes, until the potatoes are tender. Add the scallops and corn and simmer for 4 to 5 minutes until the scallops are just cooked through. Season with salt and pepper, add the parsley, and serve.

OYSTER AND GINGER BISQUE

SERVES 6 TO 8

3 dozen oysters

1 cup white wine

2 tablespoons minced shallots

¼ cup finely diced fresh ginger
(trimmings and peel reserved)

8 cups Chicken Stock (page 33) or
canned broth

3 tablespoons cornstarch

2 cups heavy cream

Salt and freshly ground black pepper

3 tablespoons chopped fresh chives

THE DIFFERENCE BETWEEN a bisque and chowder is that a bisque is a cream-based soup that is made primarily with the ingredient that gives it its flavor. For instance, oyster bisque is flavored only with oysters. If potatoes, onions, and other vegetables are added, it becomes oyster chowder. The difference between a bisque and a great bisque is the addition of the ginger, which gives it an unexpected and slightly exotic kick.

Reading old cookbooks, I was surprised to find so much ginger in recipes from New England. Then I remembered Boston was one of the points of the trade triangle of England, the West Indies, and New England, and the ships from the West Indies arrived full of tropical spices, fruits, and other exotic ingredients. Colonial recipes call for ground ginger, because that was what was available, but now we can get fresh ginger, which tastes better.

Thoroughly wash and scrub the oysters, discarding any that are not tightly closed.

Put the oysters in a large saucepan and add the wine, shallots, and reserved ginger trimmings. Cover, bring to a boil, and steam the oysters for 3 to 5 minutes, just until they open.

Remove the oysters and strain the cooking liquid through a cheesecloth-lined sieve into a bowl. Discard any unopened oysters. Remove the oysters from the shells and set aside.

Return the cooking liquid to the pan, add the chicken stock, and bring to a boil. Reduce the heat and simmer for 15 to 20 minutes, until reduced by half. (You should have about 4 cups liquid.)

Mix the cornstarch with 2 tablespoons of the cream to make a smooth paste.

Bring the reduced stock to a rapid boil, lower the heat, and stir in the rest of the cream. Raise the heat and bring to a boil, then lower the heat to a simmer and stir in the cornstarch mixture. Simmer for 3 to 4 minutes, stirring frequently.

Strain the soup through a fine sieve into a large saucepan. Season with salt and pepper and bring to a simmer. Add the ginger and oysters and simmer for about 1 minute or until the oysters start to curl. Sprinkle with the chives and serve.

MANHATTAN CLAM CHOWDER

■■■■■■■■■■■■■■■■■■■■■■■■■■■■■■■■■■■■

SERVES 6 TO 8

1 dozen cherrystone clams

6 cups clam juice or Chicken Stock (page 33) or canned broth *or* an equal mixture of clam juice and stock or broth

1 slice bacon

2 onions, diced

4 pale-green inner ribs celery, diced

2 medium potatoes, peeled and diced

1 tablespoon minced garlic

4 medium tomatoes, peeled, seeded, and chopped

2 tablespoons chopped fresh thyme

Salt and freshly ground black pepper

Dash of Tabasco

¼ cup chopped flat-leaf parsley

MANHATTAN CLAM CHOWDER always means a tomato-based chowder, but it also has to include thyme. Those two ingredients make the soup authentic—they also make a lovely taste combination. Fresh thyme is best, of course.

Thoroughly wash and scrub the clams, discarding any that are not tightly closed. Put them in a large saucepan, add the clam juice or broth, cover, and bring to a simmer. Steam for about 5 minutes, removing the clams to a bowl as they open, and set them aside to cool. Strain the broth through a cheesecloth or coffee filter to remove any sand.

Put the bacon in a large saucepan and cook over low heat, stirring until the fat is rendered, making sure the bacon does not brown. Using a slotted spoon, remove and discard the bacon. Add the onions, celery, potatoes and garlic to the bacon fat and cook gently, stirring, for about 10 minutes until the onions are translucent. Add the tomatoes and thyme and cook, stirring, for 1 minute.

Add the strained clam broth and bring to a simmer. Cook for 5 to 6 minutes, or until the potatoes are tender.

Meanwhile, remove the clams from the shells and dice. Reserve any liquid that has accumulated in the bowl.

Add the diced clams and any liquid to the chowder. Season with salt and pepper and the Tabasco. Add the chopped parsley and serve.

RICHARD'S SPICY CLAM CHOWDER

SERVES 6 TO 8

2 tablespoons olive oil

2 onions, finely chopped

1 tablespoon minced garlic

½ pound white mushrooms, trimmed, cleaned, and sliced

½ pound hot Italian sausage, casings removed and diced

8 medium tomatoes, peeled, seeded, and chopped (about 4 cups)

¼ cups tomato puree

¼ cup chopped fresh basil

3 cups clam juice

3 cups Chicken Stock (page 33) or canned broth

3 dozen littleneck clams

2 tablespoons chopped flat-leaf parsley

RICHIE D'ORAZI HAS BEEN my chef at An American Place from the beginning. He made this soup, basing it on Manhattan clam chowder and adding hot Italian sausage sautéed with mushrooms. To me, this soup is America, by way of Italy, Portugal, and, of course, New England!

Heat the olive oil in a large saucepan over medium heat. Add the chopped onions and cook, stirring, for about 5 minutes, or until softened; do not let the onions brown. Add the garlic and cook for 1 minute. Add the mushrooms and cook, stirring, for 2 to 3 minutes. Add the sausage and cook for 2 to 3 minutes more. Add the tomatoes, tomato puree, and half the chopped basil, reduce the heat to medium-low, and cook gently for 5 to 6 minutes. Add the clam juice and chicken stock and bring to a boil, then lower the heat to a simmer, skimming off any fat or foam from the surface.

Meanwhile, thoroughly scrub and rinse the clams, and discard any that are not tightly closed. Tie the clams loosely in a large square of cheesecloth to prevent any remaining sand from mixing with the soup.

Add the clams to the simmering soup and cook just until the shells open, 3 to 5 minutes. Remove the clams from the soup and discard the cheesecloth and any unopened clams.

Distribute the clams, in their shells, among individual serving bowls. Ladle the chowder into the bowls and sprinkle with the remaining basil and the parsley.

GRANDMA'S CHICKEN ESCAROLE SOUP

■■■■■■■■■■■■■■■■■■■■■■■■■■■■■■■■■■■■■■

SERVES 6 TO 8

4 chicken leg-thigh quarters (from free-range chickens, if possible)

1 onion, thinly sliced

1 carrot, peeled and thinly sliced

1 rib celery, thinly sliced

8 cups Chicken Stock (page 33) or canned broth

1 pound escarole

Salt and freshly ground black pepper

Freshly grated Parmesan cheese for serving

WHEN I WAS A CHILD, we visited my Italian grandmother every other weekend on her sprawling, self-sufficient farm near Port Jefferson on eastern Long Island. When she wasn't in the field, she was in the kitchen. She often served us a simple chicken soup made with the freshest chicken and wilted leaf vegetables. We sprinkled cheese on top and ate the soup with Italian bread. Here's my version of that memorable soup.

Place the chicken in a large saucepan and add the sliced vegetables and stock. Bring to a boil over high heat, skimming off any foam that rises to the surface. Lower the heat and simmer for 30 to 40 minutes, until the chicken is tender.

Meanwhile, wash the escarole and tear the leaves into small pieces. Discard any tough stems.

Remove the chicken from the broth and set aside to cool. You should have about 6 cups of broth remaining in the pan; if necessary, simmer the stock over medium heat until it has reduced, skimming off any fat or foam from the surface. Season with salt and pepper.

Remove the meat and discard the chicken skin. Remove and chop it.

Add the chicken and escarole to the soup, bring to a simmer, and cook for 5 to 6 minutes, until the escarole is tender. Ladle the soup into bowls, and serve with Parmesan cheese sprinkled on top.

CHICKEN NOODLE SOUP
WITH VEGETABLES

■■■

SERVES 6 TO 8

2 large chicken breast halves,
    skin removed

8 cups Chicken Stock (page 33) or
    canned broth

1 carrot, peeled and diced

2 ribs celery, diced

1 onion, diced

2 tomatoes, peeled, seeded, and diced

4 ounces noodles or wide-strand pasta,
    cooked until al dente and drained

Salt and freshly ground black pepper

2 tablespoons chopped flat-leaf parsley

CHICKEN NOODLE SOUP is something of an American classic—a warming, comforting, get well soon soup that we all grew up with in one version or another. I make mine by cooking chicken breast meat in stock, removing it from the bone, and then returning it to the broth with fresh vegetables. Although you can use canned broth, this really is far superior made with a good strong chicken stock. I cook the noodles separately and add them at the last minute, because pasta cooked in the soup releases starch that turns it cloudy. Finally, I finish the soup with lots of fresh parsley. Serve it as a first course or light meal. With a loaf of warm bread, it's a lunch.

Put the chicken breasts in a large saucepan, add the stock, and bring to a boil. Lower the heat and simmer for 18 to 20 minutes, or until the chicken is cooked, skimming off any fat or foam from the surface.

Remove the chicken breasts from the broth and set aside to cool. Bring the broth back to a boil and cook until reduced to 6 cups. Strain the stock through a fine strainer.

Rinse out the saucepan and return the stock to the pan. Add the diced vegetables and simmer for 5 to 10 minutes, or until the vegetables are tender.

Meanwhile, when the chicken is cool enough to handle, remove the meat from the bones and cut it into bite-sized pieces.

Add the chicken and noodles to the soup and bring to a simmer. Season with salt and pepper, add the parsley, and serve.

HEARTLAND CHOWDER

SERVES 6 TO 8

2 tablespoons olive oil

1 pound smoked sausage, such as kielbasa,
    cut into 2 or 3 pieces

1 small onion, finely diced

1 carrot, peeled and finely diced

2 ribs celery, finely diced

1 teaspoon minced garlic

1 pound lentils, picked over and rinsed

8 cups Chicken Stock (page 33) or canned
    broth or water

½ cup tomato puree

1 cup cooked wild rice (see Note,
    page 180)

1 cup cooked hominy or uncooked fresh
    corn kernels (from approximately
    3 ears)

1 cup spinach leaves, washed and
    coarsely chopped

Salt and freshly ground black pepper

MOST PEOPLE THINK OF SEAFOOD when they think of chowder, but actually a soup only has to include potatoes to earn its stripes as a real chowder. For this chowder, I begin with lentil soup made with potatoes, smoked sausages, tomato puree, fresh corn, and wild rice—and then finish it by wilting fresh spinach in the hot soup. Each of these ingredients makes me think of the heartland of America, and put together this way they capture some of the rich, sunny abundance of that part of America.

Heat the olive oil in a large saucepan. Add the sausage and brown lightly on all sides. Add the onions, carrot, celery, garlic, and lentils and cook, stirring, for 1 to 2 minutes. Add the stock or water and the tomato puree and bring to a boil. Lower the heat and simmer, skimming off any fat or foam from the surface, for 35 to 40 minutes, or until the lentils are tender.

Remove the sausage from the soup and cut it into cubes.

Return the sausage to the soup, along with the wild rice, hominy or corn, and the spinach. Gently simmer for a few minutes, season with salt and pepper, and serve.

ROASTED CORN AND BEEF SOUP

███

SERVES 6 TO 8

12 ears corn (in the husk)

8 cups Dark Poultry Stock (page 35) or canned beef broth

1½ pounds beef chuck, cut into ½-inch cubes

Salt and freshly ground black pepper

2 tablespoons vegetable oil

2 medium onions, finely chopped

2 tablespoons minced garlic

2 tablespoons crushed black peppercorns

¼ cup thinly sliced scallions

HELPING TO START AMERICAN SPOON FOODS meant lots of trips to Michigan. On one particularly fortuitous trip, I stopped in a Native American restaurant in Petoskey and had an authentic corn and buffalo soup that was so remarkably good it inspired me to delve into Native American cookbooks and come up with my own version. Back then buffalo was reasonably priced. The price has skyrocketed, so while you can use buffalo if you want, this soup is equally good with beef or venison. It's not only delicious, it's filling enough to be a main course.

Preheat the oven to 450°F.

Place the ears of corn directly on an oven rack and roast, turning, for 15 to 20 minutes, until the husks are evenly browned. Let cool.

When the corn is cool enough to handle, remove the husks and silk. Cut the kernels from the cobs with a sharp knife and set aside.

Chop or break the cobs into pieces and put them in a large saucepan. Add the stock and bring to a boil. Lower the heat and simmer for 20 minutes.

Meanwhile, season the meat with salt and pepper. Heat the oil in a large heavy saucepan until very hot. Add the beef and sauté over high heat until evenly browned. Add the reserved corn kernels and cook for 1 to 2 minutes. Add the onion, garlic, and crushed peppercorns and cook, stirring, for 2 to 3 minutes, until the onions soften.

Strain the stock and add it to the meat. Simmer for 30 to 40 minutes, or until the meat is tender, skimming off any fat that rises to the surface. Stir in the scallions and serve.

HEARTY DUCK SOUP WITH WILD RICE

SERVES 6 TO 8

Salt

1½ cups wild rice

2 tablespoons vegetable oil

One 4-pound duck, cut into quarters

2 onions, sliced

1 clove garlic, crushed

2 cups white wine

8 cups Dark Poultry Stock (page 35) or
   canned chicken broth

¼ cup chopped parsley

4 ounces chanterelles or other wild
   mushrooms, trimmed, cleaned,
   and sliced

Freshly ground black pepper

THIS SOUP COMES with a legend: The story goes that a flying duck dropped, by chance, a few grains from his very full bill into the cooking pot of a hungry Indian somewhere in what is now northern Minnesota. The Indian, delighted with this unexpected taste, traced the flight of the duck until he came upon the source: a field of what we now call wild rice.

To make the soup that honors this lovely legend we always use wild rice that comes from natural, uncultivated rice fields in the shallow lakes in the northern Great Lakes region. Most wild rice sold in supermarkets is cultivated in vast paddies. Real wild rice is nuttier than cultivated.

Combine 2 cups water and 1 teaspoon salt in a medium saucepan and bring to a boil. Sprinkle the wild rice into the water, reduce the heat to low, and cook, uncovered, for 35 to 40 minutes, or until the rice is tender. Drain and set aside. (The rice can be cooked up to 3 or 4 hours ahead of time and refrigerated.)

Heat the oil in a large heavy saucepan over high heat. Add the duck pieces, skin side down, and cook for 2 to 3 minutes, until nicely browned. Turn the pieces over and brown on the other side.

Remove the duck from the pan and pour off the fat. Add the onions and garlic to the pan and sauté over high heat for 1 minute. Add the duck and cook for another minute. Add the wine and stock and bring to a boil. Lower the heat to a simmer and cook, covered, for 45 to 60 minutes, until tender. Skim off any foam that rises to the surface.

When the duck is tender, carefully lift the pieces from the soup and set aside to cool. Cook the soup over high heat for 10 to 15 minutes longer, until it is reduced by one third. Skim off any fat that rises to the surface. Strain through a fine sieve. You should have about 6 cups.

Remove the duck meat from the bones. Trim off any excess fat and dice the meat.

Put the duck meat, chanterelles, and the cooked rice in a large saucepan. Stir in the strained broth, bring to a simmer, and simmer for 4 to 5 minutes. Season with salt and pepper, add the parsley, and serve.

ROAST PHEASANT AND RABBIT BURGOO

■■■■■■■■■■■■■■■■■■■■■■■■■■■■■■■■■■■■■■

SERVES 6 TO 8

One 2½- to 3-pound pheasant, cut into quarters

2 rabbit leg-thigh quarters

Vegetable oil

Salt and freshly ground black pepper

8 cups Chicken Stock (page 33) or canned broth

1 medium onion, diced

2 carrots, peeled and diced

1 large potato, peeled and diced

1 teaspoon minced garlic

2 medium tomatoes, peeled, seeded, and diced

2 cups sliced cabbage

1 cup fresh corn kernels (from approximately 3 ears)

1 small red bell pepper, cored, seeded, and diced

1 jalapeño pepper, seeded and finely diced

1 cup sliced okra

½ cup chopped flat-leaf parsley

BURGOO IS COUNTRY STEW or soup that was made famous in Kentucky. It often was made with small game that was hunted in the region, but nowadays, lots of burgoos are made with chicken. I thought chicken alone undermined the flavor of the dish, so I came up with the idea of using pheasant and rabbit.

I like to use the legs and thighs of both pheasant and rabbit because they are tougher than other meats and can stand up to this sort of cooking, but you are not locked into what is written on the page: Cooks used to toss whatever the hunters brought back with them into their burgoo, so use any type of meat or game you like.

Preheat the oven to 375°F.

Rub the pheasant and rabbit pieces with a little oil and season with salt and pepper. Put them in a baking pan and roast, turning once, for 45 to 50 minutes, until nicely browned.

Transfer the pheasant and rabbit to a large pot.

Pour off any fat from the roasting pan and add 1 cup of the chicken stock to deglaze. Strain this stock into the pot with the meat and add the remaining stock. Bring to a boil, lower the heat, and simmer for 30 to 40 minutes, skimming off any fat or foam from the surface. Add the onions, carrots, potato, and garlic and simmer for 10 minutes. Remove from the heat.

Remove the pheasant and rabbit pieces from the broth and set aside to cool slightly.

When cool enough to handle, remove the pheasant and rabbit meat from the bones, and discard the skin. Cut the meat into large dice and return to the broth. Add the tomatoes, cabbage, corn, bell pepper, jalapeño, and okra. Bring to a simmer and cook for 10 minutes. Season with salt and black pepper, add the parsley, and serve.

VENISON AND BARLEY SOUP

■■■

SERVES 6 TO 8

2 tablespoons vegetable oil

1 pound venison chuck, cut into
½-inch cubes

Salt and freshly ground black pepper

8 cups Dark Poultry Stock (page 35) or
canned chicken broth

1 onion, finely chopped

1 carrot, peeled and finely chopped

½ cup barley

3 ounces white mushrooms, trimmed,
cleaned, and thinly sliced

THIS IS A FLAVORFUL game version of beef and barley soup. If you feel like it, you can easily substitute beef or lamb for the venison.

Heat the oil in a large heavy saucepan over high heat. Season the venison with salt and pepper, add to the pan, and sear until browned on all sides. Remove with a slotted spoon and drain on paper towels.

Pour off the fat from the pan. Return the browned meat to the pan, add the onion and carrot, and sauté for 1 to 2 minutes. Add the stock and bring to a boil. Lower the heat and simmer for 30 to 40 minutes, until the meat is tender.

Meanwhile, rinse the barley and put it in a small pan. Add enough cold water to cover by 2 to 3 inches. Bring to a boil and cook over medium heat for 10 to 12 minutes, until the barley is al dente; add more water if necessary, but do not let the barley become soft and mushy. Drain the barley.

Add the mushrooms and barley to the soup and simmer for 10 minutes. Season with salt and pepper and serve.

CHICKEN STOCK

■■■

MAKES 2 QUARTS

5 pounds chicken bones, including necks
and backs, well rinsed

4 quarts cold water

2 onions, peeled and sliced

5 cloves garlic, sliced

1 carrot, peeled and sliced

2 ribs celery, sliced

1 bay leaf

Few sprigs of fresh thyme

Few sprigs of parsley

1 tablespoon salt

1 teaspoon black peppercorns

Put the chicken bones in a stockpot or 8-quart saucepan and add the cold water. Bring to a boil over medium-high heat, skimming off any foam and fat that rises to the surface. Reduce the heat to medium, add the remaining ingredients, and simmer gently for 2½ to 3 hours, skimming the surface of foam and fat occasionally.

Set a strainer over another large pot and strain the stock, pressing on the solids to extract as much liquid as possible. Discard the solids.

Bring the strained stock to a boil over medium-high heat and cook until reduced to 2 quarts. Strain and cool. Refrigerate for 2 to 3 days or freeze for up to 1 month.

FISH STOCK

■■■

**MAKES ABOUT 2
QUARTS**

1 tablespoon olive oil

3 leeks, white part only, trimmed,
    rinsed, and sliced

2 cloves garlic, sliced

1 carrot, sliced

2 ribs celery, sliced

1 cup mushroom trimmings or
    sliced mushrooms

5 to 6 sprigs parsley

2 to 3 branches fresh thyme

1 small bay leaf

2 to 3 pounds fish bones and heads, from
    flat fish such as sole, halibut, or white
    flesh fish such as cod, scrod, or
    monkfish, well rinsed

1 cup white wine

1 tablespoon honey

2 quarts cold water

1 tablespoon salt

1 teaspoon black peppercorns

In a large saucepan, heat the olive oil over low heat. Add the leeks, garlic, carrot, celery, mushroom, parsley, thyme, and bay leaf and cook for 1 to 2 minutes. Add the fish, white wine, and honey, raise the heat and simmer for 2 to 3 minutes. Add the water, salt, and peppercorns. Raise the heat and bring to a boil, skimming the surface occasionally of any foam. Reduce the heat and simmer for 35 to 40 minutes. Strain through a fine sieve into a clean bowl and set aside to cool. Cover and refrigerate for up to 3 days or freeze for up to 1 month.

SHELLFISH STOCK

■■■

MAKES 2 TO 2½ CUPS

2 tablespoons olive oil

4 pounds shells and carcasses from lobsters, shrimp, and/or crab

1 small onion, sliced

1 tablespoon minced garlic

1 teaspoon hot red pepper flakes

2 tablespoons tomato puree

1 cup dry white wine

3 cups Chicken Stock (page 33) or canned broth

In a large saucepan, heat the olive oil over medium heat. Add the shells and carcasses, increase the heat to high, and cook, stirring, for 2 to 3 minutes, until aromatic. Add the onion, garlic, and red pepper flakes and cook for 2 to 3 minutes longer.

Add the tomato puree and wine, bring to a boil, and cook for 4 to 7 minutes, until reduced by half. Add the chicken stock and bring to a boil. Reduce the heat, skim off any foam that has risen to the surface, and simmer for 8 to 10 minutes, until the flavors blend.

Strain through a fine sieve into a clean bowl. Set aside to cool. Refrigerate for up to 3 days or freeze for up to 1 month.

DARK POULTRY STOCK

■■■

MAKES ABOUT 1½ QUARTS

3 pounds chicken bones, including necks and backs, well rinsed

½ cup tomato puree

1 onion, sliced

3 cloves garlic, sliced

1 cup dry white wine

2 quarts Chicken Stock (page 33) or canned broth

Preheat the oven to 400°F.

Spread the chicken bones in a roasting pan and roast for 45 to 60 minutes, turning several times, until the bones are browned.

Pour off the fat from the pan. Add the tomato puree, onion, and garlic to the bones and stir to mix. Roast for 20 minutes longer. Remove the pan from the oven, add the wine, and stir the contents, scraping the sides and bottom of the pan to loosen any browned bits stuck to it.

Transfer the contents of the roasting pan to a stockpot or 5- or 6-quart saucepan and cook, stirring, over high heat for 2 to 3 minutes. Add the stock and bring to a simmer. Cook for about 1 hour until reduced to 1½ quarts, skimming the surface of any foam and fat occasionally. Strain through a fine sieve into a clean bowl. Set aside to cool. Refrigerate for up to 3 days or freeze for up to 1 month.

NOTE: Duck, beef, lamb, and venison recipes will be enhanced by using a dark stock made from the respective bones. Follow this method, roasting meaty bones instead of chicken bones and adding stock to them for Rich Beef Stock, Rich Lamb Stock, and Rich Venison Stock.

Native Salads

ONE SPRING WEEKEND in the early 1980s, I went with my wife to our local nursery and garden center. As we were waiting to pay for our bulbs, I happened to look up and see a poster advertising a brand of weed killers. On the poster was a chart that showed a picture of a particular weed and the product that would eradicate it. I glanced down the list of undesirable weeds: purslane, chickweed, wild dandelion, native goosefoot. "Oh my gosh!" I exclaimed to Julie. "That's my salad!"

Back then, in the age of iceberg lettuce and bottled dressing, the idea of using wild native greens or edible flowers in a salad seemed incredibly exotic. Fifteen years later, the type of salad that I originally served and called an American Field Salad is a contemporary American classic. Now supermarkets sell ten different kinds of lettuce, and farmers' markets offer a seasonal bounty of baby dandelion, chicory, field cress, zucchini blossoms, beet greens, and purslane.

As salad greens have come into their own—each with real substance, distinctive character, compelling flavor—so have salads themselves. Crisp fresh ingredients, imaginatively combined and properly dressed, can't help but produce irresistible starter salads and more substantial main course salads.

It's hard to beat the dazzling freshness of the seasonal American Field Salad lightly tossed with a tart Berry Vinaigrette. Or the harmonious pleasure of a salad that incorporates the August sweetness of plump vine-ripened beefsteak tomatoes with avocado, black beans, and a zesty chile-lime dressing. But it doesn't have to be summer to produce a satisfying salad: A traditional Southern wilted salad with winter greens like kale or collard is a lovely side dish and one I often serve with a pot roast or a hearty stew. So is a simply made Winter Fruit and Nut Conserve.

With so much to choose from today, there is no excuse for a boring salad. Or a boring dressing. The New Mexican Corn Mushroom Salad and Red Pepper and Chayote Salad are a far cry from a standard tossed salad of lettuce, tomato, and cucumber. And just as engaging are dressings with pronounced flavor, like Wild Hickory Nut Vinaigrette and Sage-Mint Vinaigrette. When you find a dressing you especially like, try it on other salads too. The sage-mint vinaigrette is as good on sliced tomatoes as it is on the New Mexican Corn Mushroom Salad. The dressings in this chapter are all quite versatile and in fact should not be reserved just for salads. The chile-lime dressing, for example, adds a piquant flavor to chilled fresh shrimp. And you might want to double the recipes so you can keep extra in the refrigerator.

Just use your imagination, concentrate on bringing out a few distinct flavors, and you'll have a repertoire of salad ideas to choose from twelve months a year.

WALDORF SALAD

■■■

SERVES 4

1 cup walnut halves

½ cup mayonnaise, preferably homemade

¼ cup plain yogurt

1 teaspoon prepared mustard

Pinch of dry mustard

Juice of ½ lemon

4 to 6 tart apples, peeled, cored, and
    diced (2 cups)

1 to 2 cups finely diced inner ribs celery
    (white part only), leaves reserved

Salt and freshly ground black pepper

2 bunches tender greens, such as arugula,
    baby kale, or pepper cress, washed
    and dried

2 tablespoons olive oil

1 tablespoon fresh lemon juice

WALDORF SALAD IS ONE of those dishes that has been slowly altered over the years until it in no way resembles the original dish. When it was first created at The Waldorf Hotel almost 100 years ago, it was prepared at tableside, fresh and perfect. The apples were crisp, firm, and slightly tart. The walnuts were lightly toasted, crisp, and golden.

How did we *ever* wind up with a salad made up in huge vats and refrigerated for days, with stringy chunks of celery drenched with commercial mayonnaise, laced with cherries, and dotted with raisins?

It is important to me to examine dishes that carry real significance in American culinary history and then try to re-create the authentic recipe or a version that captures the essence of the original. This one does.

Preheat the oven to 325°F.

Spread the walnuts on a baking sheet and toast in the oven for 4 to 5 minutes, until aromatic and lightly toasted. Let cool.

Combine the mayonnaise, yogurt, both mustards, and the lemon juice in a large bowl. Fold in the apples and diced celery and season with salt and pepper.

Put the salad greens in a large bowl. Add the olive oil and lemon juice, season with salt and pepper, and toss well. Divide the greens among four plates. Spoon the apple mixture onto the greens and sprinkle with the toasted walnuts and reserved celery leaves.

OLD-FASHIONED CAESAR SALAD

■■

SERVES 4

2 small heads romaine lettuce, outer
green leaves removed and reserved for
another use

2 cloves garlic, mashed

2 tablespoons mashed anchovies

3 tablespoons fresh lemon juice

1 large egg yolk

½ cup olive oil

1 tablespoon freshly grated Parmesan
cheese or dry-aged Monterey Jack
cheese, plus one 3- to 4-ounce piece
Parmesan or dry-aged Jack,
for shaving

Salt if necessary

2 slices lightly toasted sourdough bread,
cut into ½-inch croutons
(about 1 cup)

Freshly ground black pepper

ALTHOUGH CAESAR SALAD was created in Mexico, it's hard to imagine a more all-American favorite. The real secret to making it is very simple: Use only the inner heart of the romaine lettuce, not the dark outer leaves, and make sure the lettuce is icy-cold when you toss it with the dressing. The pale green leaves are crisp and tender and taste best with the strong dressing. If you can find whole anchovies packed in salt rather than fillets packed in oil, use them. Rinse the fish well and pull the fillets off the bone. Anchovies processed this way don't taste as strong or fishy as the others. (I do not recommend substituting anchovy paste.)

Tear or cut the romaine leaves into 1-inch pieces. Wash in ice-cold water, drain well, and pat dry. Wrap in a kitchen towel and refrigerate until chilled.

Combine the garlic, mashed anchovies, and lemon juice in a large bowl and whisk until blended. Whisk in the egg yolk. Gradually whisk in the olive oil and grated cheese. Season with a little salt if necessary. Add the lettuce and croutons, season with pepper, and toss until the lettuce is well coated.

Serve on salad plates or in bowls, topped with shaved Parmesan or aged Jack cheese.

AMERICAN FIELD SALAD

BERRY VINAIGRETTE

■■

SERVES 4 TO 6

8 heads or bunches assorted baby
    lettuces, such as red leaf, green leaf,
    red oak, chicory, Bibb, arugula, and/or
    watercress

8 ounces tender young chickweed, rinsed
    and dried (about 2 cups)

8 ounces tender young lamb's-quarter
    leaves (also called goosefoot), rinsed
    and dried (about 2 cups)

8 ounces tender young purslane sprigs,
    rinsed and dried (about 2 cups)

1/2 pint small firm berries, such as
    raspberries, blackberries, or
    blueberries

8 to 12 edible flowers, such as
    nasturtiums, pansies, or violets

Berry Vinaigrette (recipe follows)

THIS WAS MY SIGNATURE SALAD. It's as delicate and fresh and invigorating as a salad can be. It isn't always easy getting all the greens this recipe calls for—if you can only get one or two, simply increase the amounts accordingly. The salad is very good made only with watercress. Use either raspberry or blueberry vinegar for the vinaigrette, whichever you prefer; it does not have to "match" the berries used in the salad.

Break apart the lettuce and rinse and dry the leaves well. Put the lettuce and wild greens in a large bowl and add the berries.

    Add about 1/2 cup of the vinaigrette to the salad and toss gently. Sprinkle the flowers over the salad and serve. Store the remaining vinaigrette in the refrigerator.

———

BERRY VINAIGRETTE

1/2 cup raspberry or blueberry vinegar

1 cup olive oil

1 1/2 teaspoons minced garlic

1 tablespoon chopped fresh chives

1 tablespoon chopped fresh basil

Salt and freshly ground black pepper
    to taste

Combine all the ingredients in a small bowl and whisk well. The vinaigrette will keep, refrigerated in a tightly sealed jar, for 2 to 3 days.

WILTED WINTER GREENS SALAD
WARM SHERRY VINAIGRETTE

■■■

SERVES 4

½ medium or 1 small daikon radish, peeled, trimmed, and cut into 2-inch julienne

3 to 4 cups assorted winter greens, such as tender kale, white chicory, romaine, and/or turnip or beet greens, washed, dried, and large leaves torn into pieces

Warm Sherry Vinaigrette (recipe follows)

WILTED SALADS ORIGINATED in the South, where cooks have always made the most of ingredients such as kale, collards, and mustard greens. Their firm leaves stand up to the warm dressing, wilting only a little as they are tossed just before serving. Use whatever fresh winter greens are available, such as kale (I like to mix white-and-green-striped kale with red kale), frisée, or baby white chicory, and beet greens. Use cream sherry in the dressing rather than dry sherry for its smoky flavor.

Combine the daikon with the greens in a large bowl.

Toss the salad with 2 to 3 tablespoons of the warm vinaigrette. Serve on individual salad plates, with the remaining vinaigrette on the side.

———

WARM SHERRY VINAIGRETTE

1 tablespoon white wine vinegar

1½ teaspoons fresh lemon juice

1½ teaspoons prepared mustard

⅛ teaspoon minced garlic

½ teaspoon minced shallot

1 tablespoon cream sherry

¼ cup olive oil

Salt and freshly ground black pepper

1 tablespoon chopped fresh herbs, such as tarragon, chervil, basil, or oregano

In a small saucepan, combine the vinegar, lemon juice, mustard, garlic, shallot, and sherry and heat over low heat until warm. Gradually whisk in the oil and continue whisking until the vinaigrette is hot. Season with salt and pepper and add the herbs. Remove from the heat and keep warm.

CRESS WITH BABY WHITE ASPARAGUS
WILD HICKORY NUT VINAIGRETTE

■■■■■■■■■■■■■■■■■■■■■■■■■■■■■■■■■■■■■■

SERVES 4

2 bunches upland or wild watercress

One 6-ounce package pepper cress (radish sprouts)

1 bunch cultivated watercress

½ pound baby white asparagus, trimmed

1 cup mixed yellow and red cherry tomatoes or mini plum tomatoes, halved or quartered depending on their size

16 wild hickory nut halves

Wild Hickory Nut Vinaigrette (recipe follows)

2 tablespoons finely chopped chives

Freshly ground black pepper

THIS DISH WAS CREATED to highlight Michigan produce, such as upland cress—a slightly more peppery version of cultivated watercress. The recipe calls for pepper cress, cultivated cress, and upland or wild cress, but use any combination. Hickory nuts are available by mail order from American Spoon Foods, page 285 or substitute another nut such as walnuts. White Michigan asparagus has a crisp flavor that goes very well in this salad.

Clean and trim wild and pepper cress. Pick out the tender sprigs of cultivated watercress, discarding large, tough sprigs. Rinse well.

Blanch the asparagus in boiling salted water for 30 seconds. Drain and immediately plunge into ice water. When the asparagus is completely cold, drain and spread on paper towels.

Arrange bundles of the cresses on four serving plates. Place the asparagus on top and sprinkle with the tomatoes and hickory nuts. Drizzle a tablespoon or two of the vinaigrette over each salad. Sprinkle with the chives and pepper and serve. Store in the refrigerator.

———

WILD HICKORY NUT VINAIGRETTE

¼ cup olive oil

2 ounces (about ½ cup) wild hickory nut meats

¼ teaspoon minced shallot or scallion

⅛ teaspoon minced garlic

2 tablespoons dry sherry

¼ cup red wine vinegar

¼ cup peanut oil

Salt and freshly ground black pepper

Heat 1 tablespoon of the olive oil in a small sauté pan over medium heat until hot. Add the nuts and gently sauté for about 1 minute, until they begin to brown. Add the shallots or scallions and garlic and cook for 30 seconds. Add the sherry and simmer until it is reduced by half. Add the vinegar, the remaining 3 tablespoons olive oil, and the peanut oil and simmer for 1 to 2 minutes. Remove from the heat and let cool.

Put the vinaigrette in a blender and process until the nuts are ground. Season with salt and pepper.

WARM BABY GREEN ASPARAGUS SALAD

■■■■■■■■■■■■■■■■■■■■■■■■■■■■■■■■■■■■■■■

Dressing

1/2 cup olive oil

3 tablespoons red wine vinegar

1 tablespoon fresh lemon juice

2 teaspoons prepared mustard

1/4 teaspoon freshly ground black pepper

2 tablespoons chopped fresh herbs, such
as chervil, tarragon, basil, or oregano

Salad

6 new potatoes, scrubbed and cooked in
boiling salted water until just
barely tender

Olive oil for brushing

Salt and freshly ground black pepper

8 shiitake or oyster mushrooms, trimmed
and cleaned

1 red bell pepper, roasted, peeled, seeded,
and cut into strips (see Note)

1 pound baby green asparagus, trimmed

4 cups assorted lettuces, such as red leaf,
watercress, and/or arugula, washed
and dried

2 tomatoes, seeded and diced

CALLED "PENCIL" ASPARAGUS, the spears need no peeling and are blanched for only about a minute, just to warm them through. If you're lucky enough to find wild oyster mushrooms, which are in season at the same time, serve them in the salad. With the roasted red peppers, mixed lettuces, and the straightforward herb-mustard vinaigrette, this makes a refreshing beginning to a meal, or it can stand on its own as a spring luncheon.

To make the dressing, combine all the ingredients in a small bowl and whisk together. Set aside at room temperature.

Prepare a medium hot fire in a charcoal or gas grill or preheat the broiler.

Cut the potatoes in half, brush with a little olive oil, and season with salt and pepper. Season the mushrooms with salt and pepper.

Grill or broil the potatoes and mushrooms, turning once, until nicely browned on each side. Transfer to a bowl, cover loosely with foil, and keep warm.

Put the pepper strips in a small bowl and drizzle with olive oil.

Blanch the asparagus in lightly salted boiling water for 1 minute, just to warm through. Drain well and spread on a plate. Drizzle with 2 tablespoons of the dressing, and let sit for a minute or so.

Arrange the lettuces, asparagus, grilled potatoes and mushrooms, and roasted pepper strips on four serving plates. Sprinkle with the chopped tomatoes, drizzle with the dressing, and serve. Pass any remaining dressing on the side.

NOTE: To roast a bell (or other) pepper, place it under the broiler or on a grill for 10 to 12 minutes, turning it several times, until charred on all sides. Transfer to a paper bag, close, and let cool. Rub the charred black skin off the pepper. Remove the core and scrape out the seeds.

SALAD OF GRILLED CÈPES, ASPARAGUS, AND SWEET PEAS

■■■

SERVES 4

16 to 20 asparagus spears, trimmed
   and peeled

²⁄₃ cup fresh peas

8 to 12 thick slices cèpes or portobello
   mushrooms (dark undersides trimmed
   if using portobellos)

3 tablespoons olive oil

Salt and freshly ground black pepper

Two ¾-inch-thick slices farmhouse or
   other country-style bread, cut in half
   on the diagonal

1 bunch arugula, washed and dried

1 bunch watercress, washed and dried

1 teaspoon chopped shallots

2 tablespoons dry white wine

3 tablespoons unsalted butter, at
   room temperature

1 teaspoon chopped flat-leaf parsley

1 teaspoon chopped fresh tarragon

2 tablespoons fresh lemon juice

I ALSO CALL this Spring Harvest Salad; it combines the heady flavor of cèpes and the crisp sweetness of peas and asparagus.

Pour about 1 inch of water into a deep skillet and bring to a boil over high heat. Add the asparagus and cook for about 1 minute, until crisp-tender. Remove with a slotted spoon or tongs and drain on paper towels. Add the peas to the boiling water and cook for about 1 minute, until crisp-tender. Drain and set aside.

Prepare a charcoal or gas grill or preheat the broiler.

Brush the cèpes and asparagus with 2 tablespoons of the olive oil and season with salt and pepper. Grill or broil for 3 to 4 minutes, until the asparagus just begins to color and the cèpes soften slightly. Transfer to a plate and set aside. Grill the bread for about 1 minute a side, until lightly toasted.

Arrange the arugula and cress on serving plates and top with the grilled bread. Arrange the cèpes and asparagus on the bread, spooning any accumulated juices over the greens.

In a small sauté pan, heat the remaining 1 tablespoon oil over medium heat. Add the shallots and wine and cook, stirring, for about 1 minute, until the shallots begin to soften. Remove from the heat and whisk in the butter a tablespoon at a time. Stir in the peas, parsley, tarragon, and lemon juice. Return the pan to low heat and cook, stirring gently, for about 1 minute to warm the peas. Season with salt and pepper and spoon over the salads.

New Mexican Corn Mushroom Salad
Sage-Mint Vinaigrette

■■

SERVES 4

2 tablespoons olive oil

1 poblano pepper, seeded and cut into
    thin strips

1 red bell pepper, cored, seeded, and cut
    into thin strips

1 small zucchini, cut into thin strips

½ cup fresh corn kernels (from 1 ear)

¼ teaspoon minced garlic

1 pound *cuitlacoche* (corn mushrooms)

Salt and freshly ground black pepper

4 cups assorted lettuces, such as red leaf,
    green leaf, Bibb, arugula, and/or
    watercress, washed and patted dry

⅓ cup Sage-Mint Vinaigrette
    (recipe follows)

8 slices grilled peasant or country-
    style bread

NEW MEXICAN CORN MUSHROOMS, or *cuitlacoche*, are actually a fungus that attaches itself to ears of corn. Often the mushrooms have crunchy corn kernels buried in them. I like to sauté them in hot oil and eat them right away or use them in this salad. *Cuitlacoche* is very perishable, so be sure to buy it from a reputable specialty store, or order it through the mail from MMA/Earthly Delights (page 285). The mushrooms hold up well when flash-frozen for shipping.

Heat the olive oil in a large skillet over medium-high heat. Add the poblano, bell pepper, zucchini, corn kernels, and garlic and cook, stirring, for 1 minute. Add the corn mushrooms, season lightly with salt and pepper, and cook for 1 minute. Remove the pan from the heat and set aside to cool and allow the flavors to meld.

Toss the lettuces with 2 tablespoons of the vinaigrette. Divide the lettuces among four serving plates. Spoon the corn mushroom mixture over the lettuce and put 2 pieces of grilled bread on each plate. Drizzle a little of the vinaigrette over each salad and serve. Pass any remaining vinaigrette on the side.

———

SAGE-MINT VINAIGRETTE
MAKES ABOUT 1¼ CUPS

1 cup olive oil

¼ cup red wine vinegar

1 teaspoon prepared mustard

1 teaspoon minced garlic

1 tablespoon chopped fresh sage

1 tablespoon chopped fresh mint

Salt and freshly ground black pepper

Combine all the ingredients except the salt and pepper in a bowl and whisk well. Season to taste with salt and pepper and whisk again. Use immediately or store in a tightly sealed jar in the refrigerator for 2 to 3 days.

WILD RICE VEGETABLE SALAD WITH MARINATED FOREST MUSHROOMS

■■■

SERVES 6

Marinated Mushrooms

¼ cup olive oil

¾ pound assorted wild mushrooms, trimmed, cleaned, and cut into 1-inch pieces

¼ cup olive oil

1 tablespoon minced onion

1 teaspoon minced garlic

1 teaspoon fresh thyme leaves

Salt and freshly ground black pepper

¼ cup dry white wine

2 tablespoons fresh lemon juice

2 tablespoons white wine vinegar

Salad

2¼ cups Chicken Stock (page 33) or canned broth or water

¾ cup wild rice

2 tablespoons olive oil

½ cup diced zucchini

½ cup diced yellow squash

¼ cup diced carrot

¼ cup diced onion

¼ cup diced red bell pepper

1 scallion, thinly sliced

3 tablespoons minced fresh ginger

Salt and freshly ground black pepper

¼ cup chopped flat-leaf parsley

2 tablespoons chopped fresh herbs

¼ cup reserved liquid from marinated mushrooms (see above)

3 to 4 bunches assorted lettuces, such as red leaf, green leaf, Bibb, arugula, and/or watercress, washed and dried

FOREST MUSHROOM IS A TERM I use to denote cultivated "wild" mushrooms, such as shiitakes, oysters, chanterelles, and/or morels. Their woodsy flavor and chewy texture is superior to that of button mushrooms. This warm rice salad, accented with ginger and marinated mushrooms, can be served as a first course or a light meal. The mushrooms are good on their own too.

To make the marinated mushrooms, heat the oil in a large skillet over medium-high heat. Add the mushrooms and sauté, stirring briskly, for 2 to 3 minutes, until softened. Add the onion, garlic, and thyme, season with salt and pepper, and toss gently. Add the wine, lemon juice, and vinegar and carefully scrape the bottom of the pan with a wooden spoon to loosen any browned bits. Toss again and cook for 1 minute. Scrape the mushrooms and the liquid into a bowl and let cool to room temperature. Strain the cooled liquid through a fine sieve into a bowl and set the mushrooms and liquid aside separately.

To make the salad, bring the stock to a boil in a medium saucepan. Add the rice and cook, uncovered, over medium heat for 15 minutes, or until all the liquid is absorbed and the rice is tender. Transfer the rice to a large bowl and set aside.

Heat the olive oil in a large skillet over medium-high heat. Add the zucchini, yellow squash, carrot, onion, pepper, scallion, and ginger and cook, stirring, for 2 to 3 minutes, until just softened. Season to taste with salt and pepper. Add the sautéed vegetables to the rice along with the parsley, herbs, and the reserved mushroom liquid, and stir to mix. Let cool a little.

Spoon the warm rice salad into six 5- or 6-ounce soufflé molds or custard cups and press down lightly. Arrange the lettuce on six salad plates and unmold a rice salad in the center of each one. Surround with the marinated mushrooms and serve.

BLACK BEAN SALAD

■■

SERVES 4

1 cup dried black beans, picked over
    and rinsed

1 bay leaf

10 black peppercorns

2 cups Chicken Stock (page 33) or
    canned broth or water

1 teaspoon minced garlic

1 teaspoon salt

1 jalapeño pepper, seeded and finely diced

½ red onion, finely diced

2 tablespoons olive oil

2 tablespoons fresh lime juice

1 teaspoon ground cumin

1 teaspoon pure chile powder

3 tablespoons chopped cilantro
    (fresh coriander)

A few drops of Tabasco

Salt and freshly ground black pepper

Lettuce leaves for serving

Sprigs of cilantro (fresh coriander)
    for garnish

I'M ALWAYS HAPPY to find new salads to serve in the summer to vary the routine—here's one I think you'll want to add to your repertoire. It can be dressed up and served with avocados and ripe tomatoes (as it is in the following recipe), but it's a nice, uncomplicated dish on its own.

Soak the beans for at least 6 hours, or overnight, in cold water to cover by at least 2 inches.

Wrap the bay leaf and peppercorns in a small square of cheese-cloth. Drain and rinse the beans. Combine the beans, chicken stock or water, bay leaf and peppercorns, garlic, and salt in a large saucepan. Bring to a simmer and cook for about 1½ hours, until the beans are tender but not mushy. Remove the beans from the heat and allow to cool in the cooking liquid.

Drain the beans and discard the bay leaf and peppercorns. Put the beans in a bowl and add the jalapeño, onion, olive oil, lime juice, cumin, chile powder, chopped cilantro, and Tabasco. Toss well and season to taste with salt and pepper.

Arrange a few lettuce leaves on each plate and spoon the black bean salad over them. Garnish each salad with a few sprigs of cilantro and serve.

(The salad can be stored, covered, in the refrigerator for 2 to 3 days. Bring to room temperature before serving.)

AVOCADO, BLACK BEAN, AND TOMATO SALAD

CHILE-LIME DRESSING

■ ■

SERVES 4

1 large ripe California avocado, such as Hass

2 large ripe tomatoes, preferably beefsteaks, each cut into 6 slices

¼ cup olive oil

Freshly ground black pepper

Lettuce leaves for serving

Chile-Lime Dressing (recipe follows)

Black Bean Salad (page 48)

Sprigs of cilantro (fresh coriander) for garnish

WE MADE THIS SALAD in the restaurant one summer when we got a bumper crop of vine-ripened Jersey beefsteak tomatoes. Combining black beans with tomatoes and avocados makes a cool, soothing salad that is a departure from an ordinary tomato and avocado salad. The dressing is actually barbecue sauce with a little oil added and fresh lime juice.

Halve the avocado lengthwise and discard the pit. Peel the avocado, cut each half in half again, and cut each quarter into a fan, leaving the slices attached at one end.

Brush the avocado fans and tomato slices with the oil and season with pepper.

Spread a few lettuce leaves on each plate. Arrange 1 avocado fan, 3 tomato slices, and ½ cup black bean salad on the lettuce on each plate. Spoon the dressing over the salads, garnish each with a sprig of cilantro, and serve.

––––––

CHILE-LIME DRESSING

½ cup Barbecue Sauce (page 152) or American Spoon Foods or other prepared barbecue sauce

¼ cup plus 1 tablespoon fresh lime juice

3 tablespoons peanut oil or olive oil

Combine the barbecue sauce, lime juice, and oil in a bowl and whisk together. The dressing will keep, refrigerated, for 2 to 3 days.

HUDSON VALLEY CAMEMBERT CRISP
OLIVE OIL VINAIGRETTE ▪ APPLE-PEAR CONSERVE

SERVES 4

AS AN APPETIZER

Flour for dredging

1 large egg

¼ cup finely ground hickory nuts
   or pecans

¼ cup dried bread crumbs (made from
   stale bread)

2 ripe 6-ounce wheels Camembert cheese

¼ cup olive oil

4 cups assorted lettuce leaves, such as
   red leaf, Bibb, oak leaf, watercress,
   spinach and/or arugula, washed
   and dried

Olive Oil Vinaigrette (recipe follows)

Salt and freshly ground black pepper

Apple-Pear Conserve (recipe follows)

AROUND THE TIME we opened The Beekman Tavern in Rhinebeck, I met some Hudson Valley cheesemakers whose Camembert-style cheese rivaled the true Camembert of France. Eager to showcase the products of the Hudson Valley, I developed this recipe, thinking it would do more justice to the cheese than simply putting it on a cheese tray.

I use a combination of nuts and bread crumbs to bread the cheese, because nuts alone would be too intense for it. I got the idea for the apple-pear conserve from the old custom of spooning chutney over cream cheese and serving it on crackers—and cheese and fruit naturally go together.

The difference between a conserve and preserve is that a conserve usually includes dried fruit as well as fresh. There's a little vinegar in this one too, to sharpen the flavor so it complements the creamy cheese.

Spread the flour in a shallow dish. Beat the egg in another shallow dish. Combine the nuts and bread crumbs in a third shallow dish.

Cut the cheeses crosswise in half. Dredge each piece in the flour, dip in the beaten egg, and roll in the nut mixture until evenly coated.

Heat the olive oil over medium-high heat in a sauté pan large enough to hold the cheeses until very hot but not smoking. Fry the cheeses for about 2 minutes, until golden brown on the bottom. Turn the cheeses over carefully and brown on the other side. Drain on paper towels.

Put the lettuces in a large bowl, add the vinaigrette and salt and pepper to taste, and toss well.

Divide the salad among four serving plates. Spoon the conserve over the greens and put the Camembert on top.

OLIVE OIL VINAIGRETTE

MAKES ABOUT 1¼ CUPS

1 cup olive oil

¼ cup red wine vinegar

1 teaspoon prepared mustard

1 teaspoon minced garlic

Salt and freshly ground black pepper

Combine all the ingredients except the salt and pepper in a bowl and whisk well. Season to taste with salt and pepper and whisk again. Use immediately or store in a tightly sealed jar in the refrigerator.

———

APPLE-PEAR CONSERVE

MAKES ABOUT 1¼ CUPS

1 tablespoon lightly salted butter

1 Granny Smith apple, peeled, cored, and diced

1 ripe Bartlett or Bosc pear, peeled, cored, and diced

1 tablespoon cider vinegar

1 teaspoon brown sugar

1 tablespoon halved dried sour cherries

Pinch of allspice

Pinch of ground cumin

Pinch of freshly grated nutmeg

To make the conserve, heat the butter in a heavy skillet over medium heat until it begins to foam. Add the apple and pear and cook, stirring, for 2 to 3 minutes, until the apple is tender. Stir in the vinegar, brown sugar, cherries, and spices and cook, stirring, for 1 to 2 minutes. Spoon the conserve into a bowl and let cool to room temperature.

COUNTRY HAM AND SWEET POTATO SALAD WITH HONEY VINAIGRETTE

SERVES 4

Vinaigrette

3 tablespoons olive oil

1½ teaspoons red wine vinegar

1 tablespoon fresh lemon juice

1 tablespoon honey

¼ teaspoon salt

⅛ teaspoon freshly ground black pepper

Salad

2 large sweet potatoes

2 ripe tomatoes, peeled, seeded, and coarsely chopped

3 tablespoons chopped flat-leaf parsley

⅓ pound country ham such as specially aged Smithfield or Ozark hams (see mail-order sources, page 285) or prosciutto, very thinly sliced

THERE IS HAM and there is incredible, unforgettable, supernal ham. I developed this recipe in honor of the latter—the wonderful one I discovered years ago called "specially cellared" country ham. It is aged longer than other country hams and is very dry, very salty, and very, very good, with a taste similar to prosciutto. And, like prosciutto, it should be sliced extremely thin and then trimmed of the fat.

The sweet potatoes and sweet honey vinaigrette in this salad counterbalance the strong flavor of the ham. You can use any country ham or good prosciutto, but if you can mail-order specially cellared ham, try it. Don't boil it first; simply cut the meat from the bone in paper-thin slices.

To make the vinaigrette, combine all the ingredients in a bowl or blender and whisk or blend until smooth. Let stand at room temperature for at least 1 hour to blend the flavors.

Preheat the oven to 350°F.

Bake the sweet potatoes for about 30 to 40 minutes, until cooked through but still slightly firm. Let cool.

Peel the potatoes, cut them into ½-inch cubes, and put them in a bowl. Add the tomatoes, parsley, and the vinaigrette and mix together gently. Let stand for 10 to 15 minutes.

Place the salad in the center of four serving plates and surround with the sliced ham or prosciutto.

NUTTED FOIE GRAS

APPLE AND RED ONION RELISH

■■

SERVES 4

AS AN APPETIZER

Flour for dredging

½ cup milk

1 large egg

¼ cup finely chopped blanched almonds

¼ cup finely chopped pecans

¼ cup finely chopped walnuts

¼ cup fresh bread crumbs

Four ½-inch-thick slices fresh foie gras
(about 6 ounces in all)

2 tablespoons olive oil

Salt and freshly ground black pepper

Apple and Red Onion Relish
(recipe follows)

2 tablespoons finely chopped fresh chives

NOTE: The foie gras can be breaded 1 to 2 hours ahead of time and refrigerated on the waxed paper–covered tray.

WHEN AMERICAN FOIE GRAS first became available, I very much wanted to use it in new ways. So in this recipe, I coat the foie gras with a nut crust that gets crunchy when lightly browned. The apple-onion relish is a sweet-and-sour sauce that sets off rich foie gras very well—and it's very American too.

Spread the flour in a shallow dish. Beat the milk and egg together in another shallow dish. Combine the nuts and bread crumbs in a third shallow dish.

Dredge each slice of foie gras in the flour, dip it in the egg wash, and then coat evenly with the bread crumb mixture. Put the foie gras on a baking sheet covered with waxed paper.

Heat the olive oil in a large nonstick skillet over medium-high heat. Add the foie gras and cook for 1 minute, until golden brown on the bottom. Carefully turn the pieces over and brown on the other side. Drain on paper towels.

Spoon the relish into the centers of four serving plates and put the foie gras on top. Sprinkle with the chives and serve immediately.

———

APPLE AND RED ONION RELISH

1 red onion, diced	¾ teaspoon freshly ground black pepper
1 tablespoon unsalted butter	1 small red bell pepper, cored, seeded, and finely diced
2 tart apples, peeled, cored, and diced	
1½ tablespoons red wine vinegar	3 tablespoons chopped flat leaf parsley

Put the onions in a strainer and run hot water over them for 2 minutes; drain well. (This rids them of acidity.)

Heat the butter in a large skillet over high heat until it foams. Add the onions and apples and cook, stirring or tossing, for 1 to 2 minutes (apple pieces should keep their shape and be crisp-tender).

Remove the pan from the heat and stir in the vinegar and pepper. Transfer to a bowl, stir in the bell pepper and parsley, and cover to keep warm.

Grilled Marinated Quail with Chestnuts and
Wild Huckleberries, served with Wild Rice Harvest Cakes

LEFT: *Maple-Whipped Sweet Potatoes*
BELOW: *Artichoke and Potato Pancakes*

ABOVE: *Grandma's Chicken Escarole Soup*
LEFT: *Lobster and Corn Chowder*

1 cèpes
2 morels
3 shiitake
4 pompom mushrooms
5 hen-in-the-woods
6 chanterelles
7 lobster mushrooms
8 black trumpets

MUSHROOMS

While many, many different varieties of wild and cultivated mushrooms exist, photographed here are the most popular varieties of mushrooms in America.

Cèpes, the "kings of mushrooms," are prized the world over. Small, young caps are firm and crisp while large, more open caps have a nice meatiness. These mushrooms are perfect for slicing and grilling.

Morels are both black and pale. They are the prize of the spring wild harvest. They are found from Maine to Washington State from early May through July. They have a wonderful, heady, earthy flavor perfect for any mushrooms preparation.

Pompon, cremini, shiitake, and lobster mushrooms are generally cultivated as "farmed" varieties. They can be used as you would any button mushroom, but they will add more flavor to your dish. Lobster mushrooms get their name from their coloring, not their taste. They should be used like a hen-in-the-woods—cooked with some moisture.

Hen-in-the-woods gets its name from its "feathered" look. Smaller, tender mushrooms can be sautéed, but more mature ones should be sautéed, deglazed, and then stewed in a little broth.

Chanterelles grow profusely in the Northwest, from where they are shipped all over the country. The smaller East Coast chanterelles are incredible but more scarce. Chanterelles take on an earthy, apricoty flavor and are perfect for sautéing.

Black trumpets, sometimes referred to as black chanterelles, are fleshy and perfect for wilting in a sauce or soup. They have a rich, woodsy flavor.

4

5

6

7

8

ABOVE: *Roast Cod with Rosemary Oil and Cranberry Beans*
OPPOSITE: *Grilled Halibut with Stewed Fresh Tomatoes*

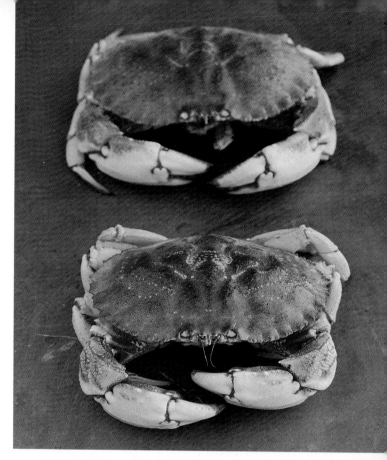

CRABS

If you have oceans, you have crabs. A regional specialty like Jonah crabmeat from Maine has become very popular since the meat is now fresh picked and shipped. Jonah crabs are "all claw meat," while blue crabs are cherished for their "lump" or body meat. Blue crabs are steamed, dumped on your table, self-cracked, and picked by people all over the Atlantic coast and Gulf states. The prized soft-shell crab of the "summer" states is uniquely American, and I always make sure to introduce it to visitors for a "taste of America." The West Coast crab is the Dungeness—large, meaty, wonderfully sweet, and a treat one should not pass up, ever!

ABOVE: *Dungeness crab*

TOP RIGHT: *Maine Jonah crabs*

RIGHT: *blue crabs*

OPPOSITE: *Maine hard-shelled lobster*

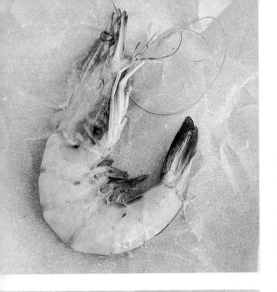

LEFT: *Gulf shrimp*

BELOW LEFT: *Caribbean pink shrimp*

BELOW: *mussels*

BELOW RIGHT: *littleneck clams*

BOTTOM RIGHT: *steamers*

OPPOSITE: *manila clams*

CLAMS

Clams, while found everywhere along America's coastlines, are perhaps most well known along the Atlantic—from soft-shelled or steamer clams, both in their shell and shucked for the famous fried clams, to hard-shelled, usually served in the half shell (cherrystones, littlenecks, topnecks, and so on). The larger quahog or chowder clam is the mainstay of New England. Regional clams of the Carolinas and northern Florida, known as sweetwaters, are wonderful. They have curved shells like the manila clams of the Northwest and are generally steamed open and served in a broth.

SHRIMP

Only two of the many types of shrimp in American waters are photographed here. America has tiny sweet Maine red shrimp; rock shrimp along the mid-Atlantic states (perfect for frying); Caribbean pinks off the coast of Florida down into the Caribbean; the most popular and readily available Gulf shrimp of gumbo fame; Baya and Monterey prawns have a clean, sweet taste; the Northwest has tiny cocktail shrimp, and, for me, the best of all, the Alaskan spot prawn—with the firm yet soft texture of lobster and an incredible sweetness.

1 *bluepoint oysters*
2 *Fanny Bay oyster*
3 *Olympia oysters*
4 *Quilicene oyster*
5 *pemaquids*
6 *Hood Canal oyster*
7 *Wellfleet oysters*

2

OYSTERS

Oysters have a very special place in American food and its history. Whether down-home style or elegantly prepared, each type of oyster has its own distinctive taste. In America, oysters are almost always named for the bay, inlet, or cove where they are harvested. Their flavor, size, and shape depend on the individual natural environment in which they grow. One can generalize by saying that Northeast oysters such as bluepoints, Wellfleets, Cotuits, and so on have a slightly salty, ocean flavor—very clean and refreshing. Oysters of the Northwest seem "fatter," with a slightly metallic, coppery aftertaste. The tiny Olympia oyster is the only true native of the West Coast; while never growing much more than an inch in size, it is a true native treat. The oysters of the Gulf are similar in size to bluepoints, but flatter and a little more plump. Gulf oysters have a grassy, freshwater flavor.

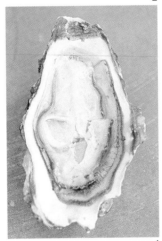

3

4

5

6

7

RIGHT: *Peconic Bay scallops on seaweed*
BELOW: *Taylor Bay scallops*

ABOVE: *Salad of Grilled Cèpes, Asparagus, and Sweet Peas*
LEFT: *An American Place Pepper Bread*
OPPOSITE: *Grilled Veal Chop and Ladies' Cabbage*

LEFT: *Cranberry-Glazed Roast Breast of Chicken with Autumn Squash*

BELOW LEFT: *Charred Rib-eye Steak and Midwest Smashed New Potatoes*

OPPOSITE: *Hudson Valley Camembert Crisp with Apple-Pear Conserve and Olive Oil Vinaigrette*

Blackberry and Apple Crisp with Crumb Topping
OPPOSITE: *Prior to baking* BELOW: *The baked crisp*

RIGHT: *Spiced Ginger Ice Cream and Sugar Cookies*
BELOW: *Old-Fashioned Strawberry Shortcake*

From America's Shores

THE AMERICAN WATERS have been blessed with an abundance of fish and seafood—from Baja to Alaska, from Appalachicola to Wellfleet, from sea to shining sea, not to mention the inland waters—the rivers, lakes, and streams. While there has always been incredible diversity and richness, now there's an availability to match. Fish markets, like farmers' markets, are prospering, boasting an impressive array of sparkling-fresh, high-quality fish.

With fish, perhaps more than anything else, the fresher the ingredients, the better the results. Because of today's incredibly efficient methods of cross-country transportation, now it's easier than ever to get a fish that's fresh when you buy it, no matter where it was caught.

Summer at the Shore

IF THERE IS ANYTHING better than summer, it is summer at the shore, where the sun is brighter, the breeze is cooler, the sky is bluer, and the seafood is abundant and sparkling fresh. From my memory of childhood trips to Maine or August weekends clamming on Long Island, summer to me is clam shacks, fishing wharves, buckets of steamers, lobster rolls.

If your memory needs a little jarring, all you need to do is try crisp and golden Fried Ipswich Clams, Fried Oysters, or old-fashioned Soft Belly Broils on Toast. They're all classic American shore favorites, in versions that celebrate the ingredients and enhance their fresh, irresistible taste.

The fried fish recipes in this chapter should remind you that frying, done properly, is a perfect way to capture and seal in flavor—not a greasy fast-food technique for disguising a nondescript fillet of fish. And if frying needs to be brought back to its rightful stature, I think cocktail sauce deserves the same consideration. People all over the country have come to believe that cocktail sauce is simply catsup combined with chili sauce. My recipe is, I think, a great deal more complex and more interesting: It's a balanced combination of catsup and horseradish with the added zing of lemon and hot pepper sauce.

After you enjoy some old favorites, I hope you'll try some destined-to-become-new favorites, such as Steamed Mussels with Orange and Fresh Basil, wonderful for company. Potato Clam Salad is a perfect choice for an afternoon picnic. And if you want a classic with just a slight twist, try serving the silken Tomato Tartar Sauce instead of regular tartar sauce with platters of fried clams and oysters. Look for the freshest clams, mussels, and oysters.

NEW ENGLAND COD CAKES
TARTAR SAUCE

■■

SERVES 4
(MAKES 12 CAKES)

3 all-purpose potatoes

2 cups flaked cooked cod (about 1 pound cod fillet)

¼ cup heavy cream

4 tablespoons unsalted butter

½ teaspoon ground ginger

1 large egg, lightly beaten

2 large egg yolks, lightly beaten

Salt and freshly ground black pepper

Flour for dusting

Tartar Sauce (recipe follows)

1 head Boston or Bibb lettuce, washed and dried

THIS A VERY SIMPLE, old-fashioned dish. I have added ginger to make it even more redolent of New England, where they have traditionally used a lot of ginger in their cooking.

In a large saucepan of lightly salted boiling water, cook the potatoes for about 20 minutes, until fork tender. Drain and cool. Peel and grate the potatoes; you should have enough to make 2 cups.

Combine the cod and potatoes in a bowl.

Combine the cream, 2 tablespoons of the butter, and the ginger in a small saucepan and bring to a boil over high heat. Pour the hot cream over the fish and potatoes, add the egg and egg yolks, and season with 1 teaspoon salt and a pinch of pepper. Stir until well mixed.

Using the palms of your hands, for each cake, form scant quarter-cups of the fish and potato mixture into balls. Lay on a baking sheet lined with waxed paper, and refrigerate at least 1½ hours, until firm.

Heat the remaining 2 tablespoons butter in a skillet over medium heat until it begins to foam. Lightly dust the chilled cod cakes with flour. Cook a few at a time for 2 to 3 minutes to a side, or until browned. Drain on paper towels, and sprinkle with salt and pepper. Serve arranged on the lettuce leaves, and pass the tartar sauce on the side.

———

TARTAR SAUCE

MAKES ABOUT 1¼ CUPS

1 cup mayonnaise, preferably homemade

1 tablespoon minced onion

1 tablespoon chopped capers

1 tablespoon chopped dill pickle

2 tablespoons chopped hard-cooked egg

2 tablespoons chopped flat-leaf parsley

1 tablespoon chopped fresh tarragon or dill

1 teaspoon fresh lemon juice

Dash of Tabasco

Salt and freshly ground black pepper, if necessary

Combine all the ingredients except the Tabasco and salt and pepper in a bowl and stir until well blended. Season to taste with Tabasco and with salt and pepper. Refrigerate for at least 1 hour before serving.

SOFT BELLY BROILS ON TOAST

SERVES 4

½ cup milk

2 large eggs

Pinch of cayenne pepper

2 cups soda cracker crumbs or cracker meal

Salt and freshly ground black pepper

½ cup unsalted butter, melted and kept warm

24 freshly shucked soft-shell clams (steamers)

4 slices good-quality white or whole wheat bread

1 lemon, halved

2 tablespoons chopped fresh herbs, such as chervil, tarragon, basil, or oregano

I AM NOT OLD ENOUGH to have had this dish when it was in its "heyday" at the turn of the century, but I know that the classic version needs no tinkering with. The only change I've made is to add fresh herbs to the clams. Serve the clams on good-quality bread—peasant bread, whole wheat, or any sort of leavened baguette. Grilling the bread adds another dimension to the recipe, but toasted bread is fine.

Preheat the broiler.

Put the milk, eggs, and cayenne in a small bowl and whisk together. Put the cracker crumbs in a second bowl and season with salt and pepper. Put the melted butter in another bowl.

Remove the tails (diggers) from the clams so that only the bellies are left. Dip the clam bellies, a few at a time, in the egg mixture and roll them in the cracker crumbs until evenly coated. Then dip in the melted butter, one at a time, and put on a baking sheet. Broil the clams 5 to 6 inches from the heat for 3 to 4 minutes.

While the clams are under the broiler, toast or grill the bread. Put 1 slice on each serving plate.

Squeeze the lemon over the cooked clams, being careful not to include any lemon seeds. Sprinkle the clams with the herbs. Use a thin spatula to loosen any clams that have stuck to the baking sheet and spoon the clams and juices over the toast. Serve at once.

NOTE: To serve as an hors d'oeuvre, place the clams on small rounds of toast.

RHODE ISLAND CLAM FRITTERS
CREAMY COCKTAIL SAUCE

■■

SERVES 4

1 cup water

1 cup clam juice

6 tablespoons unsalted butter,
    cut into pieces

1/2 cup all-purpose flour

1 cup stone-ground cornmeal

1 cup chopped quahog clams
    (about 6 clams)

2 tablespoons minced onion

1/4 teaspoon minced garlic

Salt and freshly ground black pepper

Few drops of Tabasco

2 tablespoons chopped flat-leaf parsley

3 large eggs

Peanut oil for deep-frying

Lemon wedges for serving

Creamy Cocktail Sauce (recipe follows)

THESE FRITTERS ARE ACTUALLY two dishes in one, as I combined the idea of johnny cakes and traditional clam fritters. First cook cornmeal with a little clam broth and stir in clams to make a batter, then fry the mixture. These taste especially good with a creamy cocktail sauce, made by adding sour cream to classic cocktail sauce. I don't know where the idea came from that cocktail sauce is a mixture of catsup and chili sauce: Real cocktail sauce is a balanced combination of catsup, grated fresh horseradish, and lemon juice, seasoned with salt, freshly ground black pepper, and hot pepper sauce.

Combine the water, clam juice, and butter in a medium saucepan and bring to a boil over high heat.

Combine the flour and cornmeal and slowly whisk into the clam juice mixture. Lower the heat to medium and cook, stirring, for 2 to 3 minutes, until the mixture is smooth and thick. Add the clams, onion, and garlic, and cook for 1 minute. Season with salt and pepper and the Tabasco and stir in the parsley. Remove the pan from the heat and stir in the eggs one at a time, mixing well after each addition.

In a deep-fat fryer or a deep heavy saucepan heat the oil to 350°F. Using a large soup spoon, carefully drop spoonfuls of batter into the oil, without crowding, and fry for about 1 1/2 to 2 minutes on each side, until golden and puffed. Gently lift the fritters from the oil with a slotted spoon and drain on paper towels. Sprinkle lightly with salt and keep warm in a 200°F oven.

Serve the fritters in a large breadbasket lined with a cloth napkin, with lemon wedges and the cocktail sauce on the side.

CREAMY COCKTAIL SAUCE

MAKES ABOUT 1 CUP

¾ cup catsup

⅓ cup fresh lemon juice (about 2 lemons)

2 tablespoons freshly grated horseradish

¼ cup sour cream

Salt and freshly ground black pepper

Dash of Tabasco

To make classic cocktail sauce, omit the sour cream.

In a bowl, stir together the catsup, lemon juice, and horseradish. Whisk in the sour cream and season with salt and pepper and Tabasco. Refrigerate for at least 2 to 3 hours before serving. The sauce keeps in the refrigerator for 2 to 3 days.

POTATO CLAM SALAD

SERVES 4

¾ pound red new potatoes, scrubbed but not peeled

16 littleneck clams, shucked and liquor reserved

¼ cup olive oil

1 small red onion, minced

½ teaspoon minced garlic

2 tablespoons white wine vinegar

¼ teaspoon Tabasco

½ cup coarsely chopped flat-leaf parsley

Salt and freshly ground black pepper

1 head Boston or Bibb lettuce, washed and dried

2 ripe tomatoes, sliced

AS IF WE NEED a reminder of how magical summer can be, this salad conjures it all up instantly. Originally, I made this exclusively with razor clams because I like their flavor so much. Now I use a variety of clams because razor clams are becoming hard to get. I make this rather as I would a clam sauce for linguine, but I mix it with new potatoes as a warm salad.

Cook the potatoes in boiling salted water for 8 to 10 minutes, until cooked through but still firm. Drain and let cool to room temperature.

Cut potatoes in half and then into thick slices; put in a bowl.

Cut the clams in half and set aside in a small bowl with their liquor.

Heat the olive oil in a sauté pan over medium heat. Add the onions and garlic and cook for 2 minutes, or until the onions are translucent but not browned. Add the clams and clam liquor, bring to a simmer, and cook for 1 minute. Remove from the heat and stir in the vinegar and Tabasco.

Pour the clam dressing over the sliced potatoes. Add the parsley and season with salt and pepper. Toss to coat the potatoes.

Arrange the lettuce leaves and tomatoes on individual serving plates, spoon the potato salad onto the lettuce, and serve.

FRIED IPSWICH CLAMS
TOMATO TARTAR SAUCE

SERVES 4

Peanut oil for deep-frying

1½ cups half-and-half

Dash of Tabasco

1 tablespoon freshly ground black pepper

Salt

1 quart small Ipswich or other frying
    clams, shucked (about 1½ cups)

2 cups all-purpose flour

1 cup stone-ground cornmeal

1 teaspoon cayenne pepper

Tomato Tartar Sauce (recipe follows)

THINK BACK TO THE DAYS when you could stop at little clam shacks along an ocean road and buy really great clams and oysters, fried or on the half-shell, or creamy chowder. Eating those fried clams is among my fondest memories. But with the advent of fried clam strips instead of clam bellies, the general quality of fried clams became horrible.

For a long time, fine restaurants disassociated themselves from fried foods because the public's perception was that if it was fried, it was cheap. It's really quite the contrary. Fried foods done properly are wonderful; the problem is that many places use cheap oil in the fryer, so everything tastes the same. I use a really good peanut oil that is so light it does not cover up any of the flavor of the clams. It's also important to use fresh oil each time you fry. Treat fried foods as a gourmet item, cooking only the best, most unadulterated products, and you will end up with great food.

In a deep-fat fryer or a deep heavy saucepan, heat the oil to 350°F.

Meanwhile, in a large bowl, combine the half-and-half, Tabasco, pepper, and 1 teaspoon salt. Add the clams and let them soak for 1 minute.

Combine the flour, cornmeal, 1 tablespoon salt, and the cayenne in a shallow pan. Remove the clams from the soaking liquid with a slotted spoon and toss them in the cornmeal mixture until evenly coated.

Fry the clams in small batches for about 3 minutes, until crisp and golden. Drain on paper towels, and sprinkle lightly with salt. Serve with the tartar sauce.

TOMATO TARTAR SAUCE

MAKES ABOUT 1½ CUPS

⅔ cup tomato paste

⅔ cup dry white wine

1 teaspoon minced garlic

1¼ cups mayonnaise, preferably
   homemade

2 hard-cooked eggs, chopped

2 tablespoons India relish

1½ tablespoons chopped fresh tarragon

1 tablespoon minced onion

Dash of Tabasco

Salt and freshly ground black pepper

Combine the tomato paste, wine, and garlic in a noncorrosive saucepan and bring to a boil over medium heat. Cook for 6 to 8 minutes, until reduced by half. Transfer to a bowl and let cool.

Add the mayonnaise, eggs, relish, tarragon, onion, and Tabasco to the tomato paste mixture and blend well. Season with salt and pepper. Cover and refrigerate for at least 1 hour before serving. The sauce keeps, refrigerated, for up to 2 days.

DEVILED CRAB AND OYSTER FRITTERS

12 oysters, shucked, liquor and bottom
    shells reserved

1 recipe Deviled Crab Cakes mixture
    (page 65)

1½ cups milk

2 large eggs

2 cups fresh bread crumbs

Peanut oil for deep-frying

Salt

3 tablespoons chopped flat-leaf parsley

Lemon wedges for serving

Mustard Dressing (page 66) or Tartar
    Sauce (page 58)

I GOT THE IDEA for this unusual dish from an old Southern cookbook that devoted a whole chapter to the notion of frying oysters and clams directly in their shells. I decided to incorporate the deviled crabmeat mixture for my crab cakes as well, combining it with oysters and frying both in the bottom oyster shells. The oysters must be poached first, or they will not cook through. You can make these ahead of time, then drizzle them with melted butter and warm them up in the oven before serving. They won't be quite as delicious as they are right after frying, but they are still awfully good.

Place the oysters and oyster liquor in a small saucepan and cook over low heat for 2 to 3 minutes, just until the liquor comes to a simmer and the edges of the oysters begin to curl. Immediately remove the oysters with a slotted spoon and place on paper towels to drain and cool. Strain and reserve the cooking liquid.

Wipe out the insides of the reserved oyster shells. Put about 1½ tablespoons of the deviled crab mixture into each shell and press down, making sure the shell is evenly coated. Put a cooled oyster in each shell and top each one with another 1½ tablespoons of the crab mixture, pressing it around the oyster so that it encases the oyster completely.

Beat the milk and egg together in a shallow bowl. Put the bread crumbs in another shallow bowl. Dip the filled shells in the egg mixture, one at a time, and carefully roll them in the cracker crumbs until evenly coated. Set them on a waxed paper–lined baking sheet.

In a deep-fat fryer or a deep heavy saucepan, heat the oil to 350°F.

Fry the oysters in batches for 2 to 3 minutes, until golden brown. Remove from the oil with a slotted spoon and drain on paper towels. Sprinkle with salt and the chopped parsley. Serve with lemon wedges and mustard dressing or tartar sauce.

NOTE: You can bake the oysters in a 500°F oven rather than fry them. After breading the oysters, drizzle with melted butter and arrange on a baking sheet. Bake in the center of the oven for 6 to 8 minutes, until golden brown and crisp.

DEVILED CRAB CAKES

MUSTARD DRESSING

■■

SERVES 4
AS AN APPETIZER

Crab Cakes

2 teaspoons unsalted butter

2 tablespoons mixed finely chopped red
    and green bell pepper

1½ teaspoons finely chopped onion

⅛ teaspoon minced garlic

2 tablespoons all-purpose flour

⅓ cup heavy cream

1 tablespoon spicy brown mustard

1 teaspoon dry mustard

1 tablespoon chopped fresh herbs, such as
    chervil, tarragon, basil, or oregano

¼ teaspoon cayenne pepper

Dash of Tabasco

1 large egg yolk

1½ cups fresh crabmeat, picked over for
    shells and cartilage

1 teaspoon fresh lemon juice

¼ cup fresh bread crumbs

Salt and freshly ground black pepper

1 cup milk

1 large egg

1 cup cracker crumbs or bread crumbs

Peanut oil for deep-frying

Mustard Dressing (recipe follows)

THE BEST OF DEVILED CRABS and the best of classic crab cakes meet in this felicitous combination. This is another dish that begs for really good ingredients. You have to start with fresh crabmeat and handle the cakes very carefully as they are not bound together with a lot of bread crumbs. They must be cold when fried so the cream and butter have solidified and hold them together. If you are used to crab cakes made with two cups of bread crumbs and a cup of frozen crabmeat, you are in for a delicious surprise.

To make the crab cakes, melt the butter in a large heavy skillet over medium heat. Add the peppers, onion, and garlic and cook, stirring, for 2 to 3 minutes. Stir in the flour and cook for 2 to 3 minutes, stirring constantly to make sure the flour does not burn. Slowly stir in the cream until the mixture is smooth, and cook for 2 to 3 minutes, stirring until thickened. Remove the pan from the heat.

Add both mustards, the herbs, cayenne, Tabasco, and egg yolk and mix well. Add the crabmeat, lemon juice, and bread crumbs and stir until mixed. Season with salt and pepper.

Transfer the mixture to a bowl and cover with lightly buttered waxed paper. Let cool to room temperature, then refrigerate for 3 to 4 hours, until completely chilled.

Using your hands, form the crab mixture into 4 large or 8 small oval cakes.

Beat the milk and egg together in a shallow bowl. Put the cracker or bread crumbs in another shallow bowl. Dip each crab cake into the egg wash and then roll in the crumbs until evenly coated. Set on a waxed paper–lined baking sheet.

In a deep-fat fryer or a deep heavy saucepan heat the oil to 350°F.

Fry the crab cakes, a few at a time, for 2 minutes on each side, or until golden brown. Transfer to paper towels and sprinkle lightly with salt. Serve with the mustard dressing.

continued

MUSTARD DRESSING

MAKES ABOUT 1 1/4 CUPS

1/2 cup mayonnaise, preferably homemade

1/4 cup sour cream

1/4 cup spicy brown mustard

2 tablespoons catsup

1 1/2 teaspoons white wine vinegar

Dash of Tabasco

1 tablespoon pickle relish

1 hard-cooked egg, grated

2 tablespoons chopped fresh herbs, such as chervil, tarragon, basil, or oregano

Combine the mayonnaise, sour cream, mustard, catsup, vinegar, and Tabasco in a bowl. Whisk well to blend. Stir in the relish, egg, and herbs. Cover and refrigerate for at least 1 hour before serving. The dressing will keep, refrigerated, for up to 4 days.

LOBSTER AND RICE FRITTERS

■■■■■■■■■■■■■■■■■■■■■■■■■■■■■■■■■■■■■

SERVES 4
(MAKES 12 FRITTERS)

1½ cups Fish Stock (page 34) or Chicken Stock (page 33) or canned chicken broth

¾ cup short-grain white rice

1 tablespoon unsalted butter

¼ cup diced white mushrooms

1 tablespoon minced onion

¼ teaspoon minced garlic

2 tablespoons all-purpose flour

½ cup plus 2 tablespoons heavy cream

6 ounces cooked lobster meat, diced

1 tablespoon chopped fresh tarragon

2 tablespoons chopped flat-leaf parsley

2 tablespoons fresh bread crumbs

Salt and freshly ground black pepper

Breading

1 cup all-purpose flour

1 tablespoon salt

1 teaspoon freshly ground black pepper

1 large egg

½ cup milk

2 cups fresh bread crumbs

Peanut oil for deep-frying

Salt and freshly ground black pepper

GROWING UP IN an Italian household, I ate a lot of rice balls and rice cakes. These are a take-off on my childhood favorites. Short-grain rice that's cooked until it's nice and sticky, mixed with mushrooms and lobster, garlic, and cream, shaped into ovals, and deep-fried until golden: That's all there is to it—and they're delicious.

Bring the stock to a boil in a medium saucepan. Add the rice, stir once, reduce the heat to low, and cook, covered, for 25 to 30 minutes until the liquid is absorbed and the rice is tender. Remove from the heat and set aside.

Melt the butter in a large skillet over medium-low heat. Add the mushrooms, onion, and garlic and cook, stirring, for 2 to 3 minutes. Stir in the flour, reduce the heat to low, and cook, stirring, for 2 to 3 minutes. Stir in the cream and cook, stirring, for 2 to 3 minutes longer.

Add the lobster, rice, tarragon, parsley, and bread crumbs. Stir until well combined and season with salt and pepper. Scrape the lobster mixture into a shallow dish and cover with parchment paper. Cool to room temperature, then refrigerate for 2 to 3 hours, until completely cold.

Shape the lobster mixture between the palms of your hands into 12 ovals.

To make the breading, put the flour, salt, and pepper in a shallow bowl and stir with a wire whisk to combine. Put the egg and milk in another shallow bowl and whisk lightly. Put the bread crumbs in a third shallow bowl.

Roll each fritter in the flour mixture, dip in the egg wash, and then roll in the bread crumbs. Lay the fritters on a waxed paper–lined baking pan and refrigerate until ready to fry.

In a deep-fryer or a large deep saucepan, heat the oil to 350°F.

Fry the fritters, 2 or 3 at a time, for 2 to 3 minutes on each side, until golden brown. Drain on paper towels. Sprinkle with salt and pepper and serve.

STEAMED MUSSELS WITH ORANGE AND FRESH BASIL

■■

SERVES 4

2 leeks, white parts only

4 dozen mussels, well scrubbed and debearded

1 cup dry white wine

1 cup dry white vermouth

1 cup Chicken Stock (page 33) or canned broth

2 teaspoons minced garlic

1 bay leaf

1 cup heavy cream

Zest of 1 orange, removed in long strips with a vegetable peeler or sharp knife, blanched in boiling water for 1 minute, and finely diced

2 tablespoons finely chopped fresh basil

1 tablespoon finely chopped flat-leaf parsley

GROWING UP ON LONG ISLAND, I was accustomed to cooking and eating mussels. But when I tried them in a creamy orange zest and basil broth, I was floored. It's an incredible combination, with a refreshing, delicious flavor that is the perfect counterpoint for mussels.

Wash the leeks thoroughly, making sure all the grit is removed. Slice one of the leeks and finely dice the other.

Combine the mussels, white wine, vermouth, stock, garlic, the sliced leek, and the bay leaf in a large saucepan, cover, and bring to a boil over high heat. Lower the heat and simmer for 4 to 5 minutes, just until the mussels open. Remove the mussels with a slotted spoon, discarding any that have not opened, and put them in a deep bowl. Cover with a damp cloth to keep warm.

Increase the heat under the saucepan to high and boil until the liquid is reduced by half. Add the cream, return to a boil, and simmer for 4 to 5 minutes, until thickened. Strain through a fine sieve or cheesecloth into another saucepan.

Add the orange zest, the diced leek, the basil, and parsley to the cream mixture. Bring to a simmer and cook for 1 to 2 minutes. Remove from the heat.

Meanwhile, remove the top shells from the mussels and discard. Divide the mussels on their half shells among four warm soup plates.

Spoon the hot creamy broth over the mussels and serve immediately.

FRIED OYSTERS

BACON–SOUR CREAM DRESSING

SERVES 4

1¼ cups all-purpose flour

1 cup milk

Pinch of cayenne pepper

Salt

24 oysters, shucked and bottom shells reserved

⅓ cup stone-ground cornmeal

Freshly ground black pepper

Peanut oil for deep-frying

Bacon-Sour Cream Dressing (recipe follows)

Salad greens or rock or coarse salt for lining the plates

Lemon wedges for serving

OYSTERS AND BACON have a natural affinity for each other. I like to fry the oysters and serve them with a hollandaise-type sauce made with a little bacon fat. I stir some chopped bacon into the sauce and smooth it out with sour cream—a perfect dipping sauce or dressing, also good on greens.

Put ¼ cup of flour in a small bowl. Gradually whisk in the milk to make a smooth paste. Season with cayenne and salt and add the oysters.

Combine the remaining 1 cup flour and cornmeal in a shallow pan. Season with salt and pepper.

One at a time, lift the oysters from the milk mixture and coat evenly with the cornmeal mixture. Set aside on a piece of waxed paper.

In a deep-fat fryer or deep heavy saucepan, heat the oil to 375°F.

Fry the oysters a few at a time, turning often, for 2 to 3 minutes, until golden brown. Drain on paper towels and sprinkle with salt.

Lay salad greens or arrange a bed of rock salt on each serving plate. Put 6 of the reserved oyster shells on each plate, stabilizing them on the greens or salt. Spoon 1 tablespoon of dressing into each shell and top with a fried oyster. Serve with lemon and pass remaining dressing.

BACON–SOUR CREAM DRESSING

2 tablespoons white wine vinegar

2 tablespoons water

2 teaspoons prepared mustard

3 large egg yolks

2 teaspoons warm bacon fat

1½ teaspoons sour cream

2 slices bacon, cooked and chopped (about ¼ cup)

1½ tablespoons finely chopped scallions

Dash of Tabasco

Freshly ground black pepper

Combine the vinegar, water, mustard, and egg yolks in the top of a double boiler over hot water. Whisk vigorously until thickened; the mixture should hold the whisk lines. Remove from the heat.

Whisk the bacon fat, sour cream, bacon, and scallions into the egg yolk mixture. Season with the Tabasco and pepper. Set over hot water to keep warm until ready to use.

OYSTER ROAST WITH PAN-ROAST BUTTER

■■■■■■■■■■■■■■■■■■■■■■■■■■■■■■■■■

SERVES 4

Rock or coarse salt for lining the pan

24 large oysters, scrubbed

4 tablespoons unsalted butter

2 tablespoons fresh lemon juice

½ teaspoon Worcestershire sauce

A few dashes of Tabasco

2 tablespoons chopped flat-leaf parsley

Salt and freshly ground black pepper

THE INSPIRATION FOR THIS DISH is the oyster roasts popular on Georgia's barrier islands, where the oysters grow in clusters. The people down there put a cluster directly into the fireplace and roast the oysters near the hot coals. When the oysters begin to open, they lift them from the fireplace with a shovel and set the cluster on a large platter. Everyone plucks oysters from the cluster, pops off the top shells, dips them in butter, and eats them. Even if you never eat them quite this way, it's a fantastic image to keep in mind when serving this recipe.

I suggest laying the oysters on a bed of rock salt to stabilize them during cooking and then placing the platter right on the table. I spoon a pan butter with lemon juice and Worcestershire sauce over the oysters just before serving.

Preheat the oven to 350°F.

Spread a ½- to ¾-inch-deep layer of rock or coarse salt on a baking sheet large enough to hold the oysters. Put the oysters, rounded side down, on the salt. Roast the oysters for 7 to 8 minutes, until they begin to open.

Meanwhile, melt the butter in a small saucepan over medium heat. Add the lemon juice, Worcestershire sauce, Tabasco, and parsley. Season with salt and pepper. Remove from the heat.

Take the pan of oysters from the oven and let cool for 1 minute. Then, with an oyster knife, pop off the top shells. Spoon the butter over the oysters and serve immediately, directly from the pan.

MARINATED SEAFOOD SALAD

■■

SERVES 4

½ pound salmon fillet, skinned

¼ pound striped bass fillet, skinned

8 shrimp, cooked, peeled, and deveined

8 fresh shucked oysters or clams

½ pound bay scallops, muscles removed

½ cup red bell pepper, cored, seeded, and finely diced

½ cup poblano pepper, seeded and finely diced

¼ cup minced red onions

½ cup fresh lime juice

2 tablespoons chile oil

2 tablespoons chopped fresh basil

2 tablespoons chopped cilantro (fresh coriander)

Dash of cayenne pepper

Freshly ground black pepper

½ pound baby green beans, blanched in boiling water until crisp-tender, drained, and chilled

Salt

1 head Boston or Bibb lettuce, washed and dried

FOR THIS ARTLESS and delicious recipe, I marinate the fish in lime juice and spices so that it "cooks" in the same manner as seviche. Get the freshest possible fish for the salad—it will taste fantastic. Serve it with asparagus and you have a wonderful appetizer or luncheon dish.

Using a sharp knife, trim away any dark parts from the salmon and bass fillets. Cut the fish into 1/2-inch cubes.

Put the shrimp, oysters, fish, and scallops in a bowl. Add the diced peppers, onions, lime juice, chile oil, basil, and cilantro. Season with the cayenne and pepper and toss gently. Cover tightly and refrigerate for 2 to 3 hours, tossing from time to time. (The fish should look "cooked" and have a firmer texture than when raw.)

Toss the baby green beans with the seafood salad. Season lightly with salt and pepper.

Place a few lettuce leaves on each serving plate, arrange the seafood salad on the lettuce leaves, and serve.

Shellfish

AMERICANS LOVE TO EAT shellfish, but I'm not sure we do it justice. Most home cooks are reluctant to prepare shellfish in anything but a few basic, tried-and-true ways. Boiled lobster, cold shrimp cocktail, and plain broiled scallops are dishes that come to mind. On the other hand, restaurants tend to offer elaborate presentations that seem to me unnecessarily complicated, with overly rich sauces, too many ingredients, and too little of the fresh, briny taste of the shellfish itself.

In this chapter, I've tried to demystify the art of cooking shellfish with a variety of recipes that, I hope, sound so straightforward, so inviting, and so delicious that you won't be able to resist them. Some of my favorites are unusual dishes that have evolved from early American recipes or been adapted from traditional favorites and translated into something modern.

If the name Baked Lobster Savannah conjures up a fussy, outdated American entrée that's more gooey cream sauce than lobster, you'll want to try the recipe here. It's a lovely and balanced amalgam of lightly browned lobster, velvety lobster cream, and mushrooms that, I think, restores this dish to its former glory. At the other end of the spectrum is an utterly simple and perfect summer dinner: Grilled Lobster with Herb Salad and a breezy lemon vinagrette.

With shellfish, it all comes down to being as imaginative as you want while still respecting the ingredients. Know how to combine the right flavors—like the venerable Tidewater paring of soft-shell crab and Smithfield ham. Know how to enhance the flavors you start with—like grilled sea scallops with orange, red onion, and cilantro or barbecued shrimp with a peanut sauce. And, of course, know that there are times when the scallops are so sparkling and succulent and the lobster so fresh and tender that your job will be to determine when to leave well enough alone.

SAUTÉED SOFT-SHELL CRABS WITH SPINACH AND SMITHFIELD HAM

■■

SERVES 4

4 tablespoons lightly salted butter

½ teaspoon minced garlic

4 cups fresh spinach leaves, washed and dried

Salt and freshly ground black pepper

1 cup milk

1 cup all-purpose flour

½ cup stone-ground cornmeal

½ teaspoon cayenne pepper

¼ cup vegetable oil

8 soft-shell crabs, trimmed and cleaned (see Note)

Juice of 2 lemons

2 tablespoons dry sherry

4 large thin slices aged Smithfield ham or prosciutto

2 tablespoons chopped fresh chives

FOR THIS DISH, I make a bed of spinach and garlic, lay a paper-thin piece of ham and then the crabs on it, and spoon a little sherry brown butter with chives over all. The combination of flavors is fabulous and as popular today in Maryland and Virginia as it always was.

Preheat the oven to 175°F (or the warm setting).

Heat 2 tablespoons of that butter in a large sauté pan over high heat until it foams and begins to brown. Add the garlic and spinach leaves and stir for 1 to 2 minutes, just until the spinach begins to wilt. Season with salt and pepper, and transfer to an ovenproof plate. Keep warm in the oven.

Put the milk in a shallow bowl. Combine the flour, cornmeal, 1 table-spoon salt, 1 teaspoon pepper, and the cayenne in another shallow bowl.

In a sauté pan large enough to hold 4 of the crabs, heat 2 table-spoons of the oil over high heat. One by one, dip the crabs into the milk, shake off the excess, and then dredge them in the seasoned flour. Pat off any excess flour.

Carefully put 4 of the crabs in the pan, shell side down, and cook for 2 to 3 minutes. Turn them over and cook for 2 minutes longer. Drain the crabs on paper towels, place on a baking sheet, and keep warm in the oven.

Drain off the oil and wipe out the pan. Add the remaining 2 table-spoons oil and heat it over high heat. Cook the remaining crabs, and drain on paper towels. Keep warm in the oven.

Drain off the oil and wipe out the sauté pan. Heat the remaining 2 tablespoons butter over high heat until it foams and begins to brown. Stir in the lemon juice and sherry and boil for 1 minute.

Arrange the spinach in the center of four plates, top with the ham, and lay 2 crabs on top of each slice of ham. Spoon the sauce over the crabs and sprinkle with the chives.

NOTE: Buy soft-shell crabs from a reputable fish merchant, who will trim and clean them for you.

GRILLED SOFT-SHELL CRABS WITH
SWEET POTATOES

■■■

SERVES 4

4 medium sweet potatoes, scrubbed
  but not peeled

8 scallions, trimmed

2 tablespoons olive oil

Salt and freshly ground black pepper

3 tablespoons wild beach plum jelly

1 tablespoon fresh lemon juice

½ teaspoon coarsely ground black pepper

8 soft-shell crabs, trimmed and cleaned
  (see Note, page 75)

2 tablespoons chopped fresh flat-leaf
  parsley

2 limes, cut into thick wedges

SOFT-SHELL CRABS ARE INDIGENOUS to the United States, although they are eaten in many other countries. In this recipe I have combined them with wild beach plums, another indigenous food found in the same general region. These little fruits grow on bushes along sand dunes up and down the East Coast. They are very acidic, with a noticeably tart flavor. I have thinned the wild beach plum jelly with lemon juice, another acidic ingredient, and added a little black pepper—when you brush this mixture on the crabs before grilling, it turns into a pungent sweet-and-sour glaze.

Be sure to keep the crabs high off the coals or keep the heat of the fire low enough so that the crabs do not burn; soft-shell crabs are really quite tender.

Preheat the oven to 350°F.

Bake the sweet potatoes for 25 to 30 minutes, until softened but still offering some resistance when pierced with a knife or fork. Let cool.

Slice the potatoes lengthwise into ³⁄₄-inch-thick slices. (This can be done an hour or so ahead of time. Cover and set aside at room temperature.)

Prepare a charcoal or gas grill or preheat the broiler.

Brush the potato slices and scallions with the olive oil and season with salt and pepper. Grill the scallions for 3 to 4 minutes, turning from time to time; grill the potatoes for 3 to 5 minutes to a side, or until tender. Transfer the vegetables to a plate, cover loosely with foil, and set aside to keep warm.

Combine the jelly, lemon juice, and coarsely ground pepper in a small bowl. Brush the crabs lightly with this mixture. Grill or broil the crabs for 3 to 4 minutes a side, making sure the coals are not too hot or that the crabs are far enough from the heat so that they color without burning. Baste the crabs several times with the jelly mixture as they cook.

Serve the crabs alongside the grilled vegetables, sprinkled with the parsley and garnished with lime wedges.

BLUE CRAB AND CORN PUDDING
SWEET RED PEPPER CREAM

■■■■■■■■■■■■■■■■■■■■■■■■■■■■■■■■■■■■■

SERVES 4

1½ cups corn kernels, fresh (from 4 to
    5 ears) or frozen

1 large egg

2 egg yolks

⅓ cup heavy cream

½ pound crabmeat, picked over for shells
    and cartilage

1 tablespoon all-purpose flour

1 teaspoon salt

½ teaspoon sugar

⅛ teaspoon cayenne pepper

1 tablespoon chopped flat-leaf parsley

Dash of Tabasco

Sweet Red Pepper Cream (recipe follows)

2 tablespoons chopped fresh chives

TWO AMERICAN FOODS I have always loved—crab and corn—in a winning combination. We make a lot of corn puddings at the restaurant; these crabmeat corn puddings are firm but very moist. They are served with a delicate red pepper cream. Blue crabs from the Chesapeake Bay are the best, but you can use any good crabmeat.

Preheat the oven to 350°F.

Butter four 6-ounce custard cups or soufflé dishes.

Combine the corn, egg, egg yolks, cream, and half the crabmeat in a food processor or blender and puree. Add the flour, salt, sugar, and cayenne and process for a few seconds more to blend.

Scrape the puree into a bowl. Stir in the remaining crabmeat, the parsley, and Tabasco.

Fill the prepared custard cups with the corn mixture and cover each one with foil. Set the cups in a baking pan and add enough hot water to come halfway up the sides of the cups. Bake in the center of the oven for 30 to 40 minutes. Remove the foil and bake for 5 minutes longer, until just set. Lift the cups from the pan of hot water.

To serve, run a thin-bladed knife around each pudding and unmold each one onto the center of a serving plate. Spoon the red pepper cream around the pudding, sprinkle with the chives, and serve.

SWEET RED PEPPER CREAM
MAKES ABOUT 1 CUP

1 tablespoon olive oil

1 red bell pepper, cored, seeded, and
    diced

1 red Anaheim pepper, seeded and diced

1 tablespoon minced garlic

¼ teaspoon cayenne pepper

Pinch of hot pepper flakes

1 tablespoon dry white wine or vermouth

1½ cups heavy cream

Salt and freshly ground black pepper

continued

Heat the olive oil in a medium sauté pan over medium heat until hot. Add the diced peppers and cook, stirring, for 2 to 3 minutes; do not allow to brown. Stir in the garlic, cayenne, and red pepper flakes, then add the wine and stir to deglaze the pan.

Stir in the cream and bring to a boil. Lower the heat and simmer for 2 to 3 minutes, until the cream has thickened and reduced by one third. Skim off any scum from the surface of the cream mixture, pour into a blender, and puree. Season with salt and pepper, cover, and keep warm until ready to use.

BAKED LOBSTER SAVANNAH

SERVES 4

Four 1¼-pound lobsters

1 tablespoon unsalted butter

1 red bell pepper, cored, seeded, and finely diced

½ green bell pepper, cored, seeded, and finely diced

8 to 10 mushroom caps, thinly sliced

¼ teaspoon minced garlic

Pinch of cayenne pepper

¼ cup plus 1 tablespoon bourbon

¼ cup Chicken Stock (page 33) or canned broth

1 tablespoon cornstarch

1 cup heavy cream

2 large egg yolks

2 tablespoons finely chopped fresh chives

Salt and freshly ground black pepper

½ cup fresh bread crumbs

I AM A BIG BELIEVER in maintaining our collective culinary memories. Lobster Savannah was a very popular dish—it evolved from the same school as Lobster Thermidor. In both dishes, the lobster meat was removed from the shell and mixed with other ingredients. It was then returned to the shell and the lobster was baked. Again, like Lobster Thermidor, Lobster Savannah was not prepared with great care, so its original luster faded and it greatly diminished in popularity. I think it's time to revive it! In this recipe, the lobster meat is mixed with a lobster cream, mushrooms, peppers, and garlic and then finished with egg yolks, which help it brown under the broiler. (Be sure to position the lobsters on the second rack so that they are not too near the heat.) I flavor the sauce with bourbon rather than the brandy called for in Thermidor.

Bring a large pot of lightly salted water to a boil. Add the lobsters, bring back to the boil, and cook for 5 to 6 minutes. Drain the lobsters and chill in ice water until cooled; drain.

Remove the lobster claws and small legs from the bodies. With a sharp knife, split each lobster in half lengthwise, being careful that the body and tail sections stay attached. Remove and discard the vein running down the center of each tail.

Carefully remove the tail meat from each half lobster and cut the meat from each one into 5 or 6 pieces. Set aside. Remove and discard the sacs from the heads. Remove and discard the pale green liver (tomalley). Remove any coral (dark green roe) and chop it. Set aside. Wipe out the shells with a cloth, and set aside.

Crack the lobster claws and remove the meat from them and from the knuckles. Cut the meat into large pieces.

Preheat the oven to 400°F.

Melt the butter in a large sauté pan over high heat. Add the bell peppers, mushrooms, garlic, and cayenne and cook, stirring, for 1 to 2 minutes. Add ¼ cup of the bourbon and shake the pan to mix. (The bourbon may ignite. Don't worry; let the flames die out.)

Stir in the lobster meat, and cook for 30 seconds.

Strain the contents of the pan in a sieve set over a bowl. Set the lobster mixture aside. Pour the strained liquid back into the pan and add the stock. Bring to a boil over high heat and cook for about 2 minutes, until reduced by half.

Stir the cornstarch into the cream until smooth, and add to the pan. Bring to a boil, lower the heat to a simmer, and cook for 3 to 4 minutes, until thickened. Remove from the heat.

Beat the egg yolks in a small bowl. Gradually whisk in ½ cup of the hot cream mixture to temper the eggs. Stir in the remaining 1 tablespoon bourbon.

Return the lobster mixture to the sauce in the pan, along with the chopped roe, if any. Cook over high heat for 30 seconds. Remove from the heat and stir in the tempered egg yolks and the chives. Season with salt and pepper.

Carefully spoon the lobster mixture into the cleaned half shells. Sprinkle with the bread crumbs. Using a spatula, transfer the filled shells to baking sheets.

Bake for 5 to 6 minutes. (Brown under a broiler if not golden brown from baking.) Arrange 2 half shells on each plate, and serve.

LOBSTER WITH BRAISED WHITE BEANS AND CHANTERELLES

■■

SERVES 4

Four 1-pound lobsters

2 strips bacon, diced

¼ cup minced onion

½ teaspoon minced garlic

4 ounces chanterelles, trimmed, cleaned, and sliced

1 tomato, peeled, seeded, and diced

3 cups cooked white beans

2 cups Shellfish Stock (see page 35)

Salt and freshly ground black pepper

2 tablespoons chopped fresh chives

THIS IS A REAL FALL DISH—the chanterelles give it a dark, earthy flavor. You could, of course, substitute other mushrooms, such as shiitakes or white cultivated. This is an interesting way of preparing white beans, which were the bean of colonial cooking. They used them in a stew with corn, onions, and potatoes, a forerunner of succotash. We cook the beans in a broth made with the lobster shells and serve the lobster meat out of the shell, so it's very easy to eat.

Bring a large pot of lightly salted water to a rapid boil. Add the lobsters, and simmer for 5 to 6 minutes. Take the lobsters from the pot and plunge them into a bowl of ice water to cool; drain.

When chilled, separate the lobster claws and tails from the bodies. Split the tails in half, and remove and discard the vein running down the center of each tail. Cut each tail crosswise in half. Remove the meat from the claws and knuckles. Cover and refrigerate the lobster meat until ready to use. (Use the shells and carcasses to make the shellfish broth if necessary.)

Cook the bacon in a large sauté pan over low heat just until it begins to color and render its fat. Add the onion, garlic, chanterelles, and tomatoes, and cook for 2 to 3 minutes. Add the beans and cook for 2 minutes longer. Add the stock, raise the heat, and bring to a simmer. Cook for 3 to 4 minutes.

Add the lobster meat, season with salt and pepper, and cook for 1 to 2 minutes, until the lobster meat is heated through. Ladle into shallow bowls or plates, and sprinkle with chives. Serve with warm or toasted peasant bread.

LOBSTER AND FENNEL IN CABBAGE LEAVES
BASIL OIL

■■■■■■■■■■■■■■■■■■■■■■■■■■■■■■■■■■■■■■■

SERVES 4
AS A MAIN COURSE

Two 1-pound lobsters

1 head savoy cabbage

1 bulb fennel

1 tablespoon olive oil

1 leek, trimmed, washed, and thinly sliced

Salt and freshly ground black pepper

Basil Oil (recipe follows)

2 ripe tomatoes, seeded and diced

THIS IS A DISH for late summertime, when cabbage is great and the fennel at farmstands is incredibly fresh. The coolness of the fennel is a nice balance to the cabbage and lobster.

Because it is summer, I do not fuss with a sauce but simply make an infusion of olive oil and fresh basil to drizzle over the cabbage leaves. It's wonderful. If you can get some fresh new potatoes from a farm, boil them and serve them alongside. This makes twelve pieces, and you can serve it as an appetizer, hors d'oeuvre, or a main course.

Cook the lobsters in a large pot of lightly salted boiling water for 5 to 6 minutes. Lift the lobsters from the cooking water and plunge into ice water. Keep the cooking water hot, and skim the surface of any foam.

Core the cabbage and carefully peel off 12 large leaves. Bring the cooking water back to a boil, and blanch the leaves for 1 to 2 minutes, until softened. Lift them from the boiling water and cool in ice water; drain on paper towels. Discard all but 1 cup of the cooking water.

Split the lobsters and remove the meat. Crack the claws and remove the meat from the claws and knuckles. Rinse the shells and freeze for another use, such as Shellfish Stock (page 35). Cut the lobster meat into 1/2-inch pieces.

Split the fennel bulb lengthwise, core it, and slice crosswise into 1/4-inch-thick slices. Thinly slice enough of the remaining cabbage to make 1/2 cup; reserve the remaining cabbage for another use.

Preheat the oven to 325°F.

Heat the olive oil in a large sauté pan over high heat. Add the fennel and cook for 2 to 3 minutes, until tender. Add the leek and sliced cabbage and cook for 2 minutes. Add the lobster meat, season with salt and pepper, and cook for 1 minute longer. Remove meat from the heat and let cool to room temperature.

Wipe the cabbage leaves dry and trim any tough stems. Spoon a little of the lobster mixture onto the center of each cabbage leaf, dividing it evenly among them. Fold the sides over the filling and, beginning at the stem end, roll the cabbage leaves into rolls. Lay the rolls, seam sides down, in a casserole large enough to hold them without crowding. Add the reserved 1 cup cooking water. Cover and bake for 6 to 7 minutes, until the rolls are heated through.

Lift the rolls from the casserole and drain on paper towels. Put 3 rolls on each plate and drizzle with basil oil. Sprinkle the diced tomatoes around the rolls and serve. (Store any leftover basil oil in the refrigerator.)

BASIL OIL

½ cup packed fresh basil leaves

1 cup olive oil

Salt and freshly ground black pepper

¼ teaspoon minced garlic

Chop the basil in a food processor. Add the oil and process for 1 minute. Pour into a bowl or jar and season with salt and pepper. Add the garlic. Let the oil stand for 3 to 4 hours, then strain through a fine sieve or cheesecloth.

GRILLED LOBSTER WITH HERB SALAD
LEMON VINAIGRETTE

SERVES 4

1 bunch small-leaved arugula

1 head Boston lettuce

½ cup flat-leaf parsley leaves

¼ cup cilantro (fresh coriander) leaves

¼ cup fresh thyme leaves

¼ cup fresh oregano leaves

½ cup small fresh basil leaves

Four cooked 1-pound lobsters
　(see page 81)

1 large sweet onion, cut into ½-inch-
　thick slices

2 tablespoons olive oil

Salt and freshly ground black pepper

Lemon Vinaigrette (recipe follows)

THIS IS THE SALAD to serve in the summer when you want something really elegant. Luckily, it's not all that difficult to prepare. The herb leaves should be picked off the stems, never chopped. The vinaigrette is made from a quick lemon reduction that has olive oil whisked into it. And the lobster does not take long on the grill, because it's basically already cooked—something you can do well ahead of time.

Wash and pat dry the arugula leaves and tear any large leaves into smaller pieces. Core the Boston lettuce, wash and pat dry the leaves, and tear the large leaves into smaller pieces.

Combine the lettuce leaves and herbs in a bowl, cover, and refrigerate until well chilled.

Prepare a charcoal or gas grill or preheat the broiler.

Split the lobsters and remove the meat. Crack the claws and remove the claw and knuckle meat. If using a grill, thread any smaller pieces, such as the knuckle meat, on skewers to prevent them from falling into the fire.

Brush the lobster meat and sliced onion with the olive oil and season with salt and pepper.

Grill or broil the onion slices for 2 to 3 minutes on each side. Separate them into rings, and keep warm.

Grill the lobster meat for 2 minutes on each side. Transfer to a plate and cover to keep warm.

Toss the herb salad with 2 tablespoons of the vinaigrette and a little pepper.

Arrange the salad in the center of the serving plates. Place the grilled lobster and onion rings on the salad, spoon a little more vinaigrette over them, and serve.

———

LEMON VINAIGRETTE

MAKES ABOUT ⅔ CUP

Zest of 2 lemons, removed in long strips with a knife or peeler and cut into julienne

Juice of 2 lemons

1 teaspoon prepared mustard

¼ teaspoon minced garlic

¼ cup plus 2 tablespoons olive oil

Salt and freshly ground black pepper

Bring 1 cup water to a boil in a small saucepan. Blanch the lemon zest for 30 seconds, drain, and rinse under cold water. Repeat the procedure to ensure that all the bitterness is removed from the zest.

Combine the lemon juice, mustard, and garlic in a small noncorrosive saucepan and bring to a boil. Remove from the heat and whisk in the olive oil. Add the lemon zest and season with salt and pepper. Set aside at room temperature until ready to use.

GRILLED SEA SCALLOPS WITH ORANGE, RED ONION, AND CILANTRO

■■■■■■■■■■■■■■■■■■■■■■■■■■■■■■■■■■■■■■■

SERVES 4

3 large oranges

1 red onion, halved and sliced

Salt and freshly ground black pepper

1½ pounds large sea scallops, tough side
   muscles removed

2 tablespoons olive oil

¼ cup small cilantro (fresh coriander)
   sprigs

4 leaves soft lettuce, such as Boston,
   washed and dried

GOOD NEWS FOR ALL of us who seem to spend our summer at the grill: This recipe is easy to do, light and refreshing, such a nice change of pace. The flavor combination of onions and oranges is an intriguing one, and seems perfect married with sea scallops. You could try another fish; if you do use scallops, they must be sea scallops, as bay scallops are too small to grill. Add lots of cilantro and soft lettuce leaves, toss it all together at the last minute, and you have an incredible dish.

Prepare a charcoal or gas grill or preheat the broiler.

With a sharp knife, cut the bottom and top off the oranges to expose the flesh. Stand each orange on end and slice downwards to remove the skin and bitter white pith. Working over a bowl, slice between the membranes to release the orange sections into the bowl. Add the onion and season with salt and pepper.

Brush the scallops with about 1 tablespoon of the oil and season with salt and pepper.

Grill the scallops for 2 to 3 minutes on each side, until just cooked through and opaque.

To serve, add the cilantro to the oranges and toss. Place a lettuce leaf on each plate and spoon the orange salad onto it. Arrange the grilled scallops around the salad and drizzle with the remaining olive oil.

SAUTÉED SHRIMP WITH ARTICHOKES AND MUSHROOMS

■■

SERVES 4

1 tablespoon cornstarch

1½ cups heavy cream

1½ to 2 pounds large shrimp (24 to 32 shrimp), peeled and deveined, shells reserved

Salt and freshly ground black pepper

1 tablespoon unsalted butter

½ teaspoon minced garlic

4 ounces wild mushrooms, such as morels, black chanterelles, lobster mushrooms, or shiitakes, trimmed, cleaned, and thinly sliced

2 cooked artichoke bottoms, thinly sliced (see page 146)

2 tablespoons dry white vermouth

2 tablespoons chopped fresh chives

WHEN I BECAME the chef at Regine's in New York City in the 1970s, this was one of the first dishes I put on the menu. The shrimp holds up well to the earthiness of the mushrooms and the flavor of the artichokes, and it's quick and easy to make. Although any variety of mushroom will do, I recommend wild mushrooms if possible, in particular, morels or black chanterelles.

In a medium saucepan, whisk the cornstarch into the heavy cream until smooth. Add the reserved shrimp shells and bring to a boil over medium heat. Lower the heat and simmer for 12 to 15 minutes, until the cream is reduced by one third. Skim the surface of the cream and season with salt and pepper. Strain and set aside.

Melt the butter in a large sauté pan over high heat. Add the shrimp and garlic and cook, stirring, for 1 to 2 minutes, until the shrimp turn pink. Add the mushrooms and artichoke bottoms and stir well. Add the vermouth and season with salt and pepper. Cover and cook for 2 minutes longer.

Lower the heat and, using tongs, transfer the shrimp to a bowl. Cover to keep warm. Raise the heat under the mushroom mixture and cook until most of the liquid has evaporated. Stir in the strained cream sauce, lower the heat, and simmer for 2 to 3 minutes. Remove from the heat.

Using a slotted spoon, transfer the artichokes and mushrooms to the center of a serving platter. Arrange the shrimp around the vegetables and spoon the sauce over the shrimp. Sprinkle with the chives and serve.

Sautéed Shrimp with Watercress
Grits Cakes

■■

SERVES 4

4 oval or rectangular Grits Cakes (recipe follows), about 3½ by 2½ inches

Salt and freshly ground black pepper

Flour for dusting

2 tablespoons lightly salted butter

4 bunches watercress

2 tablespoons olive oil

1½ pounds large shrimp (about 24 shrimp), peeled, deveined, and split in half lengthwise

½ teaspoon minced garlic

½ teaspoon minced fresh ginger

½ teaspoon pure chile powder

Pinch of cayenne pepper

½ teaspoon chopped fresh thyme

2 tablespoons dry white wine

½ cup Chicken Stock (page 33) or canned broth

4 tablespoons unsalted butter, at room temperature, cut into pieces

THIS HARMONIOUS DISH combines the crispness of lightly sautéed shrimp with the simple, homey taste and texture of fresh grits. When you make this dish, you can use the small stems, as most of the bitterness in watercress comes from the thicker stalks.

Preheat the oven to 175°F (or the warm setting).

Season the grits cakes with salt and pepper and dust lightly on both sides with flour.

In a large frying pan, heat the lightly salted butter over high heat until foaming and lightly browned. Carefully add the cakes and sauté for 2 minutes on each side, until golden brown. Drain the grits cakes on paper towels, then place on a baking sheet and keep warm in the oven until time to serve.

Remove the small, tender branches of watercress from the thick stalks and discard the stalks. Wash the watercress and pat dry with paper towels.

Heat the olive oil in a large sauté pan over high heat until almost smoking. Add the shrimp and sauté, gently stirring, for 2 minutes. Add the garlic, ginger, chile powder, cayenne, and thyme, stir well, and cook for 1 minute. Stir in the white wine and stock and lower the heat to medium-low. Add in the unsalted butter and stir until melted. Add the watercress and stir 1 more minute.

Place a grits cake in the center of each plate. Spoon the shrimp mixture over the cakes, and serve.

GRITS CAKES

A few of the recipes in the book call for soft corn pudding, or grits, which is similar to polenta. If you look at recipes for grits and polenta, you will find that they are essentially the same. It's interesting to note that the Italians didn't begin to make polenta until Columbus brought cornmeal back from America.

In this recipe, I stir some shredded Monterey Jack or white Cheddar into the grits and add chives and diced country ham—any nice smoky ham will do. The grits is poured into a lightly oiled pan and cooled; then it can be cut into whatever shape you want. Traditionally, grits cakes are cut into squares and sliced, brushed with butter, and grilled or sautéed. We cut them into ovals for Sautéed Shrimp with Watercress and Grits Cakes.

2½ cups milk

½ teaspoon minced garlic

½ cup plus 2 tablespoons stone-ground white grits cornmeal

½ cup finely diced country ham

½ cup shredded Monterey Jack or Cheddar cheese

2 tablespoons finely chopped fresh chives

Salt and freshly ground black pepper

Pinch of cayenne pepper

Combine the milk and garlic in a large saucepan and heat over high heat until scalding. Reduce to a simmer and, using a wooden spoon, slowly stir in the grits. Cook over low heat, stirring constantly, for 8 to 10 minutes, until the mixture is the consistency of mush. Remove from the heat and stir in the ham, cheese, and chives. Season with salt and pepper and the cayenne.

Depending on the shape you desire, pour the mixture into a lightly oiled 9-by-9-inch square pan or other shallow pan. Cover tightly with plastic wrap and cool to room temperature, then refrigerate for 2 to 3 hours, until firm.

Unmold the grits mixture and slice or cut into the desired shapes.

PEANUT BARBECUE SHRIMP

PEANUT SAUCE ▪ CHAYOTE AND RED PEPPER SALAD

▪▪▪▪▪▪▪▪▪▪▪▪▪▪▪▪▪▪▪▪▪▪▪▪▪▪▪▪▪▪▪▪▪▪▪▪▪▪▪

SERVES 4

1½ to 2 pounds large peeled and deveined shrimp (about 24 shrimp), shells reserved

1 cup Peanut Sauce (recipe follows) or American Spoon Foods Peanut Sauce

½ cup Chicken Stock (page 33) or canned broth

2 tablespoons unsalted butter, at room temperature

Chayote and Red Pepper Salad (recipe follows)

2 tablespoons chopped fresh chives

SHRIMP WITH PEANUT SAUCE has been one of the most popular dishes at the restaurant ever since I put it on the menu. I developed the combination originally for the Peanut Advisory Board, using shrimp and a chayote salad because, along with peanuts, I think of them as being Southern.

Thread 6 shrimp each on 4 skewers and set on a large plate. Brush the shrimp on both sides with ½ cup of the peanut sauce. Cover and refrigerate for 1 hour.

Prepare a charcoal or gas grill or preheat the broiler.

Combine the reserved shrimp shells and the stock in a small saucepan, bring to a simmer over high heat, and simmer for 2 to 3 minutes. Stir in the remaining ½ cup peanut sauce and return to a simmer. Remove the pan from the heat and stir in the butter until melted. Strain the sauce and keep it warm.

Grill or broil the skewered shrimp for 2 to 3 minutes on each side, basting from time to time with the sauce remaining on the plate. Slide the shrimp off the skewers onto a tray or plate.

Arrange the chayote salad in the center of four plates and spoon the warm sauce around the salad. Arrange 6 shrimp around each salad, sprinkle with the chives, and serve.

PEANUT SAUCE

MAKES 2 CUPS

2 tablespoons fresh lemon juice

1/4 cup molasses

2 tablespoons Worcestershire sauce

2 tablespoons vegetable oil

1 tablespoon plus 1 teaspoon
    cider vinegar

3/4 cup beer

1 teaspoon pure chile powder

1/2 teaspoon minced garlic

1/4 teaspoon dried oregano

1/4 teaspoon dried thyme

1/2 teaspoon dry mustard

1/2 teaspoon salt

1/8 teaspoon cayenne pepper

1 bay leaf

1/4 cup natural creamy peanut butter

Put all the ingredients in a medium saucepan and bring to a boil, stirring constantly. Lower the heat and simmer for 3 to 4 minutes. Remove the bay leaf and let cool.

Use the sauce immediately, or store in a tightly sealed container in the refrigerator for up to 3 weeks.

———

CHAYOTE AND RED PEPPER SALAD

MAKES ABOUT 2 CUPS

Chayotes are also called mirlitons or vegetable pears. Their cool spiciness makes them a great counterbalance to the peanut sauce in this dish.

2 chayotes (also called vegetable pears
    or mirlitons), peeled, cut in half, and
    pits removed

1 large red bell pepper, cored, seeded,
    and cut into julienne

1/2 teaspoon olive oil

Juice of 2 limes

Salt and freshly ground black pepper

Slice the chayotes as thin as possible and cut into julienne.

Combine the chayote and bell pepper in a bowl. Add the olive oil and lime juice and season with salt and pepper. Toss well and let sit for 15 to 20 minutes before serving.

SHRIMP ETOUFFÉE-STYLE
BAKED CORN BREAD PUDDING

SERVES 4

3 tablespoons vegetable oil or olive oil

1½ pounds large shrimp (about 24 shrimp), peeled and deveined, shells reserved

1 red bell pepper, cored, seeded, and finely chopped

1 green bell pepper, cored, seeded, and finely chopped

4 scallions, finely chopped

½ teaspoon minced garlic

½ teaspoon cayenne pepper

1 tablespoon pure chile powder

¼ teaspoon dry mustard

¼ teaspoon dried thyme

¼ teaspoon dried oregano

½ bay leaf, crushed

2 cups Shellfish Stock (page 35) or Chicken Stock (page 33) or canned broth

¼ cup all-purpose flour

Salt and freshly ground black pepper

1 tablespoon lightly salted butter

Baked Corn Bread Pudding (recipe follows)

2 tablespoons chopped flat-leaf parsley

OUT OF A SENSE OF FAIRNESS, I call this etouffée-style because I don't feel I have the right to change a classic dish such as an etouffée. I have great respect for authentic, classic recipes and for people who have spent their lives promoting and preserving their regional food.

Because I have never had great success with sauces that do not begin with a good stock, I do not start in the traditional way by making the roux and then adding the stock. I begin with the stock, skim off the fat as it comes to the top, and make a roux using the fat, then add this to the stock to thicken it and make a sauce.

Heat the oil in a large heavy saucepan over high heat. Add the shrimp shells, half the peppers, half the scallions, the garlic, and cayenne and cook, stirring, for 3 to 4 minutes. Add the chile powder, mustard, thyme, oregano, and bay leaf and cook, stirring, for 3 minutes.

Add the broth or stock and bring to a boil. Lower the heat and simmer for 10 to 12 minutes, until reduced by half. Skim off the fat as it rises to the surface and put it in a small saucepan.

Heat the fat over high heat. Slowly add the flour, stirring constantly until it is well incorporated. Lower the heat to medium and cook the roux, stirring constantly, until well browned; take care not to burn it.

Add the roux to the simmering sauce 2 tablespoons at a time and cook, stirring, for 2 to 3 minutes, until the sauce thickens. Let simmer for 5 to 6 minutes longer, then strain the sauce through a fine sieve. Season with salt and pepper and keep warm over very low heat.

Heat the butter in a large sauté pan over high heat until it begins to foam and turn light brown. Add the shrimp and the remaining peppers and scallions and cook, stirring, for 1 minute. Add the sauce, lower the heat, and let simmer for about 2 minutes. Remove from the heat.

Unmold the corn bread puddings into the centers of four plates and spoon the shrimp and sauce around them. Sprinkle with the parsley and serve.

BAKED CORN BREAD PUDDING

SERVES 4

This savory bread pudding goes very well with Southern cooking. It is basically stale corn bread crumbled and stirred into a custard along with sautéed corn and peppers, then baked. The flavor is a nice complement to the étouffée, as well as other dishes.

2 tablespoons unsalted butter, at room temperature

1/4 cup fresh or frozen corn kernels

1/2 red bell pepper, cored, seeded, and finely chopped

1 jalapeño pepper, seeded and finely chopped

1 scallion, thinly sliced

2 tablespoons chopped fresh marjoram or oregano

Salt and freshly ground black pepper

Pinch of cayenne pepper

1/2 cup heavy cream

1 egg

2 large egg yolks

1 1/2 cups crumbled stale corn bread, such as Yeast-Raised Corn Bread (page 231)

Using 1 tablespoon of the butter, grease four 4-ounce soufflé dishes or ramekins. Refrigerate to set the butter.

Preheat the oven to 350°F.

Melt the remaining 1 tablespoon butter in a medium sauté pan over medium heat. Add the corn, bell pepper, jalapeño, and scallion and sauté for 2 minutes. Remove from the heat and add the herbs. Season with salt and pepper and the cayenne.

Combine the heavy cream, egg, and egg yolks in a large bowl. Beat until well blended. Add the corn bread and the corn mixture and stir until well blended.

Spoon the mixture into the prepared dishes and cover each one with a piece of buttered foil. Set the dishes in a small baking pan and add hot water to come halfway up the sides of the dishes.

Bake in the center of the oven for 20 to 25 minutes. Remove the foil and bake for 5 minutes longer until just set. Remove the dishes from the pan. (If necessary, keep warm in the turned-off oven, leaving the door open, until ready to serve.)

To serve, gently run a thin-bladed knife around the corn puddings and unmold.

NOTE: You can also bake the pudding in a well-buttered 1-quart casserole. Cut the unmolded pudding into 4 pieces.

SAUTÉED CAROLINA ROCK SHRIMP IN BARBECUE SAUCE

CORN SALSA

SERVES 4

2 tablespoons peanut oil

1½ pounds cleaned rock shrimp or 1½ pounds other small shrimp, shelled and deveined

½ red onion, minced

2 red bell peppers, cored, seeded, and minced

1 Anaheim pepper, seeded and minced

1 jalapeño pepper, seeded and minced

1 teaspoon minced garlic

⅛ cup Worcestershire sauce

1 cup Barbecue Sauce (page 152)

Freshly ground black pepper

2 tablespoons unsalted butter

3 cups cooked rice

1 cup Corn Salsa (recipe follows)

¼ cup chopped flat-leaf parsley

I GOT THE IDEA for this dish from what is called a New Orleans barbecue. It has nothing to do with a grill but is rather a spicy shrimp dish made with barbecue sauce. I like Carolina rock shrimp, but you could use any type of shrimp or crayfish.

Carolina rock shrimp are found in waters off the southeastern coast of the United States. Because the shells are rock hard and difficult to remove, rock shrimp are usually fully shelled and cleaned. They are small with a dense, firm texture similar to lobster, but a taste like shrimp. (They cost about half as much as other shrimp, too.)

Heat the peanut oil in a large sauté pan over high heat until hot. Add the shrimp and toss, then add the onion, bell peppers, Anaheim pepper, jalapeño, and garlic and sauté for 2 to 3 minutes, stirring constantly. Add the Worcestershire sauce and cook another minute.

Stir in the barbecue sauce and season with pepper. Add the butter, lower the heat, and stir until the butter melts and the sauce is hot.

Place about ¾ cup cooked rice in the center of the dishes. Spoon the shrimp and sauce around and sprinkle generously with the corn salsa and parsley.

───

CORN SALSA

MAKES ABOUT 2 CUPS

1 cup fresh corn kernels (from 2 ears)

1½ teaspoons minced jalapeño pepper

¼ cup minced red bell pepper

¼ cup minced green bell pepper

Juice of 1 lime

2 to 3 tablespoons chopped cilantro (fresh coriander)

Freshly ground black pepper

In a large bowl, combine all the ingredients except the black pepper. Stir gently until well mixed. Season with pepper. Set aside at room temperature for at least 1 hour or up to 3 hours. The salsa will keep, covered, in the refrigerator for up to 2 days. Serve at room temperature.

Catch of the Day

I LOVE FISH. I love to catch fish, cook fish, eat fish. Most of all, I love being able to devise ways to dazzle everyone who grew up thinking that breaded halibut fillets and frozen fish sticks were how fish should be eaten. All it takes is a couple of bites of a dish like Southwest-Style Whitefish in Tortillas, topped with a spicy poblano cream sauce, or sizzling Charred Tuna.

Fish is light, healthful, varied, versatile, and willing to reward you with all sorts of miraculous tastes if you treat it right. And what a spectrum of cooking concepts and combinations is possible if you are both thoughtful and creative. What's the catch of the day? What are you in the mood for? There's an enormous range of possibilities, from the smoky assertiveness of Cedar-Planked Salmon to the nutty crunch of Panfried Lake Trout to the refreshing coolness of lime-marinated grilled mahimahi. Dishes that taste even better than they sound and recipes that are remarkably undaunting.

For me, part of the fun is discovering how to bring out the inherent flavor of a particular fish. The other part is figuring out how to enhance the flavor by adding ingredients to spice it up, cool it down, jazz it up, add texture, color, finesse—to make the whole greater than the sum of its parts.

Sometimes it's as simple as tweaking a familiar idea. My recipe for Warm Smoked Trout Salad makes that dish new again just by gently heating the trout to bring out its character. The Panfried Lake Trout, dipped in sour cream and buttermilk, then breaded with cornmeal, has all the elements of a traditional New Orleans dish, but with the contemporary jolt of a hollandaise sauce spiked with chile powder and cayenne. The Cedar-Planked Salmon with Old-Fashioned Egg Sauce marries a traditional New England fish sauce with a cooking technique originated by Pacific Northwest Indians.

Whatever you make, feel free to substitute one fresh fish for another as long as it has similar taste and texture characteristics. If you adore salmon and see an interesting recipe that calls for swordfish, it will work just as well made with salmon. No fresh salmon or swordfish that day? Use tuna instead. If you're grilling, make sure you choose a fish that's firm enough.

A note of reassurance: Fish is no mystery. There are no unfamiliar tricks you need to know or cooking techniques you have to learn. If you grew up not wanting to eat fish, let alone cook it, you will be delighted at just how easy it is to produce spectacular results.

GRILLED BASS WITH RADISHES AND ORANGE

■■■

SERVES 4

Four 6-ounce bass fillets, with skin

Salt and freshly ground black pepper

¼ cup olive oil

¼ cup chopped flat-leaf parsley

Grated zest of 1 orange

¼ cup fresh orange juice

Two 6-ounce packages radish sprouts
   (pepper cress)

8 radishes, trimmed and grated

Radish sprouts for garnish (optional)

SERVING A GRILLED BASS on a radish and orange salad enhances both the fish and the salad. A little oil drips from the fish into the salad, which tastes crisp and fresh against the fish. The salad is a holdover from salads popular in the 1950s and 1960s, when radishes were considered a little fancy. Nowadays you can buy radishes in farmers' markets, which means they are better tasting than they used to be, when all you could get were plastic bags full of red radishes that were hot without any real flavor. Always buy radishes with the greens attached; they'll be fresher and better. The pepper cress—daikon radish sprouts—extends the radish flavor.

Using a very sharp knife, lightly score the skin of each fillet. Season with salt and pepper and rub with about half of the olive oil. Lay the fish in a single layer in a glass or stainless steel pan.

Cut the sprouts so that the stems are about 1 inch long.

Combine the remaining olive oil, the parsley, orange zest, and juice in a small bowl and mix thoroughly. Add the sprouts and radishes and stir. Pour the marinade over the fish. Cover and refrigerate for no longer than 1 hour.

Prepare a charcoal or gas grill or preheat the broiler.

When the coals are medium-hot, lift the bass from the marinade and grill for 3 to 4 minutes on each side, until opaque. Serve garnished with more radish sprouts if desired.

ROAST BASS WITH OLIVE OIL AND LEMON

■■■■■■■■■■■■■■■■■■■■■■■■■■■■■■■■■■■■■■■

SERVES 4

½ cup Fish Stock (page 34) or Chicken Stock (page 33) or canned chicken broth

¼ cup fresh lemon juice

2 tablespoons chopped fresh oregano

½ teaspoon minced garlic

¼ cup plus 2 tablespoons olive oil

Salt and freshly ground black pepper

Four 6- to 8-ounce bass fillets, with skin

2 tablespoons chopped flat-leaf parsley

THIS RECIPE, which I never get tired of making, came about one day when we wanted to make an emulsified sauce using olive oil rather than butter. I realized if I used a really good olive oil, I would not need much oil, as the assertive flavor would come through.

Preheat the oven to 450°F.

Combine the stock, lemon juice, 1 tablespoon of the oregano, and the garlic in a small saucepan and bring to a boil. Cook for 2 to 3 minutes, until reduced to about 5 tablespoons.

Strain and pour the reduced liquid into a blender. With the motor running on medium speed, slowly add ¼ cup of the olive oil. Transfer the mixture to a saucepan and season with salt and pepper. Keep warm over low heat; do not let the sauce get hot.

Spread the 2 remaining tablespoons oil over the bottom of a heavy baking pan. Heat the pan in the oven for 4 to 5 minutes, until hot.

Season the bass fillets with salt and pepper and lay them skin side down in the hot pan. Roast for 5 to 6 minutes, until the skin is nicely browned. Turn the fillets and roast for 4 to 5 minutes longer.

Place the fillets on serving plates. Mix the remaining 1 tablespoon of oregano with the parsley and sprinkle the herbs over the fish. Serve with the warm lemon sauce spooned around the fish. (If the sauce has separated, return it to the blender and blend at high speed for about 30 seconds.)

SOUTHERN-FRIED CATFISH
SPICY TARTAR SAUCE ▪ CHARLESTON SLAW

SERVES 4

2 cups milk

2 ¼ cups all-purpose flour

1 teaspoon cayenne pepper

Salt and freshly ground black pepper

¾ cup stone-ground cornmeal

1½ pounds catfish fillets from small catfish, cut into eight 2- to 3-ounce pieces

Peanut oil for deep-frying

Spicy Tartar Sauce (recipe follows)

Charleston Slaw (recipe follows)

THIS RECIPE IS A REAL CELEBRATION of Southern cooking. When you buy catfish, look for nice, small, farm-raised fish. Small catfish, fried this way and served with Charleston Slaw, are fantastic. The slaw, which goes well with any fried fish, is a straightforward vegetable salad flavored with sesame seeds. The African heritage of the slaves was responsible for the popularity of sesame seeds (also called benne seeds) in Southern cooking, particularly in the area around Charleston, South Carolina.

Preheat the oven to 175° F (or the warm setting).

Combine the milk, ¾ cup of the flour, ½ teaspoon of the cayenne, 2 teaspoons salt, and 1 teaspoon pepper in a large shallow bowl and stir until smooth.

In another shallow bowl, combine the remaining 1½ cups flour, the cornmeal, and the remaining ½ teaspoon cayenne. Season with salt and pepper.

In a deep-fryer or a deep heavy saucepan, heat the oil to 350°F.

Piece by piece, dip the catfish into the milk mixture and then dredge in the seasoned flour, coating the fish evenly. Fry the fish, in batches, for 2 to 3 minutes to a side, until golden brown. Do not crowd the pan, and be sure to let the oil regain its temperature between batches. Drain the fish on paper towels, and keep warm in the oven.

Serve the fish with the tartar sauce and slaw.

continued

SPICY TARTAR SAUCE

MAKES ABOUT 1½ CUPS

1 cup mayonnaise, preferably homemade

1 teaspoon dry mustard

1 tablespoon minced onion or scallions

1 tablespoon finely chopped capers

2 tablespoons finely chopped dill pickle

¼ teaspoon cayenne pepper

1 teaspoon pure chile powder

2 tablespoons cider vinegar or wine vinegar

2 tablespoons chopped flat-leaf parsley

Combine all the ingredients in a bowl. Cover and refrigerate for at least 2 to 3 hours to give the flavors time to develop. The sauce can be refrigerated for up to 4 days.

———

CHARLESTON SLAW

MAKES ABOUT 4 CUPS

¼ head green cabbage, cored and thinly sliced (about 2 cups)

½ red onion, thinly sliced

½ green bell pepper, cored, seeded, and thinly sliced

½ red bell pepper, cored, seeded, and thinly sliced

1 Anaheim pepper, seeded and thinly sliced

1 cup snow peas, trimmed and thinly sliced

¼ cup Olive Oil Vinaigrette (page 51)

1 teaspoon sesame oil

2 tablespoons sesame seeds

Salt and freshly ground black pepper

In a large bowl, combine all the ingredients except the salt and pepper. Toss well. Season to taste with salt and pepper. Cover and let marinate for 15 to 20 minutes before serving.

ROAST COD WITH ROSEMARY OIL AND CRANBERRY BEANS

SERVES 4

1 cup olive oil

3 to 4 large sprigs fresh rosemary

Four 6- to 8-ounce cod fillet, 1½ to 2 inches thick, skinned

Salt and freshly ground black pepper

2 cups cooked cranberry beans (see Note)

½ red bell pepper, finely diced

2 ripe medium tomatoes, peeled, seeded, and diced

1 small white onion, finely diced

½ teaspoon minced garlic

2 ounces mushrooms, trimmed, cleaned, and diced (about ⅔ cup)

1 cup Fish Stock (page 34) or Chicken Stock (page 33) or canned chicken broth

NOTE: To cook beans, rinse under cold water. Put in a bowl and cover with cold water by 2 to 3 inches. Cover and soak at room temperature for 4 to 8 hours, or overnight. Change water 2 or 3 times if possible.

Drain beans, put in a heavy saucepan, and cover with cold water by 2 to 3 inches. Bring to a boil. Skim off any foam. Add whole peeled onion, carrot, and garlic cloves, and season with salt and pepper. Reduce heat and simmer, partially covered, for 1½ to 2 hours, until tender; add more water if necessary.

THIS KIND OF DISH reminds me that something healthy can also be quite delicious. A note on making this successfully: When you roast fish, you need to begin with a good thick piece so that it can stay in the oven long enough actually to roast. The cod for this dish ought to be a good inch and a half to two inches thick. Roasting the fish in a lightly oiled pan in a very hot oven makes both the top and bottom of the fish get nice and crusty. Then it's set over cooked cranberry beans and drizzled with rosemary oil.

Preheat the oven to 425°F.

Warm the oil in a small saucepan over very low heat. Add the rosemary sprigs and heat gently for 20 to 30 minutes, taking care that the oil does not get hot. Remove from the heat and let cool to room temperature. Remove the leaves from 1 sprig of rosemary and chop them fine. Discard the remaining rosemary.

Brush a roasting pan large enough to hold the cod in one layer with a little of the rosemary oil. Season the fish with salt and pepper and sprinkle with half the chopped rosemary leaves. Lay the fish in the pan and brush with a little rosemary oil. Roast for 10 to 12 minutes, until the cod is barely flaky to the touch.

Meanwhile, heat 2 tablespoons of the rosemary oil in a large sauté pan over medium heat. Add the cranberry beans, bell pepper, tomatoes, onion, garlic, and mushrooms and cook, stirring, for 2 to 3 minutes. Season with salt and pepper. Add the stock, bring to a simmer, and cook for 2 to 4 minutes. Stir in the remaining chopped rosemary.

Spoon the bean mixture onto serving plates and top with the cod. Drizzle about ½ teaspoon rosemary oil over each piece of fish and serve.

SPICY HONEY-GLAZED GROUPER WITH FIGS
FRESH CRANBERRY VINAIGRETTE

SERVES 4

8 to 12 fresh figs, preferably Black
   Mission

Salt and freshly ground black pepper

Fresh Cranberry Vinaigrette (recipe
   follows)

1 tablespoon olive oil

Four 6- to 8-ounce grouper fillets, skinned

2 tablespoons honey

1 teaspoon dry mustard

¼ teaspoon cayenne

½ tablespoon unsalted butter, at room
   temperature

2 tablespoons chopped flat-leaf parsley

ALTHOUGH I'D GRILLED duck breasts with a wildflower honey glaze, I'd never considered honey-glazing fish until I saw Mark Miller do it at my restaurant when he was on a book tour. Substitute any meaty fish, such as cod, rockfish, or salmon. The glaze is similar to the glazes used on hams—a little dried mustard bound with honey, cayenne, and butter.

Place the broiler tray under the broiler and preheat the broiler.

Cut the figs into halves or quarters, depending on their size. Season with a little salt and pepper, toss with 1 tablespoon of the vinaigrette, and set aside at room temperature.

Brush the olive oil on the preheated broiler tray. Season the grouper with additional salt and pepper and place the fish rounded side up on the tray. Combine the honey, mustard, cayenne, and butter in a small bowl and brush about half of this mixture on the fish. Broil 3 to 4 inches from the heat for 2 to 3 minutes. Brush the remaining honey mixture on the fish and broil for 2 to 3 minutes longer.

Add the figs to the broiler tray and continue to cook another minute to warm the figs.

Arrange the glazed grouper in the center of your plates and surround with the figs. Spoon 2 tablespoons of vinaigrette around each grouper, sprinkle with parsley, and serve.

———

FRESH CRANBERRY VINAIGRETTE
MAKES 2 CUPS

½ cup chopped fresh cranberries

¼ cup cranberry juice

2 tablespoons chopped shallots

1½ tablespoons chopped fresh
   rosemary

1½ teaspoons chopped flat-leaf
   parsley

2 teaspoons honey

¼ cup fresh lemon juice

¼ cup red wine vinegar

¼ cup olive oil

Salt and freshly ground black
   pepper

Combine all the ingredients and stir. Let stand 4 hours or overnight.

GRILLED HALIBUT WITH STEWED FRESH TOMATOES

■■■

SERVES 4

Four 6- to 8-ounce halibut fillets, skinned

Salt and freshly ground black pepper

¼ cup plus 1 tablespoon olive oil

¼ cup finely chopped red onion

½ teaspoon minced garlic

4 ripe large tomatoes, peeled, seeded, and chopped

¼ cup dry white wine

¼ cup chopped flat-leaf parsley

¼ cup chopped fresh basil

I DEVELOPED THIS RECIPE for the summertime, when nearly everyone has access to wonderful vine-ripened tomatoes. And it's always easy to find fresh halibut. Halibut used to be very popular in the United States, but it developed a bad reputation as being dry and tasteless. No doubt this came from mishandling, as often the fish was frozen, and if you freeze tender, flaky white fish, it dries out and loses flavor. Fresh halibut is coming back, thankfully, because it is one of the most delicious fish there is.

Prepare a charcoal or gas grill or preheat the broiler.

Season the fillets with salt and pepper and brush on both sides with about 2 tablespoons of the oil.

Heat the remaining oil in a large noncorrosive saucepan over medium heat. Add the onion and garlic and sauté for 1 minute; do not let the onion brown. Add the tomatoes and wine and simmer for 2 to 3 minutes. Add the parsley and basil and season with salt and pepper. Remove from the heat and cover to keep warm.

Grill or broil the halibut fillets for 3 to 4 minutes on each side, until just cooked through. Place on serving plates and spoon the sauce over the fillets.

GRILLED HALIBUT WITH SHRIMP AND FOREST MUSHROOM COMPOTE

■■

SERVES 4

1 tablespoon lightly salted butter

12 medium shrimp, peeled, deveined, and split in half lengthwise

1 ounce (about 1 cup) fresh wild mushrooms, such as cèpes, chanterelles, or shiitakes, trimmed, cleaned, and thickly sliced

¼ teaspoon minced garlic

2 tomatoes, peeled, seeded, and diced

Salt and freshly ground black pepper

2 tablespoons dry white wine

2 tablespoons chopped fresh herbs, such as tarragon, basil, chervil, or oregano

2 tablespoons unsalted butter

Four 4- to 6-ounce halibut fillets, skinned

2 tablespoons olive oil

THIS IS A SIMPLIFIED VERSION of a more elaborate recipe. Grilled halibut sits on a compote of shrimp and wild mushrooms for a nice, light dinner with lots of flavor.

Prepare a charcoal or gas grill or preheat the broiler.

Heat the lightly salted butter in a sauté pan over high heat until it foams and begins to turn brown. Add the shrimp, mushrooms, garlic, and tomatoes and sauté for 1 minute. Season with salt and pepper. Add the wine and cook for 2 to 3 minutes, until almost all the liquid has evaporated. Remove the pan from the heat and stir in the herbs and unsalted butter. Cover to keep warm.

Season the halibut fillet, with salt and pepper and brush on both sides with the olive oil.

Grill or broil the halibut for 3 to 4 minutes on each side, until just cooked through. Place a fillet in the center of each plate and spoon the shrimp and mushroom compote around it.

GRILLED MAHI-MAHI WITH
PINEAPPLE-CHILE BARBECUE SAUCE

SERVES 4

¼ cup chopped fresh pineapple or canned
    crushed pineapple

2 tablespoons minced jalapeño peppers

2 tablespoons brown sugar

1 cup Barbecue Sauce (page 152; see
    Note)

Four 6- to 7-ounce mahi-mahi fillets,
    skinned

2 large Walla-Walla onions or other sweet
    onions, such as Vidalia, Texas
    Sweet, or Maui

2 tablespoons olive oil

Salt and freshly ground black pepper

2 tablespoons peanut oil

2 tablespoons unsalted butter

2 tablespoons fresh lime juice

2 tablespoons chopped cilantro
    (fresh coriander)

NOTE: You can make this recipe
using 1 cup American Spoon
Foods Pineapple Chili Barbecue
Sauce; omit the pineapple,
jalapeños, and brown sugar.

IS THERE ANY OTHER FISH we cook with a name that's quite
so exotic? Mahi-mahi is dolphin fish (not the Flipper variety),
and I always associate it with Hawaii. It is similar to pompano,
but a little milder; it tastes rather like swordfish.

Pairing mahi-mahi with tropical ingredients always works
well. I happen to use Walla-Walla onions in this recipe; you
could substitute sweet Maui onions, but they are usually more
expensive. You could also use white-skinned sweet onions, but
yellow onions are a little too strong and acidic. The fish is marinated in a pineapple chile sauce, based on my barbecue sauce.

Combine pineapple, jalapeños, and brown sugar in a small noncorrosive
saucepan and cook over high heat, stirring, for 5 to 6 minutes, until the
mixture begins to caramelize. Add the barbecue sauce and cook for 1 to
2 minutes longer. Transfer the sauce to a blender or food processor and
puree. Let cool.

Place the mahi-mahi in a noncorrosive pan or dish and pour the
sauce over the fish. Cover and refrigerate for 2 to 3 hours.

Prepare a charcoal or gas grill or preheat the broiler.

Peel the onions and slice about ½ inch thick, keeping the rings
together. Brush the slices with the olive oil and season with salt and pepper.
Grill the onions for 2 to 3 minutes on each side, until cooked but still
slightly firm. Remove from the grill, cover, and keep warm.

Lift the mahi-mahi from the sauce and pat dry. Brush with the
peanut oil and season with salt and pepper. Grill the mahi-mahi for 3 to 4
minutes on each side, basting with the barbecue sauce from time to time.

Just before the fish is done, transfer the remaining sauce to a small
noncorrosive saucepan and bring to a simmer. Stir in the butter and lime
juice.

Spoon the sauce onto the serving plates and top with the grilled
fish. Break up the onion rings and top the fillets with the rings. Sprinkle
with the cilantro and serve at once.

GRILLED MAHI-MAHI WITH LIME AND AVOCADO

■■

SERVES 4

Juice of 3 limes (about ¼ cup)

2 tablespoons olive oil

½ teaspoon minced garlic

2 tablespoons chopped flat-leaf parsley

2 tablespoons chopped cilantro (fresh coriander)

1 tablespoon pure chile powder

1 teaspoon ground cumin

Four 6- to 7-ounce mahi-mahi fillets, skinned

2 ripe but firm avocados, preferably Hass

3 scallions, sliced

1 red bell pepper, cored, seeded, and finely chopped

½ jalapeño pepper, seeded, and finely chopped

2 plum tomatoes, seeded and diced

FOR THIS RECIPE the fish is marinated in a mixture of lime juice, olive oil, garlic, parsley, cilantro, chile powder, and cumin. The fish must not be left in the marinade longer than fifteen or twenty minutes, or the acid will "cook" it. Then half the marinade is used to baste the fish as it grills so that the flavors keep going, and the other half is combined with scallions, red peppers, nice ripe tomatoes, jalapeños, and avocados to make a sauce. This is light and refreshing and very flavorful, and it's not a lot of work.

Prepare a medium-hot fire in a charcoal or gas grill or preheat the broiler.

Combine the lime juice, olive oil, garlic, parsley, cilantro, chile powder, and cumin in a bowl and season lightly with salt and pepper.

Put the fish fillets in a noncorrosive pan or dish and pour the marinade over them. Cover and let marinate for 15 to 20 minutes, turning from time to time.

Remove the fish from the marinade, and season with a little salt and pepper. Pour half the marinade into a small noncorrosive saucepan and reserve the remaining marinade for basting the fish.

Grill the fillets for 4 to 5 minutes to a side, basting occasionally with the marinade.

Meanwhile, halve the avocados lengthwise, remove the pits, and peel them. Cut into cubes.

Add the scallions and peppers to the marinade in the saucepan and bring to a simmer. Immediately remove from the heat. Add the avocados and tomatoes.

Place the grilled mahi-mahi on serving plates and spoon the sauce over.

BRAISED MONKFISH WITH FRESH VEGETABLE SUCCOTASH

■■

SERVES 4

2 slices bacon, diced

2 cups fresh lima beans

1 medium tomato, peeled, seeded, and
    diced (1 cup)

1 cup fresh corn kernels (from 2 to 3 ears)

1 onion, finely diced

½ teaspoon minced garlic

2 cups Fish Stock (page 34) or Chicken
    Stock (page 33) or canned chicken
    broth

1 bay leaf

1 teaspoon chopped fresh thyme

Salt and freshly ground black pepper

2 tablespoons olive oil

Four 6- to 8-ounce pieces monkfish fillet

Flour for dusting

2 cups trimmed yellow wax beans

1 cup fresh shell beans or fresh peas

2 to 3 tablespoons chopped flat-leaf
    parsley

MONKFISH USED TO BE one of those underutilized fish sometimes called "trash fish." Fish purveyors every so often included monkfish as a bonus with a good fish order, suggesting that the staff could eat the fish. That was when I first began to appreciate its flavor and its texture: firm and flaky all at once.

Monkfish is good for sautéing and braising as it holds up well to high temperatures.

Cook the bacon in a large sauté pan over low heat just until it begins to color and render its fat; do not let brown. Add the lima beans, tomatoes, corn, onion, and garlic and cook 2 to 3 minutes. Add the stock, bay leaf, and thyme and season with salt and pepper. Raise the heat, bring to a simmer, and cook for 8 to 10 minutes, until the lima beans are tender. Remove from the heat.

In another large sauté pan, heat the olive oil over high heat until hot. Season the monkfish with salt and pepper and dust evenly and lightly all over with flour. Add the fish to the pan and brown on both sides, 2 to 3 minutes per side. Pour off the oil and add the lima bean mixture. Add the wax beans and fresh shell beans or peas.

Bring to a simmer and cook for 4 to 5 minutes. Remove and discard the bay leaf.

Place a piece of fish in the center of each plate and spoon the succotash over it. Sprinkle generously with parsley.

ALMOND-COATED POMPANO

TROPICAL RELISH

■■■■■■■■■■■■■■■■■■■■■■■■■■■■■■■■■■■

SERVES 4

1 cup all-purpose flour

1 cup milk

2 large eggs

1 cup finely ground almonds

1 cup fresh bread crumbs

Peanut oil for deep-frying

Four 4- to 6-ounce pompano fillets, skinned

Salt and freshly ground black pepper

Tropical Relish (recipe follows)

BREADING FISH WITH A mixture of bread crumbs and ground almonds produces a novel flavor. You can use almond flour too, if you can get it.

The tropical relish could also be called sweet Creole relish. This does not refer to the Creole of New Orleans but to the Creole of the Caribbean islands, which explains the tropical fruits, such as papaya, mango, and pineapple. It is seasoned with cilantro and lime juice, and the effect is that of "fire and ice," hot and chilled at the same time.

Put the flour in a shallow bowl. Mix together the milk and eggs in another shallow bowl. Combine the almonds and bread crumbs in a third shallow bowl.

In a deep-fryer or a deep heavy saucepan, heat the oil to 350°F.

Lightly dredge each fillet in the flour, dip in the milk mixture, and coat evenly with the bread-crumb mixture, shaking off any excess.

Fry the fillets for 2 to 3 minutes to a side, until golden brown. Drain on paper towels and place on serving plates. Serve with the relish on the side.

TROPICAL RELISH

MAKES ABOUT 3 CUPS

½ red bell pepper, cored, seeded, and finely chopped

1 jalapeño pepper, seeded and finely chopped

1 small red onion, finely diced

1 poblano or Anaheim pepper, cored, seeded, and finely chopped

½ cup finely diced fresh pineapple

1 cup finely diced papaya

1 cup finely diced mango

Juice of 2 limes

3 tablespoons chopped cilantro (fresh coriander)

Freshly ground black pepper to taste

Combine all the ingredients in a bowl and let stand at room temperature for at least 1 hour before serving. The relish can be made up to 4 hours ahead of time and kept covered in the refrigerator. Let come to room temperature before serving.

Store any leftover relish in a tightly covered container in the refrigerator. It will keep for 1 day.

BAKED POMPANO WITH CRABMEAT
VIRGINIA-STYLE SHERRY SAUCE

■■

SERVES 4

1 teaspoon unsalted butter

6 ounces lump or backfin crabmeat,
picked over for shells and cartilage
(about ¾ cup)

½ teaspoon minced shallots or scallions

½ cup plus 2 tablespoons dry vermouth

1 teaspoon cornstarch

½ cup heavy cream

½ teaspoon chopped fresh herbs, such as
tarragon, basil, chervil, or oregano

Salt and freshly ground black pepper

½ cup fresh bread crumbs

¼ cup coarsely ground yellow cornmeal

Four 6- to 8-ounce pompano fillets,
skinned

5 tablespoons unsalted butter, melted and
kept hot

2 to 3 tablespoons Fish Stock (page 34) or
Chicken Stock (page 33) or canned
chicken broth

Virginia-Style Sherry Sauce
(recipe follows)

¼ cup julienned country ham

2 tablespoons finely chopped fresh chives

WHAT DISTINGUISHES American cooking from European is not technique—technique does not vary much—but ingredients and how they are used. This dish came about because I thought of using pompano, a Southern fish, with crabmeat, sherry, and country ham, all common ingredients in old Southern recipes. Sherry works very well with crabmeat and country ham, but it also tastes really good with pompano.

Preheat the oven to 425°F.

Melt the 1 teaspoon butter in a medium saucepan over low heat. Add the crabmeat and shallots, cover, and cook for 3 minutes. Using a slotted spoon, remove the crabmeat and drain on paper towels.

Raise the heat under the pan to medium and add 2 tablespoons of the vermouth. Simmer for about 1 minute.

Stir the cornstarch into the cream until smooth and add to the saucepan. Bring to a simmer and cook for about 5 minutes, until thickened. Gently stir in the crabmeat and herbs. Season with salt and pepper, remove from the heat, and let cool to room temperature.

Combine the bread crumbs and cornmeal in a small bowl.

Season the fillets with salt and pepper. Put a quarter of the cooled crabmeat mixture on each fillet and spread it evenly over it. Drizzle the melted butter over the crabmeat mixture. Sprinkle the cornmeal mixture over the top of each fillet and gently pat down the crumbs so they adhere to the fish.

Lightly butter a shallow baking dish and carefully lay the pompano, coated sides up, in it. Mix the remaining ½ cup vermouth with 2 tablespoons of stock and pour into the dish. The liquid should come about halfway up the sides of the fish; add another tablespoon of stock if necessary. Bake the fish for 8 to 10 minutes, until just done. (If the crumbs are not browned, briefly place the dish under the broiler, just until the crumbs brown.)

Use a spatula to transfer the fish to serving plates. Spoon the sauce around the fish and sprinkle the julienned ham and chives over the sauce.

VIRGINIA-STYLE SHERRY SAUCE

MAKES ABOUT 1 CUP

¾ cup cream sherry

¼ cup trimmings from smoked or country ham

2 tablespoons minced shallots or scallions

1 cup Dark Poultry Chicken Stock (page 35) or canned chicken broth

About 5 ounces fish bones, from pompano or other nonoily white fish, such as sole, whitefish, or cod (see Note)

1 tablespoon cornstarch

¾ cup heavy cream

Salt and freshly ground black pepper

Combine the sherry, ham trimmings, shallots or scallions, stock, and fish bones in a medium saucepan. Bring to a boil over high heat and cook for 5 to 6 minutes, until the liquid has reduced to about 6 tablespoons; skim off any foam from the surface as the liquid reduces.

Stir the cornstarch into the cream until smooth, and add to the saucepan. Bring the mixture to a boil, and lower the heat, and simmer for 4 to 5 minutes, until the sauce is thick enough to coat the back of a spoon. Season with salt and pepper. Strain the sauce through a fine sieve and keep warm over very low heat.

NOTE: Ask the fish merchant for fish bones.

SESAME ROCKFISH WITH CRISP GINGER AND SOY

■■■

SERVES 4

Crisp Ginger

One 4- to 5-inch piece fresh ginger, peeled and thinly sliced

Peanut oil for deep-frying

Rockfish

Four 6- to 8-ounce rockfish or snapper fillets, skinned

Salt and freshly ground black pepper

½ cup sesame seeds

4 tablespoons unsalted butter, at room temperature

Soy

1 teaspoon sesame oil or olive oil

4 scallions, white and green parts, sliced

2 tablespoons grated or minced fresh ginger

¼ teaspoon minced garlic

2 tablespoons good-quality soy sauce

2 tablespoons red or white wine vinegar

IN THE GULF OF MEXICO, this fish is called redfish. Along the southern Atlantic coast, it's called rockfish. If you cannot find it, substitute snapper. Frying the ginger might seem odd, but the crisp slices are really an interesting part of the recipe.

To make the crisp ginger, bring 2 cups water to a rapid boil in a medium saucepan. Add the ginger and cook for 30 seconds. Drain and plunge into ice water. When chilled, drain on paper towels and pat completely dry.

In a deep-fat fryer or a deep heavy saucepan, heat the oil to 350°F.

Fry the ginger in batches, without crowding, for about 2 minutes, until golden brown. Use a slotted spoon or wire spider to stir the ginger gently as it fries, then lift the ginger from the oil and drain on paper towels. Set aside in a warm place.

To prepare the fish, season the fillets with salt and pepper.

Spread the sesame seeds on a piece of waxed paper or a large flat plate. Press the rounded top side of the fillets into the seeds to coat evenly.

Heat 2 tablespoons of the butter in a large sauté pan over medium heat until it begins to foam. Add the fish coated side down and cook for 2 to 3 minutes. Carefully turn the fillets and cook for 2 to 3 minutes longer, until just cooked through. Transfer to a warm platter.

Pour off the butter from the pan, add the oil, and heat for a few seconds. Add the scallions, grated ginger, and garlic and sauté for 30 seconds over medium-high heat. Add the soy sauce and vinegar and simmer for 30 seconds. Reduce the heat to low and stir in the remaining 2 tablespoons butter.

Spoon the sauce around the fish and top with the crisp ginger.

SALMON WITH CRACKED WHEAT CRUST

GRAIN MUSTARD SAUCE

■■■■■■■■■■■■■■■■■■■■■■■■■■■■■■■■

SERVES 4

¼ cup fine cracked wheat or bulgur

Four 6- to 8-ounce salmon fillets, skinned

Salt and freshly ground black pepper

1 tablespoon olive oil

3 tablespoons lightly salted butter, cut into pieces

Grain Mustard Sauce (recipe follows)

SEVERAL YEARS YEARS AGO, I tried a "new" way of cooking in America—coating fish with cracked wheat. If the cracked wheat is too coarse it will be unpleasantly crunchy; pulse the wheat in a blender or buy fine bulgur.

Spread the cracked wheat on a plate. Season the salmon fillets with salt and pepper and press the rounded sides into the wheat to coat evenly.

Heat the oil in a large sauté pan over medium heat until hot. Lay the salmon coated side down in the pan, add the butter, and cook for 3 to 4 minutes. Carefully turn the fillets over and cook for 3 to 4 minutes longer, until firm and just cooked through.

Place a fillet on a plate, spoon the sauce around, and serve.

———

GRAIN MUSTARD SAUCE

MAKES ABOUT 2 CUPS

2 teaspoons olive oil

1 onion, chopped

1 teaspoon minced garlic

½ cup dry white wine

¼ cup plus 2 tablespoons grain mustard

2 cups Fish Stock (page 34) or Chicken Stock (page 33) or canned chicken broth

8 to 12 ounces fish bones, preferably from nonoily white fish such as sole, whitefish, or cod

2 tablespoons cornstarch

1½ cups heavy cream

Salt and freshly ground black pepper

2 tablespoons chopped fresh mint

Heat the oil in a small saucepan over medium heat. Add the onion and garlic and cook, stirring for 4 to 5 minutes, until the onion is translucent but not browned. Stir in the wine and ¼ cup of the mustard. Add the stock and fish bones, raise the heat to high, and bring to a boil. Cook for 3 to 4 minutes, until reduced by half. Lower the heat to a simmer.

Stir the cornstarch into the cream until smooth, add the cream to the saucepan, and simmer 4 to 5 minutes, until thickened. Season with salt and pepper. Strain the sauce through a fine sieve, and stir in the remaining mustard and mint. Cover and keep warm until ready to serve.

CEDAR-PLANKED SALMON
OLD-FASHIONED EGG SAUCE

■■

SERVES 4

1 teaspoon salt

¼ teaspoon freshly ground black pepper

¼ teaspoon dry mustard

1 tablespoon unsalted butter, at room temperature

Four 6-ounce salmon fillets, skinned

Old-Fashioned Egg Sauce (recipe follows)

2 untreated cedar shingles or shims (available from lumber yards), 4 to 5 inches wide and about 12 inches long

THIS RECIPE COMBINES cooking from the eastern part of the country with that of the West. Egg sauce is traditionally served in New England on the Fourth of July; salmon cooked on a board is a Northwest specialty. It is a method that goes back to the Pacific Northwest Indians, who cooked salmon on planks next to open fires. Planked salmon now is served in restaurants around the country, but it wasn't on many other menus when we began serving it. Some forgotten cooking methods just need someone to rediscover them, lighten them up, and make them fun and interesting.

The salmon can be served hot or cold. If you want to serve it cold, as a change from poached fish on a buffet table, for example, stir some mayonnaise and lemon juice into the cooled egg sauce.

When I cook at big charity events, I sometimes like to prepare whole planked salmon over an open fire. I lash the fish to a large piece of cedar or oak with wire and prop it on stacked bricks near the fire; I invert the fish so that as it cooks its juices and the butter it's brushed with drip into the fire. The flames flare up and you can smell the charring wood. It's really wonderful and very visual.

Mix together the salt, pepper, and mustard. Brush the top of the salmon fillets with a little butter and then sprinkle both sides with the mustard mixture.

Preheat the broiler. Soak the shingles in cold water for 5 to 10 minutes.

Put the soaked shingles under the hot broiler, 4 to 5 inches from the heat source, for 2 to 3 minutes, until the wood is browned on the top. Carefully take the shingles from the broiler.

Immediately, so that the shingles do not cool, lay 2 salmon fillets on the browned side of each shingle. Return the shingles to the broiler and cook the fish for about 5 to 7 minutes until firm but not dry. Lift the salmon from the shingles, or serve it on the shingles if you like, with the egg sauce.

OLD-FASHIONED EGG SAUCE

¼ cup dry white wine

¼ cup Fish Stock (page 34) or Chicken Stock (page 33) or canned chicken broth

1 teaspoon minced shallots or scallions

2 tablespoons fresh lemon juice

¼ cup heavy cream

8 tablespoons unsalted butter, cut into 8 pieces

½ teaspoon Tabasco

Salt and freshly ground black pepper

2 hard-cooked eggs, coarsely grated

3 tablespoons chopped flat-leaf parsley

1 tablespoon salmon caviar (optional)

Combine the wine, stock, shallots or scallions, and 1 tablespoon of the lemon juice in a small noncorrosive saucepan. Bring to a simmer over medium heat and cook for 3 to 4 minutes, until reduced to about 2 tablespoons.

Stir in the cream and simmer for about 3 minutes, until the cream thickens slightly. Lower the heat and stir in the butter a tablespoon at a time; do not add another tablespoon until the one before it has been thoroughly incorporated.

Remove the sauce from the heat and stir in the remaining 1 tablespoon lemon juice and the Tabasco. Season to taste with salt and pepper. Strain the sauce through a fine sieve, into a bowl. Cover to keep warm until ready to serve.

Just before serving, mix the grated eggs with the parsley and caviar. Stir the mixture into the warm sauce and serve with the salmon.

GRILLED SALMON WITH PUMPKIN SEED VINAIGRETTE AND BRAISED KALE

SERVES 4

Vinaigrette

1 cup shelled pumpkin seeds (pepitas)

¼ cup fresh or solid-pack unsweetened pumpkin puree

¼ teaspoon minced garlic

½ teaspoon turmeric

½ cup plus 2 tablespoons cider vinegar

½ cup seed or nut oil, such as safflower, walnut, or peanut oil, or olive oil

Salt and freshly ground black pepper

Salmon

1 small head (about 1½ pounds) rainbow or green kale

Four 6- to 8-ounce salmon fillets

2 tablespoons unsalted butter, at room temperature

Salt and freshly ground black pepper

2 tablespoons olive oil

2 tablespoons minced onion or shallots

½ teaspoon minced garlic

½ cup Fish Stock (page 34) or Chicken Stock (page 33) or canned chicken broth

THIS RECIPE TAKES very American ingredients, salmon and pumpkin, and turns them into something special. The salmon is grilled, although it certainly could be broiled. The vinaigrette includes toasted hulled pumpkin seeds, called pepitas, which are easy to find at health food stores or any market with an extensive selection of nuts and seeds. (These are not the whole seeds, but rather the inside part of the seed.)

Be sure to buy unsweetened solid-pack pumpkin puree for the vinaigrette, not pumpkin pie filling, which is sweetened and seasoned. The turmeric simply adds color; it doesn't provide much flavor but brightens up the vinaigrette. Kale is a good alternative to spinach or cabbage. Small heads that weigh about a pound and a half have tender leaves that cook quickly.

To make the vinaigrette, preheat the oven to 325°F.

Spread the pumpkin seeds in a shallow pan and toast in the oven for 3 to 4 minutes, until lightly browned. Remove from the oven.

Put half the toasted seeds in a small noncorrosive saucepan, reserving the remaining seeds for garnish. Add the pumpkin puree, garlic, turmeric, and ½ cup of the vinegar and bring to a boil over medium heat. Remove the pan from the heat and whisk in the oil. Stir in the remaining 2 tablespoons vinegar and season with salt and pepper.

Transfer the vinaigrette to a blender or food processor and puree for 1 minute. Set aside and keep warm.

Prepare a charcoal or gas grill or preheat the broiler.

Separate the kale leaves and remove the tough center ribs. Tear the leaves in half, wash and set aside.

Brush both sides of the salmon fillets with the butter and season with salt and pepper. Grill or broil for 5 to 6 minutes, without turning.

Meanwhile, in a large sauté pan equipped with a tight-fitting lid, heat the olive oil, uncovered, over high heat. Add the onion or shallots and the garlic and sauté for 30 seconds. Add the kale and cook for 2 minutes, stirring constantly. Add the stock and season with salt and pepper. Cover, reduce the heat to low, and cook for 2 to 3 minutes, until the kale is tender. Drain any liquid from the kale.

Make a nest of braised kale in the center of each plate and top with a salmon fillet. Spoon the vinaigrette around the fish and sprinkle with the reserved toasted pumpkin seeds.

GRILLED SMOKED SALMON WITH CAPERS

■■

SERVES 4
AS AN APPETIZER

Four 4-ounce pieces good-quality, moist smoked salmon (ask the market to cut it in 1 thick slice and then into 4 medallions), at room temperature

2 tablespoons olive oil

Freshly ground black pepper

2 tablespoons finely chopped fresh chives

2 tablespoons drained tiny capers

½ cup Grain Mustard Sauce (page 111)

GRILLING SMOKED SALMON is an unusual technique. You need to start with smoked salmon that is really fresh and moist. The fish is not sliced paper-thin in the regular way, but instead is cut into thick medallions, then grilled over a very hot fire. You can use a gas grill if that is what you have, but a charcoal or wood fire gives the best flavor. The grilling is only for flavor, so the salmon should not be left on the fire for more than a minute a side.

Prepare a very hot charcoal or wood fire or a hot fire in a gas grill, or preheat the broiler.

Rub each piece of salmon generously with the olive oil. Grill or broil the fish for 1 minute on each side. Place on individual plates, sprinkle with pepper, the chives, and capers, and spoon the sauce around the salmon.

SPENCER OVEN-FRIED FILLET OF SCROD

■■■■■■■■■■■■■■■■■■■■■■■■■■■■■■■■■■■■■■■

SERVES 4

About ⅓ cup peanut oil or other light
vegetable oil

1 cup half-and-half

Salt and freshly ground black pepper

3 cups stale fine bread crumbs

1½ pounds scrod fillet, skinned and cut
into 1¼- to 1½-inch pieces

Lemon wedges for serving

Spicy Tartar Sauce (page 98) for serving

THIS METHOD OF COOKING FISH has an interesting history. It was developed in the 1930s by a woman named Evelyn Spencer who, while working for the Department of Fisheries to promote fish consumption, came up with a way to cook fish that was appealing to home cooks. The fish is breaded, placed in a lightly oiled pan, drizzled with a little oil, and then baked in a very hot oven. It emerges crispy, as if it were fried, but the house does not smell of frying fish and oil. Even today people are reluctant to fry fish at home, and this technique provides an ingenious way around it. We use scrod but you could use cod or any fish that is good for frying. (If you use sole, be sure to trim the tail pieces, as the fish should be uniformly sized.)

Preheat the oven to 500°F. Generously brush a baking pan large enough to hold the scrod without the pieces touching with about half the oil.

Pour the half-and-half into a shallow bowl and season lightly with salt and pepper. Put the bread crumbs in another shallow bowl.

One by one dip the scrod pieces in the half-and-half, lay them in the bread crumbs, and roll them in the crumbs until completely coated. Place the breaded fish in the oiled pan, making sure the pieces of scrod are not touching one another.

Using a brush, drizzle the fish with the remaining oil. Bake in the center of the oven for 8 to 10 minutes, until the fish is golden brown and crisp. Lift from the hot pan with a spatula, and serve with lemon wedges and the tartar sauce.

BAKED NEW ENGLAND SCROD IN CIDER VINEGAR SAUCE

SUMMER SQUASH

■ ■

SERVES 4

3 tablespoons unsalted butter

1 tablespoon finely chopped scallion

½ teaspoon minced garlic

2 tablespoons chopped fresh sage

1 tablespoon chopped flat-leaf parsley

Juice of 1 lemon

1½ cups dried bread crumbs

Salt and freshly ground black pepper

Four 6- to 8-ounce scrod fillets, skinned

⅓ cup Fish Stock (page 34) or Chicken Stock (page 33) or canned chicken broth

Summer Squash (recipe follows)

BECAUSE SCROD FILLETS are so thin, they can overcook and dry out very easily. Coating them with a bread-crumb topping serves to keep them moist. And while the fish bakes, the bread crumbs turn golden brown and crunchy. In this dish, the scrod is served on a bed of squashes, sliced paper-thin and cooked briefly.

Preheat the oven to 375°F.

Melt the butter in a small sauté pan over low heat. Stir in the scallions, garlic, sage, and parsley and cook for 1 minute. Add the lemon juice and remove the pan from the heat.

Put the bread crumbs in a bowl, pour the melted butter over them and stir until well mixed. Season lightly with salt and pepper. Pat an even coat of the bread crumbs over the top of each fillet.

Lightly butter a baking dish large enough to hold the fillets and lay them in it. Pour the stock into the dish. Bake for 10 to 12 minutes, until most of the broth has evaporated and the bread crumbs are golden. (If you desire, brown the fish under a hot broiler.) Spoon the squash and sauce onto the plates and top with the scrod.

SUMMER SQUASH

1 shallot, sliced

½ tart apple, cored and sliced

½ cup cider vinegar

1 cup Chicken Stock (page 33) or canned broth

1 tablespoon cornstarch

½ cup heavy cream

1 tablespoon fresh lemon juice

Salt and freshly ground black pepper

2 zucchini, halved

2 yellow squash, halved

Put the shallot, apple, and vinegar in a small noncorrosive saucepan and bring to a boil over high heat. Cook for 2 to 3 minutes, until reduced by about two thirds. Add the stock, bring to a boil, and cook for 2 to 3 minutes longer, until reduced by half. Lower the heat to a simmer.

continued

Stir the cornstarch into the cream until completely smooth. Add the cream mixture to the saucepan, bring to a simmer and cook for 3 to 4 minutes. Add the lemon juice and season with salt and pepper. Strain through a fine sieve and set aside.

Using a spoon, scrape out the seeds from the halved zucchini and yellow squash. Slice the squash into paper-thin half-moons and put in a sauté pan. Pour the sauce over the squash and bring to a simmer. Cook for 2 minutes. Then remove from the heat and cover to keep warm.

BAKED SNAPPER IN LOBSTER BROTH WITH PASTA

SERVES 4

One 1- to 1¼-pound lobster

2 tablespoons olive oil

1 small onion, sliced

1 small carrot, peeled and sliced

1 rib celery, sliced

3 medium tomatoes, seeded and chopped

2 jalapeño peppers, chopped, or
    1 teaspoon hot pepper flakes

1 tablespoon minced garlic

½ cup plus 2 tablespoons dry white wine

2 tablespoons tomato puree

4 cups Chicken Stock (page 33) or
    canned broth

Four 6-ounce red snapper fillets, with skin

Salt and freshly ground black pepper

½ pound linguine, preferably fresh

1 cup fresh peas, blanched in lightly
    salted boiling water until al dente

2 tablespoons chopped fresh basil

EVERYONE LOVES THIS DISH—it's somehow both satisfying and luxurious yet simple and non-guilt-provoking. I came up with this when I was trying to develop a light summery dish for the restaurant. We make a delicate lobster broth, season it with fresh basil, add sweet fresh peas and diced lobster meat, and spoon it over baked snapper.

Preheat the oven to 375°F.

To kill the lobster instantly, insert a sharp knife through the cross mark on its head, about an inch behind its eyes. Twist off the tail and claws. Split the body in half. Remove the sac from the head. Remove and discard the tomalley (pale green liver). If there is dark green roe, leave it in the shell.

Heat 1 tablespoon of the olive oil in a large saucepan over high heat until hot. Add all the lobster pieces and sauté for 2 minutes. Add the onion, carrot, celery, tomatoes, jalapeños, and garlic and cook for 2 to 3 minutes. Add ½ cup of the wine and the tomato puree, lower the heat to medium, and cook, stirring, for 2 minutes.

Add the stock and bring to a boil. Lower the heat and simmer for 5 minutes. Remove the lobster tail and claws with a slotted spoon and set aside to cool slightly. Cook the stock for 5 to 10 minutes longer, until reduced by half.

As soon as the lobster tail and claws are cool enough to handle, remove the meat and return the shells to the reducing broth. Cut the lobster meat into small cubes and set aside.

Season the lobster broth with salt and pepper. Strain it twice through a fine sieve. Then line the sieve with a coffee filter to trap any grit, and slowly strain the stock into a medium saucepan. Cover and keep warm over very low heat.

Lightly brush a shallow baking pan with a little of the olive oil. Season the snapper with salt and pepper and lay it skin side up in the pan. Brush the skin with the remaining olive oil. Add the remaining 2 tablespoons wine and 2 tablespoons of the lobster broth to the pan. Bake for 5 to 6 minutes.

Meanwhile, cook the pasta in lightly salted boiling water until al dente; drain.

Add the pasta to the lobster broth, bring to a simmer, and heat the broth and pasta. Add the peas, fresh basil, and reserved lobster meat.

Using tongs, arrange the pasta in four shallow soup bowls. Lay the snapper on top of the pasta and spoon the broth over it.

GRILLED STURGEON AND OYSTERS IN BARBECUE

■■

SERVES 4

Eight 3-ounce sturgeon fillets, no thicker than ¾ inch thick

1½ cups Barbecue Sauce (page 152) or American Spoon Foods or other prepared barbecue sauce

12 oysters, scrubbed

Olive oil for brushing

Freshly ground black pepper

1 tablespoon unsalted butter

2 tablespoons chopped flat-leaf parsley

STURGEON USED TO BE a popular fish, being common in fresh-water lakes and rivers, but because of pollution, they had become less available. Fortunately, aquaculture is doing a lot to change this, as has the popularity of sturgeon roe as caviar, prompting better conditions for raising sturgeon. Although smoked sturgeon is easier to find, more and more frequently fresh sturgeon is available in the markets as well.

Sturgeon is mild and picks up the flavors of whatever it is cooked with. Its texture is firm and it grills well. Be sure not to buy the fish cut too thick—small medallions are nice—and do not overcook it, or it will turn dry and tough.

I like to serve grilled sturgeon with grilled oysters (grilling oysters in their shells is an idea I got from Jim Beard). Just put the oysters on a rack over the coals, cover the grill, and cook them until the tops pop open.

Put the sturgeon fillets in a noncorrosive pan or dish and pour the bar-becue sauce over them. Let marinate for 15 to 20 minutes.

Prepare a medium-hot fire in a charcoal or gas grill or preheat the broiler.

Lay the oysters on the grill rack, flat side up, cover the grill, and grill for 3 to 4 minutes, just until the oysters begin to open or broil the oysters for 3 to 4 minutes. Carefully remove the oysters from the heat and set them aside in a dish to cool slightly. When cool enough to han-dle, flip open the top shells and scrape the oysters and their liquor into a small bowl.

Lift the sturgeon from the barbecue sauce and brush lightly with oil. Season lightly with pepper.

Grill or broil the sturgeon for about 2 minutes to a side; do not overcook.

Meanwhile, transfer the barbecue sauce to a small saucepan and bring to a simmer. Stir in the butter until melted, then add the oysters and their liquor and heat through.

Arrange the sturgeon fillets on serving plates and spoon the oysters and sauce over the fish. Sprinkle with the parsley and serve at once.

GRILLED SWORDFISH

RED PEPPER VINAIGRETTE ▪ SOFT CORN PUDDING

■■

SERVES 4

Four 6- to 8-ounce swordfish steaks,
   2 inches thick

Salt and freshly ground black pepper

Red Pepper Vinaigrette (recipe follows)

About 1½ cups Soft Corn Pudding
   (recipe follows)

3 tablespoons chopped flat-leaf parsley

SOFT, CREAMY CORN PUDDING makes the perfect foil for the grilled fish and the vinaigrette. Any firm-fleshed fish that holds together well, such as swordfish or tuna, would work here. The recipe is a good example of how to use vinaigrettes as "new age" sauces rather than more old-fashioned cream sauces. Vinaigrettes are simply a combination of oil and vinegar with other ingredients added for flavor; you can add oil and vinegar to any vegetable puree and serve it with fish or poultry or whatever as a sauce. Here, we use red bell pepper; you can also use yellow or green bell peppers, charred tomatoes (see page 129) or pumpkin seeds (see page 160). You could also omit the oil entirely and just add vinegar to taste to the puree.

Prepare a medium-hot fire in a charcoal or gas grill or preheat the broiler.

Season the swordfish with salt and pepper, and brush each steak on both sides with about 1 tablespoon of the red pepper vinaigrette.

Grill the swordfish for 3 to 4 minutes on each side for medium; do not overcook it.

Spoon the corn pudding into the center of the plates and top with the swordfish. Spoon the vinaigrette around the fish, sprinkle with the chopped parsley, and serve.

RED PEPPER VINAIGRETTE

MAKES ABOUT 4 CUPS

1/4 cup plus 2 tablespoons olive oil

2 red bell peppers, cored, seeded, and
sliced

2 red jalapeño peppers, seeded and sliced

1 teaspoon minced garlic

1/4 cup red wine vinegar

2 tablespoons fresh lemon juice

Salt and freshly ground black pepper

Heat 3 tablespoons of the olive oil in a medium sauté pan over medium heat. Add the bell peppers, jalapeños, and garlic and cook for 2 to 3 minutes, until the peppers are tender. Add the remaining 3 tablespoons oil, the vinegar, and lemon juice and cook for 1 minute. Remove from the heat and let cool to room temperature.

Puree the pepper mixture in a food processor or blender and season with salt and pepper.

————

SOFT CORN PUDDING

MAKES ABOUT 2 1/2 CUPS

2 cups milk

1/2 teaspoon minced garlic

1/2 cup corn kernels, fresh (from 1 ear)
or frozen

2/3 cup stone-ground cornmeal

Salt and freshly ground black pepper

Pinch of cayenne pepper

1 tablespoon unsalted butter

2 tablespoons finely chopped fresh chives

Combine the milk, garlic, and corn in a medium saucepan and bring to a boil over high heat. Lower the heat to a simmer and cook for 2 to 3 minutes. Slowly add the cornmeal, stirring continually, and cook, stirring, for 3 to 4 minutes, until the pudding is the consistency of cornmeal mush or Cream of Wheat. Season with salt and pepper and the cayenne and stir in the butter until melted. Remove from the heat and keep warm.

Just before serving, stir the chives into the pudding.

SEARED TROUT WITH PUMPKIN SEED BROWN BUTTER

SOFT PUMPKIN-CORN PUDDING

■■■■■■■■■■■■■■■■■■■■■■■■■■■■■■■■■■

SERVES 4

Four 8- to- 10-ounce trout, left whole and boned (see Note)

Salt and freshly ground black pepper

1 cup buttermilk

1 cup all-purpose flour

¼ cup olive oil

6 tablespoons lightly salted butter, cut into pieces

¼ cup shelled pumpkin seeds (pepitas)

2 tablespoons cider vinegar

2 tablespoons chopped fresh chives

Soft Pumpkin-Corn Pudding
(recipe follows)

THIS DISH CELEBRATES the harvest of flavors of New York's Hudson Valley—in particular, wonderful farmed trout that I buy from Eden Brook Farms. I serve the trout with soft corn pudding mixed with pumpkin puree and top the fish with browned butter made with hulled pumpkin seeds, or pepitas. The browned butter is similar to traditional almondine browned butter, but the pumpkin seeds add their own wonderful nuttiness and give the butter a slight green tint.

Carefully check each trout to see that all the bones have been removed; remove any you find with tweezers. Season each trout inside and out with salt and pepper.

Pour the buttermilk into a shallow bowl. Put the flour in another shallow bowl. Dip each trout in the buttermilk and then dredge in the flour, shaking off the excess.

In a sauté pan large enough to hold all the trout, heat the oil over high heat. When hot, carefully add the fish and cook for 2 to 3 minutes on each side, until browned and crisp. Lift the trout from the pan with a spatula and put on warm serving plates or a platter.

Pour off the oil from the pan. Add the butter and heat it over medium heat until it begins to foam and turn brown. Add the pumpkin seeds and stir for 1 minute. Add the vinegar, raise the heat, and bring to a boil. Spoon the sauce over the trout and sprinkle with the chives. Serve with the corn pudding.

NOTE: When buying the trout, ask for butterflied boneless trout.

SOFT PUMPKIN-CORN PUDDING

SERVES 4

2 tablespoons lightly salted butter

1 tablespoon minced garlic

1 cup corn kernels, fresh (from 2 to 3 ears) or frozen

2 cups milk

1 cup fresh pumpkin puree or unsweetened solid-pack canned puree

1¼ cups stone-ground cornmeal

Salt and freshly ground black pepper

Heat the butter in a large saucepan over medium heat until it begins to foam and turn light brown. Add the garlic and corn and cook for 2 to 3 minutes. Add the milk and pumpkin puree and bring to a simmer.

Stirring continuously, slowly add the cornmeal to the pan. Lower the heat and cook, stirring, for 5 to 6 minutes longer, until the pudding is the consistency of thick oatmeal or Cream of Wheat. Season with salt and pepper. Spoon the pudding into a serving bowl or onto serving plates.

WARM SMOKED TROUT SALAD

SERVES 4

½ cup sour cream

¼ cup freshly grated horseradish

1 tablespoon fresh lemon juice

Salt and freshly ground black pepper

½ pound small new potatoes (about the size of golf balls), scrubbed but not peeled

1 kirby cucumber, peeled

2 tablespoons minced onion

¼ cup olive oil

2 tablespoons white wine vinegar

2 tablespoons chopped flat-leaf parsley

4 smoked trout fillets (about 4 ounces each)

1 small head Boston or Bibb lettuce, rinsed and dried

SOMETIMES JUST A SLIGHT RETHINKING of a dish can make an enormous difference. Cold smoked trout can be a little boring—but try warming it and you'll bring out its appealing smokiness and true trout flavor. You have to be careful only to warm it. Don't let it get hot; after all, the fish is already cooked.

Mix the sour cream with the horseradish and lemon juice. Season with salt and pepper and let stand at room temperature for at least 1 hour before serving.

Cook the potatoes in lightly salted boiling water for 8 to 10 minutes, until cooked through but still slightly firm. Drain and let cool slightly.

When the potatoes are cool enough to handle, cut them in half and then into ¼-inch-thick slices. Put the potatoes in a bowl.

Cut the cucumber in half, scoop out the seeds with a spoon, and cut into thin slices. Add to the potatoes along with the onion, 3 tablespoons of the olive oil, the vinegar, and parsley. Season with salt and pepper and toss well. Set aside in a warm place.

Preheat the broiler.

Brush the trout fillets with the remaining 1 tablespoon oil and season lightly with pepper. Put the fillets on a baking sheet and warm under the broiler for 2 minutes. Be careful not to overheat the trout, or it will dry out.

Arrange the lettuce leaves on individual serving plates and top with the potato salad and trout fillets. Spoon some horseradish cream over each fillet, and serve the remainder in a sauceboat.

PANFRIED LAKE TROUT

CHILE HOLLANDAISE

■■■■■■■■■■■■■■■■■■■■■■■■■■■■■■■■■■■■■

SERVES 4

1 cup sour cream

1/2 cup buttermilk

1/2 teaspoon Tabasco

1 tablespoon plus 1 teaspoon spicy brown mustard

2 large egg yolks

Salt and freshly ground black pepper

1 cup all-purpose flour

1/2 cup stone-ground cornmeal

1/2 teaspoon cayenne pepper

Four 6- to 8-ounce lake trout fillets, skinned

Peanut oil for frying

1 cup Chile Hollandaise (recipe follows)

ALL TROUT HAS A DISTINCTIVE, clean flavor, but lake trout is a little more flavorful than river trout. Lake trout, also called salmon trout, has pink flesh that indicates its diet includes tiny crustaceans. Any sort of trout works well in this recipe, or you could even substitute catfish. Just be sure to buy really fresh fish from a reputable market. (Larger trout are easier to bone than small ones, so you might base your decision on the size of the fish available.)

This recipe is fashioned after one from New Orleans. The fish is dipped in a mixture of sour cream and buttermilk, breaded with cornmeal, and then panfried until crisp. I serve it with a chile hollandaise, classic hollandaise jazzed up with onions, garlic, peppers, chile powder, and cayenne.

Combine the sour cream, buttermilk, Tabasco, mustard, egg yolks, 1 teaspoon salt, and 1/2 teaspoon pepper in a shallow bowl. Stir until well mixed.

Combine the flour, cornmeal, cayenne, 1 tablespoon salt, and 1 tablespoon pepper in another bowl. Mix well.

Dip each fillet in the sour cream mixture and let the excess drain off. Dredge the coated fills in the flour mixture, coating them evenly. Set aside on a waxed paper–lined baking sheet.

Pour about 1/2 inch of oil into a large deep frying pan and heat the oil to 350°F.

Fry the fillets for 2 to 3 minutes a side, or until golden brown. Drain on paper towels, and serve hot with the chile hollandaise.

CHILE HOLLANDAISE

MAKES ABOUT 2 1/2 CUPS

6 tablespoons unsalted butter

2 tablespoons finely chopped red bell pepper

2 tablespoons finely chopped green bell pepper

1/2 onion, finely chopped

1 clove garlic, minced

1 1/2 teaspoons pure chile powder

1/4 teaspoon cayenne pepper

1/4 teaspoon dried oregano

Salt and freshly ground black pepper

2 tablespoons dry white wine

1/2 cup Chicken Stock (page 33) or canned broth

2 large egg yolks

1 teaspoon fresh lemon juice

Melt 1 tablespoon of the butter in a saucepan over low heat. Add the bell peppers, onion, and garlic and cook, stirring, for 1 to 2 minutes, until softened. Add the chile powder, cayenne, and oregano and season with salt and pepper. Cook for 1 to 2 minutes longer. Add the wine and stir to deglaze the pan. Add the stock, bring to a simmer, and cook for about 10 minutes, until the sauce is thick and syrupy.

Meanwhile, melt the remaining 5 tablespoons butter in a medium saucepan. Set aside.

Put the reduced sauce in the top of a double boiler over low heat. Add the egg yolks and whisk for about 5 minutes, until the sauce begins to thicken. Be careful not to overheat the sauce, or it will curdle.

Remove the pan from the heat and slowly whisk in the melted butter. Whisk in the lemon juice and season to taste with salt. Keep the sauce warm over hot water until ready to serve; do not let it get hot, or it will break.

TUNA WRAPPED IN BACON WITH CLAMS CASINO SAUCE

■■■■■■■■■■■■■■■■■■■■■■■■■■■■■■■■■■■

SERVES 4

Eight 3- to 4-ounce pieces yellowfin tuna, 1½ inches thick and 2½ to 3 inches across

Freshly ground black pepper

9 slices bacon, preferably smoked

1 red bell pepper, cored, seeded, and finely diced

1 green bell pepper, cored, seeded, and finely diced

1 small onion, finely diced

¼ teaspoon minced garlic

Reserved clam liquor (see below), mixed with enough clam juice or Chicken Stock (page 33) or canned broth if necessary to equal ½ cup liquid

¼ cup plus 2 tablespoons fresh lemon juice

16 littleneck clams, scrubbed, shucked, and cut in half, liquor reserved

3 tablespoons unsalted butter, cut into pieces, at room temperature

1 teaspoon Tabasco

2 tablespoons chopped flat-leaf parsley

1½ teaspoons olive oil

IT PROBABLY DOESN'T sound very chic or modern to admit it, but I really like Clams Casino. And I have always thought the recipe in *The Joy of Cooking* is about as good as you can get. Here I've broken down the classic dish to use the ingredients in other ways. Wrapping the bacon around the tuna gives it a nice smokiness. The clam sauce is flavored with both sweet and hot peppers and the rendered bacon fat.

Season the tuna generously with pepper. Wrap a slice of bacon around the thickest part of each piece overlapping the ends by about ½ inch. Trim off the excess bacon and reserve it, and secure the bacon on the tuna with toothpicks or string. Cut the remaining 1 slice of bacon and the trimmings into ½-inch pieces.

Cook the bacon pieces in a sauté pan over high heat until they begin to color and render their fat. Pour off all but 1 tablespoon of the fat. Add the peppers, onion, and garlic to the pan and cook over medium heat, stirring, for 1 minute.

Add the reserved clam liquor, and ¼ cup of the lemon juice. Bring to a boil over high heat and cook for 2 to 3 minutes, until reduced by half. Stir in the clams and cook for 30 seconds. Reduce the heat to low and stir in the butter, a piece at a time. Stir in the Tabasco, the remaining 2 tablespoons lemon juice, and the parsley. Remove from the heat and set aside in a warm place.

Heat the olive oil in a large nonstick sauté pan over high heat. Add the tuna and cook, turning frequently, until the bacon is browned. Stand the tuna on its edge for 30 seconds. Turn it onto the other edge and cook for 30 seconds longer.

Remove the toothpicks or string and place 2 pieces on each plate. Spoon the clam sauce around the tuna and serve.

CHARRED TUNA

SPICY CHARRED TOMATO VINAIGRETTE

■■■■■■■■■■■■■■■■■■■■■■■■■■■■■■■■■■■■

SERVES 4

Four 6- to 8-ounce tuna steaks, at least
  1½ inches thick

2 tablespoons olive oil

Salt and freshly ground black pepper

Spicy Charred Tomato Vinaigrette
  (recipe follows)

CHARRING GIVES both the tuna and the tomatoes a nice smoky flavor. If you have great vine-ripened tomatoes, you could transfer the whole thing to the grill, but the recipe works well in the kitchen, in a cast-iron or other heavy skillet.

Brush both sides of the tuna steaks with the oil. Season lightly with salt and pepper. Heat a large cast-iron or other heavy skillet over high heat until hot. Add the tuna and cook for 2 to 3 minutes to a side, for rare to medium rare. Put a tuna steak in the center of each plate and spoon the warm tomato vinaigrette around it.

———

SPICY CHARRED TOMATO VINAIGRETTE

3 large ripe tomatoes, cut into
  thick slices

¼ cup plus 2 tablespoons olive oil

Freshly ground black pepper

1 sweet onion, thickly sliced

1 jalapeño pepper, seeded and sliced

½ cup red wine vinegar

Salt

2 to 3 tablespoons chopped fresh basil

Using 2 tablespoons of the oil, brush both sides of the tomato slices with oil, and season generously with pepper.

Heat a large heavy skillet over high heat until hot. Lay half the tomato slices in the pan, in one layer, and cook for 2 to 3 minutes on each side, until charred. Transfer to a plate and repeat with the remaining slices.

Add the onion slices to the pan and cook over high heat, stirring, for 2 to 3 minutes, until the onions begin to brown. Add the jalapeño pepper and garlic, return the tomato slices to the pan, and cook stirring, for 2 to 3 minutes. Transfer to a bowl, add the vinegar and the remaining ¼ cup olive oil, and season with a little salt. Let stand for 5 to 10 minutes.

Pass the tomato mixture through a food mill into a bowl to remove the seeds and skins (or press through a strainer). Add the basil. Keep at room temperature. Store in the refrigerator if making ahead.

SOUTHWEST-STYLE WHITEFISH IN TORTILLAS

POBLANO CREAM

SERVES 4

1 tablespoon olive oil

1 small red onion, thinly sliced

1/2 red bell pepper, cored, seeded, and thinly sliced

1/2 green bell pepper, cored, seeded, and thinly sliced

1 jalapeño pepper, seeded and finely chopped

1 teaspoon minced garlic

Salt and freshly ground black pepper

3 tablespoons chopped cilantro (fresh coriander)

1/4 cup Barbecue Sauce (page 152) or American Spoon Foods or other prepared barbecue sauce

Four 7-inch flour tortillas

Four 6- to 8-ounce whitefish fillets, skinned

2 tablespoons unsalted butter, melted

Poblano Cream (recipe follows)

SINCE EVERYONE LOVES the flavors of the Southwest these days, I decided to do a zippy down-home version of a fancier *en papillote* whitefish. In this, I use a flour tortilla to hold in the flavors of the vegetables and fish as they cook. Poblano peppers, the mildly spicy peppers from New Mexico, pureed with a little cream and garlic, make the perfect sauce.

Preheat the oven to 375°F.

Heat the olive oil in a large sauté pan over high heat. Add the onion, bell peppers, jalapeño, and garlic and saute for 1 minute. Season with salt and pepper and remove from the heat. Stir in the cilantro and barbecue sauce.

Season the fish lightly with salt and pepper.

Lay the tortillas out on a work surface and spoon the vegetable mixture into the center of each, spreading it into a 3- to 4-inch circle. Lay a whitefish fillet on top of each round of vegetables and fold over the sides of each tortilla. Fold over the bottom and top, make a neat package and turn the tortillas seam side down. Lightly brush the tops of the tortillas with about half of the melted butter.

Brush a shallow baking pan with the remaining butter and lay the tortilla packets in it, leaving a little space between them. Cover with foil and bake for 10 to 12 minutes. Remove the foil and bake for 2 to 3 minutes longer.

Serve the tortillas with the poblano cream spooned over them.

POBLANO CREAM

1 tablespoon olive oil

3 poblano peppers, seeded and chopped

1 teaspoon minced garlic

1 cup Fish Stock (page 34) or Chicken
    Stock (page 33) or canned chicken
    broth

1 tablespoon cornstarch

1/2 cup heavy cream

Salt and freshly ground black pepper

Heat the oil in a small saucepan over medium heat. Add the poblanos and sauté for 2 to 3 minutes. Add the garlic and sauté for 1 minute. Add the stock, raise the heat to high, and bring to a boil. Cook for 2 to 3 minutes, until reduced by half. Lower the heat to a simmer.

Stir the cornstarch into the cream until completely smooth, then add the cream to the saucepan and bring to a simmer. Cook for 2 to 3 minutes. Season with salt and pepper.

Pour the sauce into a blender or food processor and puree. Serve warm.

WISCONSIN-STYLE FISH BOIL

SERVES 4

1 large potato, peeled and thickly sliced

1 turnip, peeled and thickly sliced

2 pale-green inner ribs celery, peeled and
    cut into 3-inch lengths

8 to 12 small white or pearl onions, peeled

4 cups Fish Stock (page 34)

1 cup milk

2 tablespoons unsalted butter

Salt and freshly ground black pepper

1 1/2 pounds thick whitefish or perch
    fillets, skinned and cut into 4 pieces

2 tablespoons chopped fresh dill

THIS DISH INCORPORATES MUCH of what was available to the early settlers and, later, the farmers in the Wisconsin area: potatoes and turnips, milk and butter, and freshwater white fish. Dill reflects the strong Scandinavian influence there.

It's not a soup, it's more like a stew. Serve it in shallow bowls with the vegetables spooned over the fish.

Put the potato, turnip, celery, onions, and fish stock in a large saucepan and bring to a boil. Lower the heat and simmer for 5 to 6 minutes, until the vegetables are tender. Add the milk and butter and return to a simmer. Season with salt and pepper and remove from the heat.

Lay the fish in a large, deep skillet. Season with salt and pepper. Ladle the vegetables and broth over the fish, bring to a simmer, and cook for 4 to 5 minutes, until the fish just flakes at the touch.

Carefully lift the fish from the broth and put in a large shallow soup bowls. Ladle the vegetables and broth over the fish, sprinkle with the dill, and serve.

From Forests and Farms

OUR SPRAWLING WOODLANDS and vast farmlands have given us a diverse and unparalleled bounty. Discovering how best to prepare that bounty has happily occupied America's cooks for over 200 years. Frankly, what is amazing and gratifying to me is how many traditional game, poultry, and meat dishes are still part of our cooking repertoire today. My recipes for these dishes are refinements of the originals, as Roast Turkey with Maple Corn Sauce and Country Corn Samp, Pan-Roasted Venison with Dried Cranberry Sauce and Maple Whipped Sweet Potatoes, Grilled Spring Lamb with Rhubarb and Dandelion, Roast Goose with Plum Glaze and Appalachian Dressing are simple, satisfying, well-conceived recipes that have stayed true to their roots. Little has changed except for our increasing admiration and appreciation for the cooks who got it so right in the first place.

Chicken, Turkey, Duck, and Goose

THE FIRST TIME I saw a supermarket that carried free-range chickens, I knew we had come a long way! Now that it's getting so easy to find poultry that's raised organically, it's that much easier to ratchet up the taste level of just about any recipe. Happily, the superb quality of today's chickens, ducks, geese, and turkeys opens up taste possibilities that haven't existed in this country for half a century.

If you can get free-range chicken to make my sautéed Chicken à la King, you'll see what I mean. Starting with really succulent chicken, then sautéing it instead of poaching it, produces a luxurious dish that is so full of flavor it can't help but give Chicken à la King a good name again! For a newer and lighter dish, there's Grilled Chicken with Summer Vegetable Compote, which combines the sweet ripeness of summer with simply grilled chicken basted with basil puree.

Few foods feel as all-American as chicken. We all remember the Sunday roast chicken we ate at our grandmother's, the fried chicken we took on picnics, the barbecued chicken our fathers grilled in the backyard. Is it possible to improve on our old favorites? I think my Cranberry-Glazed Roast Breast of Chicken with Autumn Squash, my Buffalo-Style Chicken Salad, my slow-roasted "oven-barbecued" chicken all show how to add taste and relevance without losing the integrity of a dish. And there's certainly nothing as traditional as Roast Turkey with Maple Corn Sauce, but what's new in this case is the cooking technique. I've found that roasting the turkey on its side keeps it moister and juicier than any other method.

Of course, if the refrain in your house is "We're having chicken *again*?" duck is a nice change of pace. Fresh, farm-raised

Long Island duck, also called Peking duck, is full of flavor, and just as versatile as chicken. (Chicken, by the way, can be used for any of the duck recipes in this chapter.) Crisp Roast Duck with Wildflower Honey Glaze is a great and easy recipe. If you want to do something completely different, try the festive Adobo-Style Duck with an adobo chile sauce. One elegant dish I know you'll want to try is the overwhelming favorite at our house: Crisp Breast of Duck Julie Anne, which I developed when I was at the Connaught and named after my wife.

GRILLED BREAST OF CHICKEN WITH STICKY RICE CAKES

CREAMY CHIVE SAUCE

■■■■■■■■■■■■■■■■■■■■■■■■■■■■■■■■■■■■■■

SERVES 4

5 tablespoons unsalted butter

2 cups finely diced chanterelles or other wild mushrooms

½ onion, finely diced

1 cup short-grain brown rice

2 cups Chicken Stock (page 33) or canned broth

3 scallions, halved lengthwise and finely chopped

½ cup diced country ham

1 large egg yolk

2 tablespoons fresh bread crumbs

¼ cup chopped flat-leaf parsley

Salt and freshly ground black pepper

Four 5- to 6-ounce boneless, skinless chicken breasts

Oil for brushing

Creamy Chive Sauce (recipe follows)

DOING SOME READING ON RICE, I came upon a story about Thomas Jefferson smuggling short-grain rice into this country in his vest pockets. Those few grains were the beginning of the profitable short-grain rice industry in the Carolinas and Virginia. Today we grow mostly long-grain rice, but short-grain rice, once all we ate, is still raised as well. It's not as soft as some Asian short-grain rices, but is sufficiently starchy so that it has a soft, creamy texture, perfect for rice cakes.

Melt 3 tablespoons of the butter in a medium saucepan over medium heat. Add the mushrooms and onions and cook, stirring, for about 5 minutes, until the onions are softened and translucent. Add the rice and stir until well coated with butter. Stir in the stock, cover the pan, and bring to a simmer. Lower the heat and cook for 25 to 30 minutes, until all the liquid is absorbed and the rice is tender. Remove from the heat and stir in the scallions, ham, egg yolk, bread crumbs, and parsley. Season with salt and pepper.

Scrape the rice mixture into a shallow dish or tray, cover with parchment or waxed paper, and let cool. Refrigerate for 2 to 3 hours, until cold.

Shape the cold rice mixture into 4 large oval patties, slightly larger than the chicken breasts. Lay them on a waxed paper–lined tray, cover, and refrigerate until ready to cook.

Prepare a charcoal or gas grill or preheat the broiler.

Lightly brush the chicken breasts with oil and season with salt and pepper. Grill or broil the chicken for 4 to 5 minutes on each side, until cooked through. Transfer to a plate and cover to keep warm.

Melt the remaining 2 tablespoons butter in a large sauté pan. Add the rice cakes and cook for about 2 minutes on each side, turning them carefully, until golden brown.

Put a rice cake in the center of each serving plate. Top with the chicken breasts and spoon the chive sauce over the chicken.

continued

CREAMY CHIVE SAUCE

MAKES ABOUT 1 CUP

2 tablespoons vegetable oil

2 cups chopped chicken bones, preferably necks and backs

1 small onion, sliced

1 teaspoon minced garlic

¼ cup dry white wine or vermouth

1 cup Chicken Stock (page 33) or canned broth

1 teaspoon cornstarch

1 cup heavy cream

Salt and freshly ground black pepper

2 tablespoons chopped fresh chives

Heat the oil in a heavy skillet over high heat until smoking hot. Carefully add the chicken bones and brown on all sides, 6 to 8 minutes.

Pour off the oil, leaving just a film of oil in the pan. Lower the heat to medium, add the onion and garlic, and sauté for 2 minutes, being careful not to burn the garlic.

Add the wine, raise the heat to high, and stir to deglaze the pan, scraping up any browned bits clinging to the bottom. Add the chicken stock, bring to a boil, and cook for 4 to 6 minutes, until reduced to about 2 tablespoons.

Stir the cornstarch into the cream until smooth and add to the pan. Bring to a boil, lower the heat, and simmer for 4 to 5 minutes, stirring occasionally, until thickened. Season with salt and pepper and strain through a fine strainer. Stir in the chives and serve.

GRILLED CHICKEN WITH SUMMER VEGETABLE COMPOTE

■■

SERVES 4

Compote

1 cup thinly sliced eggplant

1 cup thinly sliced zucchini

1 cup thinly sliced mushrooms

¼ cup plus 2 tablespoons olive oil

¼ teaspoon minced garlic

1 tablespoon chopped fresh basil

2 large ripe tomatoes, peeled, seeded, and chopped

½ cup Chicken Stock (page 33) or canned broth

Salt and freshly ground black pepper

3 ounces Crowley or Monterey Jack cheese, grated

Chicken

½ cup olive oil

¾ cup fresh basil leaves

1 clove garlic

Salt and freshly ground black pepper

Two 2½-pound chickens, split in half, backbone and wing bones removed

MY FAMILY IS ALWAYS PLEASED when I serve this summer favorite. It features vegetables at their peak: zucchini, eggplant, and tomatoes. You can sauté them ahead and put them in a casserole with the cheese grated over the top; refrigerate until about thirty minutes before you're ready to heat it through in the oven.

I use Crowley or Monterey Jack cheese, but any hard cheese, such as Cheddar, will do; don't, however, use a dry cheese like Parmesan. When it's time to eat, just grill the chicken and heat the compote; the sauce requires no cooking at all.

Lightly oil a 1-quart casserole. To make the compote, blot the moisture from the eggplant, zucchini, and mushrooms with paper towels. Heat the oil in a large sauté pan over medium heat. Add the vegetables and cook, stirring occasionally, for 2 to 3 minutes. Add the garlic, basil, tomatoes, and chicken stock, season to taste with salt and pepper, bring to a simmer, and cook for 2 to 3 minutes to blend the flavors. Transfer the vegetables to the prepared casserole and allow to cool to room temperature. Sprinkle evenly with the cheese, cover, and set aside until ready to grill the chicken.

Prepare a charcoal or gas grill or preheat the broiler. Preheat the oven to 350°F.

To prepare the chicken, combine the olive oil, basil, garlic, and salt and pepper to taste in a blender and puree. Transfer to a bowl.

Season the chicken all over with salt and pepper. Brush about a tablespoon of the basil puree on each side of each chicken half.

Grill or broil the chicken for 6 to 7 minutes on each side, or until cooked through, basting occasionally with the remaining basil puree.

Meanwhile, heat the vegetable compote in the oven for 10 to 12 minutes, until the cheese is melted and bubbling.

Serve the chicken with the vegetable compote on the side.

ROAST SPRING CHICKEN WITH BARBECUED ONIONS

■■

SERVES 4

Four 1-pound spring chickens or cornish game hens, necks and wing bones reserved

Salt and freshly ground black pepper

2 tablespoons olive oil

2 large sweet onions or red onions, halved and cut into ½-inch-thick slices

½ cup Barbecue Sauce (page 152) or American Spoon Foods or other prepared Barbecue sauce

2 cloves garlic, thinly sliced

¼ cup cream sherry

1½ cups Dark Poultry Stock (page 35) or canned broth

¼ cup chopped fresh chives

SPRING CHICKENS—small young chickens—are becoming more and more popular. They usually weigh between one and one and a quarter pounds. Before chickens were raised commercially, spring chickens were the young chickens born in the spring—similar to baby lamb, which also used to be available only in the springtime. I have had luck finding spring chickens at good farmers' markets. Sometimes they are sold boned; if you are lucky enough to find them boned, remember that they will cook far more quickly. Boned spring chickens are also great for grilling. If you cannot find spring chickens, substitute Cornish game hens. The sauce is a barbecue sauce with onions added for flavor and texture and stock added to thin it to the proper consistency.

Preheat the oven to 375°F.

Truss the birds with kitchen twine and season them with salt and pepper.

Brush a roasting pan with the oil. Heat it in the oven for 3 to 4 minutes, until hot. Lay the chickens on their sides in the pan and roast for 5 minutes. Turn the chickens onto their other sides and roast for another 5 minutes. Turn the birds breasts up, add the necks and wing bones to the pan, and roast for 6 to 8 minutes.

Transfer the chickens to a platter, cover loosely with foil, and set them aside in a warm place. Add the onions and garlic to the pan, stir in the barbecue sauce, and return the pan to the oven for 4 to 5 minutes.

Remove and discard the necks and wing bones and scrape the sauce mixture into a medium noncorrosive saucepan. Stir in the sherry, bring to a boil over high heat, and cook for 2 to 3 minutes. Add the stock, bring to a boil, and cook for 3 to 4 minutes, until reduced by half. Remove from the heat.

Remove the twine from the chickens. Serve them whole or cut into serving pieces. Arrange on serving plates, spoon the sauce over, and sprinkle with the chives.

CRANBERRY-GLAZED ROAST BREAST OF CHICKEN

AUTUMN SQUASH

SERVES 4

Cranberry Glaze

2 tablespoons American Spoon Foods Cranberry Catsup or whole-berry cranberry sauce

1 tablespoon cider vinegar

2 teaspoons freshly ground black pepper

Two 16- to 18-ounce whole chicken breasts

Salt

Autumn Squash (recipe follows)

THIS DISH WAS INSPIRED by colonial New England recipes that relied on fruit catsups for flavoring. Cranberry catsup, like plum catsup, is a savory mixture of fruit and spices. (If you must, substitute chunky cranberry sauce for the catsup.)

Preheat the oven to 350°F.

Combine the cranberry catsup, the cider vinegar, and pepper in a bowl and stir well.

Season the chicken breasts with salt and brush generously with some of the glaze. Put the breasts in a shallow roasting pan and roast, brushing with the remaining glaze from time to time, for about 40 minutes, until cooked through.

Cut the breast meat off the bone in slices. Spoon the squash into the center of the serving plates and top with the chicken. Spoon the sauce over and serve.

AUTUMN SQUASH

1 cup julienned acorn squash (about ¼ pound)

1 cup julienned pumpkin or Hubbard squash (about ¼ pound)

1 cup julienned butternut squash (about ¼ pound)

1 cup Chicken Stock (page 33) or canned broth

2 tablespoons cider vinegar

Salt and freshly ground black pepper

2 tablespoons American Spoon Foods Cranberry Catsup or whole-berry cranberry sauce

4 tablespoons unsalted butter

Combine the squash, stock, vinegar, and salt and pepper in a medium sauté pan. Cover and cook over medium-high heat, stirring 2 or 3 times, for about 5 minutes, until tender. Remove from the heat.

Pour the liquid from the squash into a small saucepan and boil over high heat until reduced by half. Lower the heat and whisk in the cranberry catsup or sauce and then the butter. Serve warm.

SAUTÉED BREAST OF CHICKEN À LA KING

■■

SERVES 4

Four 6- to 8-ounce boneless chicken breasts

Salt and freshly ground black pepper

Flour for dusting

2 tablespoons vegetable oil

3 tablespoons unsalted butter

¾ cup sliced white mushrooms

½ cup chopped roasted red bell pepper (see page 44)

¼ cup finely chopped green bell pepper

1 scallion, thinly sliced

¼ cup dry sherry

½ cup Chicken Stock (page 33) or canned broth

1 teaspoon cornstarch

½ cup heavy cream

¼ cup chopped flat-leaf parsley

EARLY IN THE CENTURY, casserole-style chicken dishes were popular in restaurants. At one time Chicken à la King must have tasted very good—otherwise, it would not have been around for eighty years, even in its current state, which is not very good most places. The original dish most likely used poached chicken. I prefer to sauté it in butter; if you don't use too much butter and drain the chicken well, you don't add very much fat but you do add a great deal of flavor. I am certain the chicken used eighty years ago was more flavorful than most chicken available today, so do try to find free-range chicken. The cream sauce is basically true to the original.

Season the chicken breasts with salt and pepper and dredge lightly in flour.

Heat the oil in a large skillet over medium-high heat. When the oil is hot, add 2 tablespoons of the butter. When the butter melts, add the chicken and sauté for 2 to 3 minutes, until lightly browned. Turn the breasts over and cook for 2 to 3 minutes more. Using a slotted spoon or tongs, transfer the chicken to a plate and set aside.

Pour off the fat from the pan. Return the pan to the heat and add the remaining 1 tablespoon butter. When the butter melts, add the mushrooms, bell peppers, and scallion and cook, stirring, for 5 to 8 minutes, until the vegetables are soft but not browned. Stir in the sherry, scraping the bottom of the pan to loosen any browned bits. Add the stock and bring to a boil. Reduce the heat and simmer for 3 to 4 minutes, until reduced to about ¼ cup.

Stir the cornstarch into the cream until smooth, and add to the pan. Bring to a boil, reduce the heat, and simmer for 2 minutes.

Return the chicken breasts to the pan and heat through, about 1 minute. Put a chicken breast in the center of each serving plate and spoon the sauce over. Sprinkle with the parsley and serve.

SAUTÉED BREAST OF CHICKEN WITH BACON, MUSHROOMS, AND WILTED SPINACH

■■■■■■■■■■■■■■■■■■■■■■■■■■■■■■■■■■■■■■■

SERVES 4

4 large boneless, skinless chicken breasts

Salt and freshly ground black pepper

3 tablespoons olive oil

2 cups sliced white mushrooms

4 strips smoked bacon, coarsely chopped, cooked just until crisp, and drained on paper towels

½ teaspoon minced garlic

¼ cup dry white wine

½ cup Chicken Stock (page 33) or canned broth

1 tablespoon cornstarch

¾ cup heavy cream

4 cups lightly packed spinach leaves, washed and dried

¼ cup chopped flat-leaf parsley

THIS IS A VARIATION on the American-style spinach salad, which always includes bacon and mushrooms (although I call for white mushrooms, you may use wild mushrooms such as shiitakes or oyster instead). Just before serving, the spinach leaves are tossed in hot olive oil with garlic, salt, and pepper only until they wilt, then the chicken breasts are set on top of the spinach and the sauce spooned over them.

Season the chicken breasts with salt and pepper.

In a large sauté pan heat 2 tablespoons of the oil over medium-high heat, until hot. Add the chicken to the pan, lower the heat to medium, and cook until lightly browned, 2 to 3 minutes on each side. Transfer the chicken breasts to a plate and set aside.

Add the mushrooms, bacon, and garlic to the pan and cook, stirring, for 2 to 3 minutes. Add the wine and stock, bring to a boil over high heat, and cook for 4 to 6 minutes, until reduced by half.

Stir the cornstarch into the cream until smooth, and add to the pan. Bring to a simmer, stirring, and add the chicken breasts. Simmer for 2 to 3 minutes until the sauce is thickened. Remove from the heat and cover to keep warm.

In a large skillet, heat the remaining 1 tablespoon oil over medium-high heat until hot. Add the spinach, season with salt and pepper, and increase the heat to high. Cook, stirring, for 1 minute, until the spinach is just wilted. Drain the spinach on paper towels.

Divide the spinach among four serving plates, and place the chicken breasts on top. Bring the sauce to a boil and season to taste. Spoon the sauce over the chicken and sprinkle with the parsley.

SAUTÉED BREAST OF CHICKEN
PONTALBA HASH BROWNS

■■

SERVES 4

4 large boneless, skinless chicken breasts

Salt and freshly ground black pepper

1 tablespoon olive oil

¼ cup white wine vinegar

¼ cup white wine

1 cup Chicken Stock (page 33) or
    canned broth

1 tablespoon cornstarch

¾ cup heavy cream

Pontalba Hash Browns (recipe follows)

2 tablespoons chopped fresh tarragon

CHICKEN PONTALBA is an old New Orleans recipe for a casserole containing hash browns, chicken, and béarnaise sauce. Most people don't eat like that anymore, but because I have always liked the idea of the potatoes in the casserole, this dish uses sautéed boneless chicken breasts in a light tarragon sauce instead of the béarnaise. The hash browns are more like diner hash browns, creamier than those in the original dish. But when everything is assembled, the flavors and spirit of the "real thing" are maintained.

Season the chicken breasts with salt and pepper.

In a large sauté pan, heat the oil over medium-high heat until hot. Add the chicken, lower the heat to medium, and brown the chicken for 2 to 3 minutes on each side. Transfer the chicken to a plate and set aside.

Pour off any oil remaining in the pan, and set the pan over high heat. Add the vinegar and white wine, bring to a boil, cook for 1 to 2 minutes, until slightly reduced. Add the chicken stock, bring to a boil, and cook for 5 to 6 minutes, until reduced to about ¼ cup.

Stir the cornstarch into the cream until smooth, and add to the pan. Bring to a simmer, stirring, reduce the heat to low and add the chicken breasts. Simmer for 2 to 3 minutes, until the chicken is cooked through.

Spoon the hash browns into the centers of four serving plates and place the chicken breasts on top. Stir the tarragon into the sauce, and spoon the sauce around the hash browns. Serve immediately.

PONTALBA HASH BROWNS

1 tablespoon lightly salted butter

2 baking potatoes, cooked in boiling
    salted water until just tender,
    drained, peeled, and coarsely chopped

4 scallions, thinly sliced

½ cup diced country ham (½-inch dice)

8 white mushrooms, trimmed, cleaned,
    halved, and sliced

½ teaspoon minced garlic

Salt and freshly ground black pepper

Heat the butter in a large nonstick sauté pan over medium heat until it
begins to foam and turn brown. Add the potatoes and cook for 5 to 7
minutes, stirring occasionally, until browned. Add the scallions, ham,
mushrooms, and garlic and cook, stirring, for 2 minutes. Season with
salt and pepper and serve.

BREAST OF CHICKEN WITH ARTICHOKE SAUCE

■■■■■■■■■■■■■■■■■■■■■■■■■■■■■■■■■■■■■■■

SERVES 4

4 artichokes, with stems

1 to 2 tablespoons fresh lemon
   juice or vinegar

4 boneless chicken breasts, with skin

Salt and freshly ground black pepper

1 tablespoon olive oil

¼ teaspoon minced garlic

1 cup Dark Poultry Stock (page 35) or
   canned broth

2 tablespoons sweet vermouth

1 tablespoon cornstarch

¾ cup heavy cream

1 tablespoon unsalted butter

½ cup chopped, peeled, and seeded
   tomato

1 tablespoon chopped flat-leaf parsley

A NATURAL ELEGANCE makes this dish a stand-out. I use the entire artichoke to flavor the sauce. The little bit of artichoke flesh on the leaves, which people customarily bite or scrape off, has a lot of flavor but would be awkward to cook with—so I use the whole leaves to make the base for the sauce. Then the artichoke bottoms are grated and sautéed in browned butter for intense flavor.

Trim the tough outer leaves from the artichokes, leaving the stems intact.

Bring a large noncorrosive pot of water to a boil over high heat and add the lemon juice or vinegar. Add the artichokes, lower the heat, and simmer for 8 to 10 minutes, until the bottoms of the artichokes are cooked but still firm. Remove the pan from the heat and let the artichokes cool in the cooking water.

Remove the cooled artichokes from the water with a slotted spoon, and reserve the cooking water. Peel off the artichoke leaves and remove the chokes, reserving the leaves. Put the artichoke bottoms, with their stems intact, in a noncorrosive saucepan. Add just enough of the reserved cooking water to cover, and set aside.

Season the chicken breasts with salt and pepper.

Heat the olive oil in a large deep skillet. Add the chicken breasts skin side down and sauté for 2 to 3 minutes on each side, until browned. Transfer the chicken breasts to a plate and set aside.

Add the reserved artichoke leaves and the garlic to the skillet and sauté for 2 to 3 minutes, until the leaves are lightly browned. Add the stock and vermouth, bring to a boil, and simmer for 8 to 10 minutes, until reduced to about ¼ cup.

Stir the cornstarch into the cream, until smooth, and add to the saucepan. Bring to a boil, reduce the heat, and simmer for 3 to 4 minutes, or until the sauce is slightly thickened. Strain the sauce through a fine sieve and set aside.

Drain the artichoke bottoms and pat dry with paper towels. Using a cheese grater or a food processor fitted with the grating attachment, grate the bottoms and stems.

In a large skillet, heat the butter until it foams and begins to brown. Add the grated artichokes, season with salt and a generous amount of pepper, and cook, stirring, for 1 to 2 minutes. Add the chicken breasts, the strained sauce, the tomato, and parsley and simmer for 2 to 3 minutes.

Put a chicken breast in the center of each serving plate. Spoon the sauce around the chicken and serve immediately.

BREAST OF CHICKEN WITH HERB BUTTER
FRIED GREEN TOMATOES

■■■■■■■■■■■■■■■■■■■■■■■■■■■■■■■■■■■■

SERVES 4

4 boneless chicken breasts, with skin

Salt and freshly ground black pepper

2 tablespoons olive oil

¼ cup dry white vermouth

1 cup Chicken Stock (page 33) or canned broth

4 tablespoons unsalted butter

2 tablespoons chopped fresh herbs, such as tarragon, basil, parsley, and thyme

2 tablespoons fresh lemon juice

1 head butter lettuce, such as Boston or Bibb, washed, dried, and torn into small pieces

Fried Green Tomatoes (recipe follows)

THESE CHICKEN BREASTS are served with a light lettuce and herb sauce that you make while deglazing the pan. When you add the butter, stock, and herbs to the pan, you also toss in broken pieces of soft lettuce and let them wilt. As soon as they are wilted, the sauce is ready.

Season the chicken breasts with salt and pepper.

Heat the oil in a large skillet over high heat until hot. Add the chicken skin side down and sauté for 2 to 3 minutes, until browned. Turn the breasts over and sauté for 2 to 3 minutes more. Transfer the chicken to a plate and cover to keep warm.

Pour off the oil from the pan. Stir in the vermouth, scraping up any browned particles from the bottom and sides of the pan. Add the stock and bring to a boil over high heat. Reduce the heat and simmer for 3 to 4 minutes, until reduced to about ¼ cup. Lower the heat and whisk in the butter 1 tablespoon at a time, then add the herbs and lemon juice and season lightly with salt and pepper. Add the lettuce and cook, stirring, for 30 seconds, until wilted.

Put a chicken breast in the center of each serving plate, spoon the sauce over the chicken, and serve with the fried green tomatoes.

FRIED GREEN TOMATOES

SERVES 4

Fried green tomatoes are a classic farm-style American dish that has many variations. Although it was devised as a way to use up the green tomatoes left on the vine at season's end, it is akin, in a way, to chow-chow—another green tomato–based dish. Anyone living north of the Mason-Dixon Line knows about the piles of green tomatoes that must be picked from the garden when it gets too cold for them to ripen. This recipe is a way to eat them.

2 large green tomatoes, each cut into 4
    thick slices

½ cup milk

½ cup all-purpose flour

¼ cup stone-ground cornmeal

½ teaspoon cayenne pepper

Salt and freshly ground black pepper

Peanut oil for shallow-frying

Put the tomato slices in a shallow dish and pour the milk over them.

Combine the flour, cornmeal, and cayenne in a shallow dish and add salt and black pepper to taste.

Lift the tomato slices from the milk and dredge thoroughly in the seasoned flour. Dip each slice in the milk again and then dredge again in the flour, making sure each slice is evenly coated. Set on a wire rack or plate.

Heat ¼ inch of oil in a frying pan over medium-high heat. Fry the tomato slices in batches, for 1 to 2 minutes on each side, until golden brown. Drain the tomatoes on paper towels, season to taste with salt and pepper, and serve hot.

BUFFALO-STYLE CHICKEN SALAD
BLUE CHEESE DRESSING

■■■

SERVES 4

Peanut oil for deep-frying

8 boneless, skinless chicken thighs, each cut into 4 strips

8 cups assorted lettuces, such as arugula, Bibb, red leaf, endive, and/or hearts of romaine

1 tablespoon Olive Oil Vinaigrette (page 51)

Freshly ground black pepper

2 tablespoons unsalted butter, at room temperature

1/4 teaspoon cayenne pepper

2 teaspoons fresh lemon juice

2 teaspoons chopped flat-leaf parsley

1/2 teaspoon Tabasco

Salt

6 pale-green inner ribs celery, cut into 2 1/2- by 1/4-inch-thick sticks

2 tomatoes, seeded and diced

1/2 cup celery leaves from pale-green inner ribs

Blue Cheese Dressing (recipe follows)

BUFFALO CHICKEN WINGS were first served at the Anchor Bar in Buffalo as simple food intended to attract drinking customers. The owners set out bowls of blue cheese dressing to cool the spicy wings and served celery sticks alongside.

This salad includes all the elements of real Buffalo chicken wings, with boneless, skinless thigh meat cut into strips instead of wings. Like the Buffalo wings, the meat is deep-fried and then coated with a mixture of butter, cayenne, lemon juice, Tabasco, and parsley. For more spiciness, add a little more Tabasco; for less, hold back.

In a deep-fryer or a deep heavy skillet, heat the oil to 375°F. Add the chicken strips and fry for 4 to 5 minutes, until very crisp and golden brown. Drain on paper towels.

Toss the lettuces with the olive oil vinaigrette and pepper to taste. Arrange the lettuce on serving plates.

Put the still-warm chicken in a bowl. Add the butter, cayenne, lemon juice, parsley, Tabasco, and salt and pepper to taste, and toss until the chicken pieces are well coated. Arrange the chicken strips and celery sticks on the lettuce and sprinkle with the diced tomatoes and celery leaves.

Measure 1 cup of the blue cheese dressing and drizzle it over the salads. Serve the remaining dressing on the side.

BLUE CHEESE DRESSING

1/3 cup crumbled blue cheese, such as Maytag

2 tablespoons hot water

1/3 cup mayonnaise

1/3 cup sour cream

1/4 teaspoon freshly ground black pepper

A few drops of Tabasco

Put the cheese in a bowl, add the hot water, and stir until quite smooth. Stir in the remaining ingredients. Cover and refrigerate.

BARBECUED CHICKEN

BARBECUE SAUCE ▪ CREAMY POTATO SALAD

▪▪▪

SERVES 4

4 large chicken leg-thigh quarters

2 cups Barbecue Sauce (recipe follows) or American Spoon Foods or other prepared barbecue sauce

1 cup Chicken Stock (page 33) or canned broth

1 head Boston or other soft-leaved lettuce, washed and dried

3 to 4 tablespoons Olive Oil Vinaigrette (page 51)

Creamy Potato Salad (recipe follows)

½ sour pickle, cut into julienne

I'M AS HAPPY TRYING to improve on a simple picnic dish as I am trying to develop something far more elaborate. How you cook this barbecued chicken can make a big difference. People have come to use the terms barbecue and grill interchangeably, when in fact they are quite different. Barbecuing means cooking in a covered environment at a very low temperature, usually over wood. The slow cooking prevents shrinkage and keeps the food moist because, or so the theory goes, if the juices in the meat never boil, they won't seep out of the meat.

You can slow-cook meat in an oven as well as in a barbecue pit or covered grill, but you will not get the smoky flavor from the wood. When "oven-barbecuing," set the meat on a rack in a shallow pan and add a little liquid, such as stock, to the pan. And during cooking, baste the meat with barbecue sauce. This way, the food stays nice and moist.

When I barbecue chicken, I use only the legs and thighs. The breast is too lean and not well suited to slow roasting.

Put the chicken pieces in a shallow noncorrosive pan or dish and pour 1 cup of the barbecue sauce over them. Cover and marinate in the refrigerator for at least 8 to 10 hours, or overnight.

Preheat the oven to 300°F.

Remove the chicken pieces from the marinade and put them on a rack in a roasting pan. Reserve the marinade for basting the chicken. Pour the chicken stock into the roasting pan, and roast the chicken for 1½ hours, basting every 15 to 20 minutes with the reserved marinade.

Turn the oven temperature up to 500°F and roast the chicken for about 15 minutes more, until the skin is crisp.

Transfer the chicken pieces to a plate and set aside to cool. Pour the stock and drippings from the roasting pan into a small bowl. Stir in the remaining 1 cup barbecue sauce.

continued

Place the chicken pieces on a cutting board, skin side down, and bone them, taking care not to tear the skin.

Lightly toss the lettuce with the vinaigrette. Arrange the lettuce on the serving plates and top with the barbecued chicken and potato salad. Sprinkle with the julienned pickle and serve, passing the sauce separately.

———

BARBECUE SAUCE
MAKES ABOUT 4 CUPS

This recipe is based on one that was developed before sugar, ketchup, and vinegar were considered standard additions. It's far more interesting and complex, with most of its wonderful flavor coming from the peppers. Because there is no sugar, the sauce does not burn as easily as store-bought sauce.

1 cup olive oil	2 teaspoons dried oregano
4 cloves garlic, chopped	1/4 cup red wine vinegar
1 small onion, chopped	1/2 cup tomato juice
1 jalapeño pepper, seeded and chopped	1/2 cup tomato puree
1 small red bell pepper, cored, seeded, and chopped	1 tablespoon prepared mustard
1 poblano chile	1 tablespoon Worcestershire sauce
1/4 teaspoon cayenne pepper	1 tablespoon salt
3 tablespoons pure chile powder	1 teaspoon freshly ground black pepper
	Juice of 4 limes

In a noncorrosive saucepan, combine the olive oil, garlic, onion, jalapeño, red bell pepper, poblano chile, cayenne, chili powder, and oregano and cook over low heat for 5 to 6 minutes, being careful not to burn the vegetables. Add the remaining ingredients, except the lime juice, bring to a simmer, and cook for about 5 minutes, until the flavors blend. Stir in the lime juice. Transfer to a blender or food processor fitted with the metal blade and process until smooth. Transfer to a bowl, cover, and refrigerate up to 1 week.

CREAMY POTATO SALAD
SERVES 4 TO 6

It's important that the potatoes are still hot when they are tossed with the herbs and dressing to make this salad. If cold, they will not absorb the flavors of the other ingredients or have a nice, creamy texture. Everyone has tasted salads of sliced cold potatoes slipping around in mayonnaise. It doesn't matter whether you are mixing the potatoes with a vinaigrette or a mayonnaise-based dressing: If the potatoes are not warm when tossed with the dressing, they will not feel creamy in your mouth.

Homemade mayonnaise is best for this classic salad, but there is no reason why you can't make it with store-bought mayonnaise. The salad has chopped hard-cooked eggs and a little cucumber, too, as an interesting alternative to the ubiquitous celery. The cilantro is certainly not traditional, but its flavor goes so well with the barbecue sauce for the chicken.

Dressing

1 cup mayonnaise, preferably homemade

$1/4$ cup sour cream

2 tablespoons milk

$1 1/2$ teaspoons white wine vinegar or cider vinegar

A few drops of Tabasco

1 teaspoon prepared mustard

Pinch of sugar

Salad

2 large potatoes, scrubbed but not peeled

$1/2$ cup finely chopped peeled and seeded cucumber

2 tablespoons finely chopped scallions

1 hard-cooked egg, chopped

2 tablespoons chopped cilantro (fresh coriander)

2 tablespoons chopped flat-leaf parsley

Salt and freshly ground black pepper

To make the dressing, combine all the ingredients in a bowl. (The dressing can be made ahead, covered, and refrigerated for a day or two.)

Bring a large pot of lightly salted water to a boil. Add the potatoes and boil for 20 to 25 minutes, until cooked but still firm. Pour off the hot water and add tepid water to the pan. Let the potatoes stand in the water first until cool enough to handle; drain.

Peel the potatoes and cut them lengthwise into quarters. Cut each quarter crosswise into $1/4$-inch slices.

Put the warm potato slices in a large bowl and add the cucumber, scallions, egg, cilantro, and parsley. Season to taste with salt and pepper, toss gently, and let stand for a few minutes.

Pour the dressing over the potatoes and toss gently. Season again with salt and pepper if necessary. Serve the potato salad at room temperature or chilled.

ROAST TURKEY WITH MAPLE CORN SAUCE
COUNTRY CORN SAMP

■■■■■■■■■■■■■■■■■■■■■■■■■■■■■■■■■■■■■■■

SERVES 8 TO 10

One 12- to 13-pound fresh turkey, neck reserved

1 onion, cut into quarters, plus ¼ cup finely chopped onion

1 tablespoon minced garlic

2 carrots, coarsely chopped

Salt and freshly ground black pepper

3 tablespoons vegetable oil

3 cups Chicken Stock (page 33) or canned broth

2 cups fresh corn kernels (from 3 to 4 ears) or frozen or drained canned corn

¼ cup bourbon

¼ cup maple syrup

2 tablespoons cider vinegar

1 tablespoon cornstarch

¾ cup heavy cream

Country Corn Samp (recipe follows)

I FIRST COOKED THIS RECIPE for Craig Claiborne about ten years ago at his Long Island house. Roasting turkey on first one side and then the other keeps it moist.

Preheat the oven to 450°F. Cut the wing tips off the turkey and set aside. Cut the neck into 4 pieces and set aside.

Put the quartered onion, the garlic, and carrots in the turkey cavity and season with salt and pepper. Sprinkle the outside of the turkey with salt and pepper and rub all over with 2 tablespoons of the oil.

Brush the bottom of a large roasting pan with the remaining 1 tablespoon oil. Put the turkey on its side in the pan and distribute the neck and wing pieces around it. Roast for 40 minutes. Turn the turkey onto its other side and roast for 40 minutes longer, basting frequently.

Remove the turkey from the pan. Pour off 1 tablespoon of fat and reserve; pour off and discard the remaining fat.

Return the turkey to the pan, breast side up. Add 2 cups of the stock and bring to a boil over high heat. Return the pan to the oven. Roast for about 1¾ hours, basting the turkey occasionally with the pan juices, until the juice runs clear when the thigh is pierced or a meat thermometer inserted in the thigh registers 180° to 185°F. Transfer the turkey to a platter and cover loosely with aluminum foil.

Pour the contents of the roasting pan into a saucepan. Using a spoon, remove the vegetables from the turkey cavity and add them to the saucepan. Add the remaining 1 cup stock and bring to a boil, skimming any fat from the surface. Cook for 8 to 10 minutes, until reduced to about 1 cup. Strain the broth through a fine sieve and set aside.

Heat the reserved 1 tablespoon turkey fat in a skillet over medium-high heat. Add the chopped onion and the corn and cook, stirring until the onion is softened. Add the bourbon, maple syrup, and vinegar, and cook, stirring, for about 2 minutes, or until reduced by half. Add the strained broth, bring to a boil, and cook for about 3 minutes.

Stir the cornstarch into the cream until smooth and add to the pan. Bring to a simmer and cook, stirring occasionally, for 3 to 4 minutes, until slightly thickened. Season with salt and pepper, and remove from the heat. Carve the turkey and serve.

COUNTRY CORN SAMP
SERVES 8 TO 10

For years, I'd read about samp in old cookbooks. I first came across it at a farm stand on Long Island and although I could figure out how to cook it, I was not sure exactly what it was. The farmer's description sounded like dried whole hominy but when I described dried whole hominy, he talked about samp—it took us a few minutes to figure out we were discussing the same thing!

Hominy, or samp, is made from fresh corn that is soaked so that the sugar converts to starch. The starch expands and pops off the yellow outer husk, leaving behind little cushions of pure starch. When dried, these are hominy. If you grind hominy, it becomes grits. If you grind it further, it becomes corn flour.

Canned cooked whole hominy is sold in specialty stores, particularly in the South. Its texture is creamy and it's easy to use. Simply drain and rinse it before further cooking. It works fine here; eliminate the soaking step. Jim Beard loved the soft, dumpling-like quality of canned whole hominy.

$\frac{1}{2}$ pound (about 1$\frac{1}{4}$ cups) corn samp (dried hominy)

$\frac{1}{2}$ pound smoked sausage, such as kielbasa, cut into 4 pieces

1$\frac{1}{2}$ teaspoons minced garlic

2 Anaheim peppers

1 onion, peeled

Salt and freshly ground black pepper

4 tablespoons lightly salted butter

1 red bell pepper, cored, seeded, and finely diced

$\frac{1}{4}$ cup finely chopped flat-leaf parsley or cilantro (fresh coriander)

Pick through the samp and discard any yellow pieces. Soak the samp overnight in cold water to cover by 1 inch.

Drain the samp, put it in a large pot and add 10 cups cold water. Add the sausage, garlic, Anaheim peppers, and onion and season lightly with salt and pepper. Bring to a boil, lower the heat, and simmer for 50 to 60 minutes, until the samp is tender. Drain in a colander, remove the sausage, peppers, and onion and let cool slightly.

Cut the sausage into $\frac{1}{4}$-inch dice. Seed and chop the peppers. Finely chop the onion.

Melt the butter in a large deep skillet over medium heat. Add the bell pepper, Anaheim peppers, sausage, and onion and cook, stirring, for about 1 minute. Add the drained samp and cook, stirring, for 1 minute longer or until the samp is heated through. Add the parsley or cilantro and season with salt and pepper.

ROAST TURKEY AND PAN GRAVY

SAUTÉED BRUSSELS SPROUTS WITH MUSTARD SEED

SERVES 8 TO 10

1 cup stone-ground cornmeal

½ pound unsalted butter, softened

One 12-pound fresh turkey, neck reserved

1 large onion, coarsely chopped

4 cloves garlic

1 bay leaf

4 to 5 sprigs fresh thyme

Salt and freshly ground black pepper

6 cups Chicken Stock (page 33) or canned broth

2 tablespoons cornstarch

Sautéed Brussels Sprouts with Mustard Seed (recipe follows)

A MIXTURE OF STONE-GROUND cornmeal and butter inserted beneath the turkey skin makes it wonderfully crispy and imbues the meat with the full flavor of ground corn.

Preheat the oven to 350°F.

In a bowl, combine the cornmeal and 8 tablespoons of the butter and stir until smooth.

Chop the turkey neck into 1-inch pieces and set aside.

Wipe the turkey cavity with a damp cloth. Lift up the neck flap and loosen the breast skin by inserting your fingers or a spoon between the skin and flesh; be careful not to tear the skin. Spread the cornmeal mixture between the skin and the breast meat. Put the onion, garlic, bay leaf, and thyme in the turkey cavity, and truss the turkey. Season with salt and pepper and rub all over with the remaining 8 tablespoons butter.

Lightly oil a roasting pan and heat it in the oven for 2 to 3 minutes. Put the turkey on its side in the hot roasting pan, scatter the neck pieces around, and roast for 40 minutes. Turn the turkey onto its other side and roast for 40 minutes more, basting occasionally with the pan drippings.

Transfer the turkey to a platter and pour off the fat from the pan, reserving 2 tablespoons. Add the stock to the roasting pan, return the turkey to the pan, breast side up, and roast for 2 hours more, or until the juice runs clear when the thigh is pierced or a meat thermometer in the thigh registers 180° to 185°F.

Transfer the turkey to a platter. Remove the onion, garlic, bay leaf, and thyme from the turkey cavity and add them to the roasting pan. Cover the turkey with aluminum foil, and set aside in a warm place.

Using a wooden spoon or spatula, scrape up the browned particles from the bottom and sides of the roasting pan. Pour the cooking juices into a medium saucepan and bring to a boil, skimming any fat from the surface. Lower the heat and simmer, uncovered, for 8 to 10 minutes, until slightly reduced.

Mix the cornstarch with the reserved 2 tablespoons turkey fat to make a smooth paste, and slowly whisk the paste into the stock. Bring back to a simmer and cook for 3 to 4 minutes, skimming any fat from the surface. Strain the gravy through a fine sieve.

Carve the turkey and serve with gravy and Brussels sprouts.

SAUTÉED BRUSSELS SPROUTS WITH MUSTARD SEED

SERVES 8 TO 10

4 pints small Brussels sprouts

4 tablespoons salted butter

1 tablespoon yellow mustard seeds

¼ cup grain mustard

1 teaspoon salt

Freshly ground black pepper

Trim the bottoms from the sprouts and cut a small cross in the base of each.

Bring a large pot of salted water to a boil, add the sprouts, and cook for 5 to 8 minutes, until tender but still slightly firm. Drain.

Heat the butter in a large skillet over medium heat until it foams and turns light brown. Add the mustard seeds and cook, stirring, over low heat for 1 minute. Add the cooked sprouts and toss gently. Stir in the mustard, salt, and pepper to taste and cook for 1 minute more. Spoon the sprouts into a serving dish and serve immediately.

LEFTOVER-TURKEY PEMMICAN

SERVES 4 TO 6

2 cups shredded leftover dark roasted turkey meat

3 tablespoons turkey drippings

¼ cup whole-berry cranberry sauce

PEMMICAN IS a Native American invention that is a mixture of dried meat, rendered animal fat or lard, and acidic berries. Native American hunters took balls of pemmican with them on hunting expeditions to eat as they traveled, tying it in skins or cloth and hanging it from their belts. The berries acted as a preservative and the fat kept the meat moist.

My version uses leftover dark turkey meat mixed with pan drippings and cranberry sauce. It's mashed together until creamy and then "preserved" in the refrigerator. Try it as a sandwich spread for hot buttered toast or shape into little patties, lightly dredge in flour, and panfry.

Put the meat in the bowl of a stand mixer and beat with the paddle attachment at low speed for 2 to 3 minutes, until it begins to form a cohesive, chunky mixture. Increase the speed to medium and gradually add the turkey drippings and cranberry sauce. Beat for 3 to 4 minutes more, until the mixture is smooth enough to hold together. Use at once, or spoon into a covered container and refrigerate for up to 3 days.

Serve at room temperature with hot buttered toast. Or shape into small patties, dredge with flour, and sauté to serve for breakfast.

HOMEMADE DUCK SAUSAGE

MAKES ABOUT 1½ POUNDS (2 SAUSAGES)

1¼ pounds uncooked duck meat, cubed (from a 5- to 6-pound duck)

4 ounces country ham, cubed

2 ounces fat from a country ham or 2 ounces slab bacon, cubed

3 large egg whites

6 tablespoons unsalted butter, at room temperature

1 cup finely chopped leeks

2 tablespoons chopped mixed fresh herbs, such as chervil, tarragon, basil, and/or oregano

Salt and freshly ground black pepper

THIS RECIPE IS AN ADAPTATION of a terrine we served at the Connaught Hotel in London back in the 1970s. Because the sausage, which can be made with almost any meat—including chicken, game bird, venison, and lamb—does not contain a lot of fat, it must be poached and then chilled before it is used. If you cooked it as you would other sausage, on a grill or in a frying pan, the texture would be mealy. (The fat in the sausage is mainly provided by butter. Poaching and chilling gives the butter an opportunity to mix with the small amount of animal fat in the sausage during cooking and then, during cooling, to draw back into the sausage and make it moist.)

I don't usually cook this sausage again after it has been poached and chilled, although it can be heated briefly on the grill to bring out its flavor and brown it slightly. It is just as good served cold or at room temperature.

A meat grinder gives the best texture, but you can use a processor if necessary. It's important to mix the cubed meat and fat in a bowl before grinding or processing it, to ensure that all the ingredients are well mixed.

Combine the duck, ham, and fat and mix well. Grind the mixture in a meat grinder fitted with the small cutting blade. Transfer to a bowl, cover, and refrigerate until chilled. (Alternatively, grind the mixture in a food processor fitted with the metal blade.)

Put half of the chilled meat mixture in a medium bowl and set aside.

Put the other half of the meat in a food processor fitted with the metal blade. With the machine running, add the egg whites one at a time and process until incorporated. Add the butter and process to incorporate. Scrape the pureed mixture into the bowl with the ground meat. Add the leeks and herbs, season to taste with salt and pepper, and stir to blend well.

Lightly butter two 16- by 9-inch sheets of aluminum foil. Divide the sausage mixture in half. Place one half of the sausage about 1 inch from a long edge of one piece of foil and roll up tightly to form a sausage-shaped cylinder 2 1/2 to 3 inches thick and 10 to 12 inches long. Fold and crimp the edge of the foil securely. Repeat with the remaining sausage.

Bring a large pot of water to a simmer over medium heat. Drop the wrapped sausages into the simmering water and gently poach for 20 to 25 minutes, until their internal temperature reaches 140°F; do not allow the poaching water to boil (it should remain at approximately 160°F). Remove the pan from the heat and let the sausages cool in the poaching liquid. Using tongs, carefully lift the sausages from the liquid and refrigerate overnight, still wrapped in the foil.

To serve, unwrap the sausages and cut them into slices.

ROAST DUCK CAKES WITH TOASTED PUMPKIN SEEDS

SERVES 4

2 tablespoons lightly salted butter

2 tablespoons minced onion

2 tablespoons finely diced wild or cultivated mushrooms

1/2 teaspoon minced garlic

3/4 cup diced cooked duck meat

1 tablespoon chopped flat-leaf parsley

1 tablespoon chopped fresh sage

Salt and freshly ground black pepper

3/4 cup coarsely chopped cooked potato (1 large potato)

1 to 2 tablespoons cooked foie gras or natural foie gras pâté (optional)

1 large egg yolk

Flour for dusting

1 tablespoon olive oil

4 cups spinach leaves, stemmed, washed, and patted dry

1/2 cup Pumpkin Seed Vinaigrette (page 114)

2 tablespoons toasted pumpkin seeds (pepitas)

THIS IS, ESSENTIALLY, a classy hash, made with duck meat. It's a great way to use leftover potatoes and duck. You can substitute chicken, turkey, or even goose—and the foie gras is absolutely optional. Shelled pumpkin seeds, also called pepitas, are easy to find at health food stores.

Heat 1 tablespoon of the butter in a skillet over medium heat until it begins to foam. Add the onions, mushrooms, and garlic and cook for 2 to 3 minutes. Stir in the duck meat, parsley, and sage and season with salt and pepper. Remove from the heat and let cool for a few minutes.

Put the potatoes, foie gras, if using, and the egg yolk in a bowl and mash together with a fork. Add the duck mixture and mix well. Season with salt and pepper. Form the mixture into 4 oval cakes, wrap in plastic or waxed paper, and refrigerate for about 2 hours, until completely firm.

Dust the chilled duck cakes with flour.

Heat the remaining 1 tablespoon butter in a large skillet over medium heat until it begins to foam. Add the cakes and cook for about 2 minutes on each side, until browned and heated through. Drain on paper towels.

Heat the olive oil in a large sauté pan over medium heat. Add the spinach, season with salt and pepper, and cook, stirring, for 2 to 3 minutes, until the spinach is slightly wilted.

Spoon the spinach into the center of four serving plates and put a duck cake on top. Spoon the vinaigrette over and around the cakes and sprinkle with the pumpkin seeds.

Duck Sausage with Lentil Salad and Cottage-Fried Sweet Potatoes

■■

Serves 4

1 cup dried lentils, picked over and rinsed

1 ham hock or 2- to 3-inch chunk of country ham

1 small onion, diced

1 carrot, peeled and diced

½ teaspoon minced garlic

1 bay leaf

3 cups Chicken Stock (page 33) or canned broth or water

2 sweet potatoes, scrubbed but not peeled

¼ cup Olive Oil Vinaigrette (page 51)

Salt and freshly ground black pepper

2 tablespoons unsalted butter

Twelve ¾-inch slices Homemade Duck Sausage (page 158)

2 bunches small-leafed arugula or tender dandelion greens, washed and dried

THIS MAKES A great appetizer or lunch dish. Cottage fries are thick-sliced potatoes parboiled and then shallow-fried. Made with sweet potatoes, they develop a wonderful brown crust.

Put the lentils, ham hock or ham, onion, carrot, garlic, bay leaf, and stock or water in a large saucepan and bring to a boil over medium heat, skimming off any foam from the surface. Lower the heat and simmer for 35 to 45 minutes, until the lentils are tender.

Meanwhile, bring a large saucepan of water to a boil. Add the sweet potatoes and cook for 20 to 25 minutes, until just tender. Drain and set aside to cool.

Drain the lentils in a colander and remove the ham or ham hock and bay leaf. Transfer the lentils to a bowl and cover to keep warm.

Remove the meat from the ham hock and finely dice, or dice the country ham. Discard the bay leaf. Add the ham to the lentils. Add 3 tablespoons of the vinaigrette, toss well, and season to taste with salt and pepper. Set aside in a warm place.

Peel the sweet potatoes and cut them into ¾-inch slices.

Heat the butter in a large skillet over medium heat until foaming. Add the potato slices in a single layer and cook, turning once, until browned on both sides. (You may have to do this in batches.) Transfer the potatoes to a plate and keep warm.

Add the sliced duck sausage to the pan and cook for 1 minute on each side.

Toss the greens with the remaining 1 tablespoon vinaigrette and arrange on serving plates. Spoon the lentil salad on top and arrange the potato and sausage slices around it.

PASTA WITH GRILLED DUCK SAUSAGE AND WILD MUSHROOMS

■■

SERVES 4

3 tablespoons olive oil

6 ounces wild mushrooms, such as shiitakes, chanterelles, or morels, trimmed, cleaned, and cut into 1-inch pieces (about 2 cups)

Freshly ground black pepper

2 tablespoons thinly sliced scallions

1 tablespoon finely chopped jalapeño peppers

¼ teaspoon minced garlic

2 tablespoons fresh lemon juice

2 tablespoons dry white wine

1 tablespoon fresh thyme leaves

Salt

Twelve ¾-inch slices Homemade Duck Sausage (page 158)

About 2 tablespoons unsalted butter, softened

8 ounces fresh linguine or fettuccine

2 tablespoons chopped flat-leaf parsley

HERE THE DUCK SAUSAGE is grilled very briefly to bring out the flavor; be careful not to overcook it.

Prepare a charcoal or gas grill or preheat the broiler.

Heat the oil in a large skillet over high heat until very hot. Add the mushrooms, season lightly with pepper, and cook, stirring, for 2 minutes. Lower the heat to medium, add the scallions, jalapeño, and garlic and cook for 1 minute. Add the lemon juice, wine, and thyme, cover, and simmer for 3 to 4 minutes. Remove from the heat and season with salt and pepper to taste. Let cool slightly.

Bring a large pot of water to a boil. Add salt and the pasta and cook for 3 to 4 minutes, until just tender. Drain, and toss the pasta with the mushroom mixture.

Brush the sausage slices with a little butter and season with salt and pepper.

Grill or broil the sausages for 1 minute on each side. Cut each slice into 3 strips and toss with the pasta. Spoon the pasta into bowls. Sprinkle with the parsley and serve.

GRILLED BREAST OF DUCK WITH CRACKLIN' SAUCE

■■■

SERVES 4

Two 4½- to 5-pound Long Island (Peking) ducks

Olive oil

2 onions, sliced

2 cloves garlic, crushed

½ cup dry white wine or vermouth

2½ cups Dark Poultry Stock (page 35), Chicken Stock (page 33) or canned broth

2 bay leaves

Pinch of dried thyme

Salt and freshly ground black pepper

A LOT OF THE good duck flavor comes from the skin, but because it is so fatty, we tend to skin duck breasts. I saved some skin to make into cracklin's and sprinkled them on top of the grilled duck breasts. When the cracklin's mixed naturally with the sauce I served, I took the idea a step farther and made a cracklin' sauce.

Preheat the oven to 450°F. With a sharp knife, remove the leg and thigh sections from the ducks, and reserve for another use. Remove the breasts from the carcasses and chop the carcasses into 2-inch pieces.

Lightly oil a roasting pan and heat it in the oven until very hot. Add the chopped carcasses and roast for about 45 minutes, stirring occasionally, until evenly browned.

Pour off the fat from the pan, add the onions and garlic, and stir well. Roast for 15 minutes. Add the wine, scraping the bottom and sides of the pan to dislodge any browned particles, and pour the contents of the pan into a large saucepan.

Add the stock to the saucepan and bring to a boil over high heat, skimming off any foam that rises to the surface. Add the bay leaves and thyme, reduce the heat, and simmer for about 25 minutes, until the sauce is reduced by two thirds. Strain the sauce into another saucepan.

Meanwhile, prepare a charcoal or gas grill or preheat the broiler.

Using a small sharp knife, remove the skin and fat from the duck breasts. Cut the skin and fat into small pieces and put them in a large sauté pan with ¼ cup water. Cook over medium heat until the skin is crispy and the fat is rendered. Remove the cracklin's from the pan with a slotted spoon and drain on paper towels. Set aside in a warm place.

Using a mallet, gently flatten the duck breasts to prevent shrinking during grilling. Rub with olive oil and season with salt and pepper.

Grill or broil the duck breasts for 3 to 4 minutes on each side for medium rare. Cut the breasts into thin slices and arrange on serving plates. Stir the cracklin's into the sauce and spoon the sauce over duck.

ADOBO-STYLE DUCK WITH SALAD

ADOBO SAUCE

■■

**SERVES 2
AS AN ENTREE,
4 AS AN APPETIZER**

One 4½- to 5-pound duck, quartered

2 cups Adobo Sauce (recipe follows)

½ cup plain yogurt

½ cup loosely packed cilantro (fresh coriander) leaves

1 tablespoon fresh lime juice

Pinch of sugar

Salt and freshly ground black pepper

1 tablespoon olive oil

1 Anaheim or other mildly hot chile pepper, seeded and thinly sliced

1 small red bell pepper, cored, seeded, and thinly sliced

1 small red onion, sliced

4 cups assorted lettuces, such as red and green leaf, Bibb, and/or arugula, washed and dried

2 to 3 tablespoons Olive Oil Vinaigrette (page 51)

2 ounces pine nuts, toasted

ADOBO IS A MEXICAN style of cooking that incorporates two or more dried chiles. I add fresh chiles, too, to give the dish even more dimension. (That also explains why I call this adobo-style, because it is not absolutely authentic.)

The duck is slowly roasted to the point where the meat just about falls from the bones and then the meat is pulled apart and served on a bed of lettuces. The sauce is aggressive but not hot, just very full flavored with a pleasing spiciness.

Put the duck in a noncorrosive pan and pour 1½ cups of the adobo sauce over it. Cover and marinate in the refrigerator for 8 to 10 hours, or, preferably, overnight, turning the duck occasionally.

Preheat the oven to 300°F.

Remove the duck pieces from the marinade and put them on a rack in a roasting pan. Pour 1 cup water into the pan. Roast the duck for 1¼ hours, basting every 15 to 20 minutes with the marinade. Increase the oven temperature to 375°F and roast the duck for 15 minutes more.

Remove the duck from the oven and set aside to cool slightly. When cool enough to handle, remove the meat from the bones and cut into large pieces.

Put the yogurt and cilantro leaves in a blender. Add the remaining ½ cup adobo sauce, the lime juice, and sugar. Season with salt and pepper and process to a puree.

Heat the olive oil in a saucepan over high heat until almost smoking. Add both peppers and the onion and cook, stirring, for 1 minute, until slightly softened. Remove from the heat.

Put the lettuces in a bowl and toss with the vinaigrette. Season with freshly ground black pepper. Divide the lettuces among four plates.

Sprinkle the onion-pepper mixture on top of the lettuce. Arrange the duck pieces on the salads and drizzle some of the adobo-yogurt sauce over. Sprinkle with the toasted pine nuts and serve. Pass the remaining sauce on the side.

ADOBO SAUCE

MAKES ABOUT 4 CUPS

3 cloves garlic, unpeeled

5 to 6 ancho chile peppers

2 to 3 pasilla chile peppers

1 chipotle chile packed in adobo sauce

3 cups Chicken Stock (page 33) or canned broth, at room temperature

1/4 teaspoon dried thyme

1/4 teaspoon dried marjoram

1/4 teaspoon ground cumin

Pinch of ground cloves

3/4 teaspoon freshly ground black pepper

1 tablespoon red wine vinegar

1 tablespoon olive oil

1 Anaheim or poblano pepper, seeded and sliced

1 bay leaf

1 tablespoon sugar

Preheat the oven to 300°F.

Place the garlic cloves in a small baking dish and roast for 20 to 25 minutes, or until quite soft. Let cool slightly and peel.

Meanwhile, spread the anchos and pasillas on a baking sheet and toast in the oven for 3 to 4 minutes. Remove from the oven and split in half while still warm. Remove the seeds, reserving 1 tablespoon and discarding the rest.

Put the anchos, pasillas, and reserved tablespoon of seeds in a bowl and pour the chicken stock over them. Let soak for 20 to 25 minutes, or until softened. Drain the peppers, reserving the stock.

Put the anchos and pasillas in a food processor or blender. Add the chipotle chile, thyme, marjoram, cumin, cloves, pepper, roasted garlic, and the vinegar. Process the mixture to a thick paste.

Heat the olive oil in a noncorrosive saucepan over high heat until almost smoking. Add the Anaheim peppers and cook, stirring, for 30 seconds. Add the ancho puree, bay leaves, and sugar and cook, stirring frequently, for 3 to 4 minutes. Add the reserved stock, bring to a boil, reduce the heat to medium-low, and simmer for 10 minutes. Using a coarse strainer, strain the sauce. Let cool.

GRILLED DUCK BREAST GLAZED WITH MOLASSES AND BLACK PEPPER
SPICY SWEET POTATO HASH BROWNS

SERVES 4

Sauce

2 tablespoons vegetable oil

Reserved duck bones (see Duck below)
   chopped

1 onion, sliced

1 clove garlic, coarsely chopped

½ cup cider vinegar

¾ cup Chicken Stock (page 33) or canned
   broth

½ cup heavy cream

1 teaspoon cornstarch

Salt and freshly ground black pepper

Duck

3 tablespoons molasses

2 tablespoons fresh lemon juice

2 tablespoons coarsely ground black
   pepper, plus more to taste

4 boneless, skinless duck breasts, from
   two 4½- to 5-pound Long Island
   (Peking) ducks, breast bones reserved

Salt

Apples

2 large tart apples

1 tablespoon vegetable oil

Salt and coarsely ground black pepper

Spicy Sweet Potato Hash Browns
   (recipe follows)

WHEN I BEGAN making this dish, I used ducks that were farm-raised for hunting preserves, which meant their wings were not clipped and they could fly. Their flesh was very dark, almost purple, and the breasts very meaty. The legs were so small we didn't use them at all and served only the breasts. You don't have to seek out this sort of duck, however—make the dish with Peking or Long Island duck. Long Island and Peking duck are the same thing; Peking ducks have traditionally been farmed on Long Island and these are the ducks you find in the meat section of the supermarket. (I refer to them this way to differentiate them from mallards, or wild ducks.)

The breasts are marinated in molasses and black pepper cut with a little lemon juice and then grilled and served with a sauce made from the pan drippings and a good, strong apple cider, tart enough to offset the sweetness of the molasses glaze. The hash browns are flavored with onions, peppers, and jalapeños, which counteract their natural sweetness in turn. For this recipe, I parboil the sweet potatoes in their jackets before sautéing them. This helps develop their wonderful flavor more fully than if they were peeled first.

To make the sauce, heat the oil in a heavy skillet over medium-high heat. Add the bones and cook until well browned. Add the onion and garlic and cook, stirring, for 2 to 3 minutes. Drain the bones, onion, and garlic in a strainer to remove any oil and return to the pan.

Add the cider vinegar to the pan, bring to a boil over high heat, and cook for 2 to 3 minutes, until the liquid is reduced by half. Add the stock, bring to a boil, and cook for 3 to 4 minutes, until reduced by half.

Mix 1 tablespoon of the cream with the cornstarch to make a smooth paste.

Add the remaining cream to the pan and return to a simmer. Stir in the cornstarch paste and bring to a boil. Lower the heat and simmer for 2 to 3 minutes. Strain the sauce into a small saucepan and skim off any fat. Season with salt and pepper.

Using a mallet or cleaver, gently flatten the duck breasts slightly to prevent shrinking during grilling.

Combine the molasses, lemon juice, and coarse black pepper in a shallow glass bowl. Add the duck breasts and marinate for at least 20 minutes, turning once or twice. While the duck marinates, prepare the hash browns and the apples.

Prepare a charcoal or gas grill or preheat the broiler.

Cut the apples lengthwise in half and remove the cores. Cut each apple half into 4 or 5 slices. Brush lightly with the oil and season lightly with salt and coarse pepper.

Broil the apple slices for barely 1 minute on each side. Remove from the heat and cover to keep warm.

Remove the duck from the marinade, shake dry, and sprinkle with salt and ground black pepper. Grill the breasts for 2 to 3 minutes on each side for medium rare.

Meanwhile, gently reheat the sauce.

Put a duck breast on each serving plate (sliced if desired). Arrange the grilled apple slices and the hash browns around the duck. Spoon a little of the sauce onto each plate and pass the remaining sauce.

———

SPICY SWEET POTATO HASH BROWNS

2 large sweet potatoes, scrubbed but not peeled

2 tablespoons vegetable oil

1 small onion, finely diced

2 jalapeño peppers, finely diced

1 red bell pepper, cored, seeded, and finely diced

1 green bell pepper, cored, seeded, and finely diced

Salt and freshly ground black pepper

Cook the sweet potatoes in a large saucepan of lightly salted boiling water for 10 minutes; they should still be quite firm. Drain.

When the potatoes are cool enough to handle, peel them and chop into small dice. Heat the oil in a large skillet over medium-high heat. Add the onion and both peppers and cook, stirring, for 1 to 2 minutes. Add the sweet potatoes and cook for 5 to 6 minutes, until nicely browned. Season to taste with salt and pepper and serve warm.

CRISP BREAST OF DUCK JULIE ANNE

■■

SERVES 4

Two 4½- to 5-pound Long Island (Peking) ducks

2 tablespoons olive oil

1 bunch fresh mint, leaves only, coarsely chopped

1 clove garlic, finely minced

¼ cup plus 1 tablespoon Cointreau

1 cup dry white wine

2 cups Dark Poultry Stock (page 35) or Chicken Stock (page 33) or canned broth

2 tablespoons unsalted butter, at room temperature

1½ teaspoons cornstarch

Zest of 2 oranges, removed in long strips and cut into julienne

Salt and freshly ground black pepper

2 medium carrots, peeled and cut into julienne

2 medium turnips, peeled and cut into julienne

THIS IS A DISH I'm especially proud of. It's the first dish I remember doing as a special that was added to the menu at the Connaught Hotel in London, where I trained. I named it after my wife, Julie Anne. Although there is orange zest and Cointreau in the sauce, it is not a typical "duck à l'orange" with a sweet, gooey sauce; the sauce is more of a mint sauce with orange undertones.

With a sharp knife, remove the leg and thigh sections from the ducks, and reserve for another use. Carefully cut the breasts away from the carcass, keeping the skin intact. Score the skin lightly with criss-cross cuts and set the breasts aside. Chop the carcasses into 2-inch pieces.

In a medium heavy-bottomed saucepan, heat the oil over medium-high heat until very hot. Add the chopped carcasses and cook, stirring occasionally, for 6 to 7 minutes, until the bones are well browned. Pour out any excess fat from the pan. Reserve 2 tablespoons of the mint for the sauce, and add the garlic and the remaining mint to the pan. Cook, stirring, for 2 minutes. Add ¼ cup of the Cointreau and cook for 1 minute. Stir in the white wine and simmer for 2 to 3 minutes to reduce slightly. Add the stock and bring to a boil, skimming the surface of any oil or foam. Cook for 5 to 6 minutes, until the liquid is reduced by half.

Meanwhile, in a small bowl, combine 1 tablespoon of the butter and the cornstarch and mix to make a smooth paste.

Stir the cornstarch paste into the sauce and simmer for 2 to 3 minutes, until the sauce thickens. Strain the sauce through a fine strainer into a small saucepan. Set aside.

In a small pan, combine the orange zest and 1 cup cold water. Bring to a boil over high heat, then immediately drain the zest in a fine strainer. Rinse with cold water to stop the cooking, drain, and set aside.

Season the duck breasts with salt and pepper and place skin side down in a large nonstick sauté pan. Add enough cold water to come to the level where the fat and meat meet and bring to a boil over medium-high heat. Lower the heat to keep the water at a gentle boil and cook until all the water has evaporated. (The water will evaporate, drawing the fat from the skin; if all the water evaporates and the duck still looks fatty, add a few more tablespoons of water and continue cooking.) Continue cooking the duck in its fat for 2 to 3 minutes, until the skin is browned and crisp. Pour off the fat and turn the breasts over. Cook for 1 minute longer for medium. Drain on paper towels, then place on a platter and keep warm.

Wipe out the sauté pan and add the carrots, turnips, orange zest, the remaining 1 tablespoon Cointreau, 2 tablespoons water, and the remaining 1 tablespoon butter. Season to taste with salt and pepper. Cook over high heat for about 2 minutes, shaking the pan occasionally. Stir in the sauce and the reserved mint, and remove from the heat.

To serve, spoon the vegetables into the centers of four serving plates. Place the duck breasts on top and spoon the sauce around.

CRISP ROAST DUCK WITH WILDFLOWER HONEY GLAZE

NEW POTATO–AVOCADO HASH

■■

SERVES 4

Two 4½- to 5-pound Long Island (Peking) ducks

2 medium onions, sliced

2 medium carrots, peeled and sliced

4 cloves garlic, sliced

¼ cup wildflower honey

1 teaspoon fresh lemon juice

1 teaspoon cream sherry

Salt and freshly ground black pepper

2 cups Dark Poultry Stock (page 35) or Chicken Stock (page 33) or canned broth

2 teaspoons sweet butter, at room temperature

2 teaspoons cornstarch

New Potato–Avocado Hash (recipe follows)

THIS DUCK IS PREPARED the way a roast duck ought to be: roasted until the skin is brown and crispy and the meat is fully cooked but tender. Wildflower honey is mild and light-colored and provides a gentle sweetness. We discovered it during a trip to a wildflower farm in Michigan, where we noticed bee boxes all through the fields. The farmer explained that the honey the bees produced was usually mixed with clover or another dark honey and sold to large commercial honey companies. This prompted us to contact a beekeeper who agreed to keep honey made from wildflowers separate and sell it exclusively to American Spoon Foods. You can use any sort of honey, but I recommend a pale-colored, mild-tasting one. Finally, the duck is served on a bed of hash browns to which diced avocado is added at the last minute, giving the potatoes interesting flavor and a creamy texture.

Preheat the oven to 350°F.

Trim the ducks of excess fat and cut off the wings. Chop the necks (if included) and wings into pieces. Spread the chopped necks and wings, the onion, carrot, and garlic in a roasting pan and set aside.

Lift the skin at the neck end of one of the ducks and gently push your fingers between the skin covering the breasts and the fatty covering just below it to loosen all the breast. Repeat with the other duck.

Combine the honey, lemon juice, and sherry in a small bowl. Rub half of this mixture under the skin of the ducks, spreading it as evenly as you can. Season each duck all over with salt and pepper.

Set the ducks on top of the vegetables and bones in the roasting pan. Add enough water to cover the bones and loosely cover the pan with aluminum foil.

Roast the ducks for 40 minutes. Remove the foil and carefully pour or spoon off the grease from the pan. Increase the oven temperature to 425°F and roast for 25 to 30 minutes, until, the skin is crisp and the juices run clear when the thighs are pricked with a fork. Lift the ducks from the pan and set them aside to keep warm. (Leave the oven on.)

Pour off the grease from the pan. Add the stock and stir with a wooden spoon, scraping up any brown bits from the bottom. Transfer the mixture to a large saucepan and bring to a boil, skimming the surface of any fat. Reduce the heat and simmer for 6 to 7 minutes, until the sauce is reduced by half. Mix the butter and cornstarch into a paste, and stir into the sauce. Let simmer another 3 to 4 minutes. Strain the sauce and season to taste with salt and pepper. Set aside in a warm place.

Cut off the leg-thigh sections from the ducks. Cut off the breast halves. Place breasts and leg-thigh sections in a baking pan and brush with the remaining honey mixture. Bake for 2 to 3 minutes to glaze.

Arrange a breast half and a leg-thigh section on each plate, with the avocado hash next to them. Spoon the sauce around and serve.

NEW POTATO-AVOCADO HASH

SERVES 4

1½ pounds small red new potatoes, scrubbed but not peeled

Salt

1 ripe avocado

1 tablespoon olive oil

2 tablespoons minced onion

1½ teaspoons minced garlic

½ cup heavy cream

Freshly ground black pepper

2 tablespoons chopped cilantro (fresh coriander)

Put the potatoes in a large saucepan and add water to cover. Season with salt and bring to a boil. Lower the heat and simmer for 10 to 15 minutes, until the potatoes are tender but still slightly firm. Drain and let cool slightly. When cool enough to handle, cut into ½-inch pieces.

Halve and peel the avocado and cut it into ½-inch dice.

Heat the olive oil in a large nonstick frying pan over high heat until hot. Add the potatoes and cook, tossing, for 8 to 10 minutes, until lightly browned. Add the onions and garlic and cook for 1 minute. Add the avocado and stir gently, then add the cream and simmer for 2 to 3 minutes, until the cream begins to thicken. Season with salt and pepper and stir in the cilantro. Serve at once.

CHILE DUCK PILAF

■■

SERVES 4

1 tablespoon peanut oil

1 small onion, diced

1 red bell pepper, cored, seeded, and diced

1 green bell pepper, cored, seeded, and diced

1 jalapeño pepper, seeded and diced

1 teaspoon minced garlic

2 cups diced cooked duck

2 tablespoons pure chile powder

½ teaspoon cayenne pepper

1 cup medium-grain brown rice

2½ cups Dark Poultry Stock (page 35) or Chicken Stock (page 33) or canned broth

2 tablespoons chopped cilantro (fresh coriander)

Salt and freshly ground black pepper

THIS IS ONE of those recipes that give leftovers a good name, in this case, leftover duck. Good cooks try to use every scrap of food in some way or another, and when I realized that we were serving an inordinate number of duck breasts and leaving behind the duck legs and thighs, I came up with the idea to use the "leftover" meat in this chile-flavored rice dish. It also works well with any leftover poultry or meat. Use a medium-grain brown rice with good, nutty flavor, and serve this for brunch, lunch, or supper, or as a buffet dish.

Heat the oil in a large saucepan over medium heat. Add the onion, bell peppers, jalapeño, and garlic and cook for 2 to 3 minutes, until the vegetables are just tender. Add the meat, chile powder, and cayenne and cook, stirring, for 2 minutes.

Stir in the rice, add the stock, and bring to a simmer. Scrape down the sides of the pan, making sure all the rice is covered by stock, cover, and cook over low heat for 25 to 30 minutes, until the rice is tender and the liquid has been absorbed. Remove the pan from the heat and let stand, covered, for 5 minutes.

Stir the chopped cilantro into the pilaf, season with salt and pepper, and serve.

ROAST GOOSE WITH PLUM GLAZE

APPALACHIAN DRESSING

■■

SERVES 6

¼ cup plus 2 tablespoons American Spoon Foods Plum Catsup or plum preserves

¼ cup fresh orange juice

1 tablespoon plus 1½ teaspoons coarsely ground black pepper

One 10- to 12-pound fresh goose

Salt

2 onions, sliced

2 cloves garlic, sliced

2 carrots, peeled and sliced

4 cups Chicken Stock (page 33) or canned broth

⅛ cup cornstarch

⅛ cup port

Freshly ground black pepper

Appalachian Dressing (recipe follows)

HOLIDAY AND TRADITION and taste all come together here. I first made this celebratory recipe for a family Christmas one year. It's simply a roast goose jazzed up with plum catsup, a spicy, fruity mixture reminiscent of the fruit catsups used widely during colonial days. Alongside the goose, I serve a corn bread–based dressing that includes toasted pecans, country ham, and fresh herbs, as well as plenty of butter to keep the corn bread moist.

Preheat the oven to 375°F.

Put the plum catsup or preserves, the orange juice, and pepper in a small noncorrosive bowl and stir to combine.

Trim the excess fat from the goose and rinse the goose under cold running water. Reserve the liver and giblets for another use, or discard.

Pat the goose dry and brush the cavity with a few tablespoons of the plum catsup mixture. Truss the goose, folding under the wings and tying the legs together. Put the goose breast up on a rack in a roasting pan and rub all over with salt. Roast for 30 minutes.

Remove the goose from the oven and prick the skin all over with a fork. Loosely cover the goose with aluminum foil and roast for 1½ hours longer, pouring or spooning off the fat from the pan every 30 minutes.

Transfer the goose to a platter, remove the rack from the pan, and pour off all the fat. Spread the onions, carrots, and garlic in the roasting pan and set the goose on top. Brush the goose all over with about one third of the remaining plum catsup mixture, and roast for 20 minutes.

Add the chicken stock to the pan, baste the goose with half of the remaining catsup mixture, and roast for 15 minutes longer.

Transfer the goose to a platter, cover loosely with foil, and let it rest in a warm place. Strain the contents of the roasting pan into a medium saucepan, pressing the solids to release the liquid. Add the remaining catsup mixture and bring to a boil over high heat, skimming off any fat. Lower the heat slightly and simmer for 6 to 7 minutes, until the sauce is reduced by about one third.

continued

Combine the cornstarch and port to make a smooth paste and stir into the sauce. Bring to a simmer and cook for 2 to 3 minutes until slightly thickened. Season the sauce with salt and pepper, and remove from the heat.

Set the goose on a carving board to be carved at the table, and serve with the sauce and Appalachian dressing.

APPALACHIAN DRESSING

SERVES 6

8 tablespoons lightly salted butter

½ cup chopped pecans

½ cup thinly sliced scallions

1½ cups finely diced country ham

3 tablespoons chopped fresh thyme

¼ cup chopped flat-leaf parsley

Freshly ground black pepper

3 cups crumbled stale corn bread, such as Yeast-Raised Corn Bread (page 231)

½ cup Chicken Stock (page 33) or canned broth

Preheat the oven to 350°F.

Heat 2 tablespoons of the butter in a large skillet over medium-high heat until foamy. Add the pecans and sauté for 1 minute. Stir in the scallions and ham. Lower the heat to medium and stir in the thyme and parsley. Season with freshly ground black pepper and cook for 2 to 3 minutes. Remove from the heat and stir in the remaining butter until melted. Set the crumbled corn bread in a bowl and stir in the pecan mixture and stock. Spoon the dressing into a casserole dish and bake for 15 minutes. Serve.

Pheasant, Quail, Partridge, and Venison

FOR ME, THERE'S NO BETTER WAY to celebrate autumn than to welcome game and game birds back into my cooking. It's great when it's finally cold enough to work up the kind of appetite you need to enjoy something as hearty as a roast pheasant with creamy wild rice sauce. And as much as game celebrates specific seasons, it also celebrates America. I can't think of any other American food that is so directly connected to—and so remarkably unchanged from—the past.

True, most of our game is now domesticated, not wild, but the cooking techniques we use—roasting, braising, grilling—are the same ones they've always been. The results are the same, too—full-flavored, aromatic, robust, and deeply satisfying dishes that evoke country kitchens, snow-covered barns, simmering cast-iron pots on oversized hearths. The recipes in this chapter feature a cross-section of native game— partridge, quail, venison, and pheasant—served with traditional accompaniments like native wild rice, dried cranberries, and forest mushrooms.

Stolid seasonal vegetables like parsnips, butternut squash, Jerusalem artichokes, and Brussels sprouts, as well as spices like fresh ginger and nutmeg, are assertive enough to stand up to the very distinct flavors of game. Because many of the ingredients and techniques I use are so traditional, even dishes like the maple glaze for the quail and the Wild Rice Harvest Cakes feel like they've always been part of our heritage.

Farm-raised game and game birds are not as gamey as

175

their unpenned relatives, so the excuse for not trying a roast pheasant because of gaminess is no longer valid. To ensure that it starts and stays tender and juicy, buy it fresh if possible, not frozen. And when you're cooking it, remember that because game has a low fat content (game, except for squab, is lower in fat, cholesterol, and calories than chicken), it shouldn't be overcooked.

If you can't get it fresh where you live, it's easy to mailorder the highest-quality game. On the other hand, if you have the opportunity to try a wild game bird—like Scottish pheasant or grouse—that is only available frozen, it's worth trying. And if you love one of these game bird recipes, but don't feel like cooking game, you can always substitute chicken or Cornish hens.

New England Harvest
Roast Pheasant

SERVES 4

Two 2- to 2½-pound pheasants

Salt and freshly ground black pepper

2 tablespoons olive oil

2 tart apples, peeled and cored, 1 thinly sliced and 1 cut into julienne

1 onion, sliced

Sprig of fresh thyme

12 small new potatoes

16 Brussels sprouts, trimmed

¼ cup apple cider vinegar

1½ cups Dark Poultry Stock (page 35) or Chicken Stock (page 33) or canned broth

½ cup apple cider

1 tablespoon cornstarch

½ cup heavy cream

½ small butternut squash, peeled and cut into julienne

2 tablespoons unsalted butter

12 roasted chestnuts, shelled (see Note)

2 tablespoons chopped flat-leaf parsley

BECAUSE IT INCORPORATES so many of the native foods that make me think of New England in the fall, this colorful dish is one of my all-time favorites. I've been preparing it for years, and while I generally use pheasant, the recipe is just as good with another game bird or with chicken. Butternut squash, new potatoes, apples, apple cider, and chestnuts: Just thinking about these ingredients conjures up shopping at farm stands when the air turns cool and the leaves begin to color. Sometimes you can even find American-grown chestnuts, which is heartening, because for many years the American chestnut tree was considered practically extinct, after the chestnut blight in the early 1900s. However, stands of trees have been discovered in the Great Lakes states, planted by Native Americans in the last century when they were "displaced" from their homes and forced to move to other parts of the country. Evidently, they carried some chestnuts with them and planted the trees in areas of the country not affected by the blight. European chestnuts, however, are botanically identical to American chestnuts and can be used in this recipe.

Preheat the oven to 400°F.

Cut off the pheasant wings and necks and coarsely chop. Truss the pheasants, rub with a little olive oil, and season with salt and pepper.

Pour the 2 tablespoons of olive oil into a roasting pan and heat the pan in the oven until the oil is hot. Lay the pheasants on their sides in the pan and roast for 15 minutes. Turn the birds over on their other sides and roast for 15 minutes more. Pour off any fat from the pan and turn the birds breast sides up. Add the chopped wings and necks along with the sliced apples, onion, and thyme; roast for another 30 minutes, until the pheasant juices run clear when the thighs are pricked with a fork.

continued

Meanwhile, cook the potatoes in a large saucepan of boiling salted water until just tender, 8 to 10 minutes. Drain and set aside.

Cook the Brussels sprouts in a large pan of simmering salted water until tender, about 4 to 5 minutes. Drain and refresh in ice water. Set aside.

Transfer the pheasants to a platter, cover loosely with foil, and set aside in a warm place. Pour off the oil in the pan and set the pan on top of the stove. Add the vinegar and bring to a boil over high heat, scraping up any bits that stick to the bottom. Transfer the contents of the pan to a saucepan and add the stock and cider. Bring to a boil and cook for 8 to 10 minutes, skimming off any foam that rises to the surface, until reduced to about $1/2$ cup. Stir the cornstarch into the cream until smooth, and add to the saucepan. Bring to a simmer, and cook, skimming off any foam that rises to the surface, for about 5 minutes, until the sauce is thick enough to coat the back of a spoon. Strain into a clean saucepan.

Add the squash to the sauce, bring to a simmer over medium heat, and cook for 1 minute. Add the julienned apple and simmer for 30 seconds. Cover and set aside to keep warm.

In a medium saucepan, melt the butter with 1 tablespoon water. Add the potatoes, Brussels sprouts, and chestnuts, season to taste with salt and pepper, and sprinkle with the parsley. Cook, stirring, for about 5 minutes, until heated through.

Carve the pheasants and arrange in the center of a large platter (see Note). Spoon the sauce, with the apples and squash, over the meat. Arrange the potatoes, Brussels sprouts, and chestnuts around the meat and serve immediately.

NOTE: To roast chestnuts, use a sharp knife to cut an X on the flat side of each nut. Spread them in a single layer on a baking sheet and roast in a preheated 425°F for 10 to 15 minutes. Transfer to a plate to cool. Peel the shells from the chestnuts, using your fingers.

Pheasant legs contain a lot of cartilage and therefore are best left unserved.

ROAST PHEASANT WITH WILD RICE AND GLAZED PEARL ONIONS

SERVES 4

Two 2- to 2½-pound pheasants, livers and giblets discarded

Olive oil for roasting

Salt and freshly ground black pepper

1 onion, sliced

1 clove garlic, crushed

3 cups Dark Poultry Stock (page 35) or Chicken Stock (page 33) or canned broth

1 cup heavy cream

2 teaspoons cornstarch

½ cup cooked wild rice (see Note)

¼ cup lightly toasted pecans, chopped

1 scallion, finely sliced

20 pearl onions, peeled

4 tablespoons unsalted butter

¼ cup sugar

THIS DISH, made with wild rice, pecans, and pheasant (although you can substitute chicken), speaks of America. Adding the rice to the sauce makes it wonderfully creamy and nutty-tasting, and the starch from the rice acts as a thickener. Use real wild rice, not a packaged wild rice mix or paddy-grown "wild" rice. Authentic wild rice is expensive but its flavor is incomparable. Toasting the pecans for a few minutes in the oven or a hot skillet activates their natural oils and brings out their full, rich flavor. As the onions cook, they caramelize in the butter and sugar, and their sweetness is a delicious counterpoint to the pheasant and sauce.

Preheat the oven to 400°F.

Cut off the pheasant wings and necks and coarsely chop them. Truss the pheasants, rub with olive oil, and season with salt and pepper.

Pour 2 tablespoons olive oil into a roasting pan and heat in the oven until the oil is hot. Lay the pheasants on their sides in the pan and roast for 15 minutes. Turn the pheasants over onto the other side and roast for 15 minutes longer. Remove the pheasants from the pan and pour off any fat, then return the birds to the pan, breast side up. Add the chopped wings and neck, the onion, and garlic to the pan and roast, stirring the vegetables from time to time, for about 30 minutes more, until the juices run clear when the pheasant thighs are pricked with a fork. Transfer to a platter, cover loosely with foil, and set in a warm place to keep warm.

Add the chicken stock to the roasting pan and stir to deglaze, scraping up any browned particles from the bottom and sides of the pan. Pour the contents of the pan into a medium saucepan, bring to a boil over medium-high heat, and cook for about 15 minutes, until reduced to about 1 cup.

In a small bowl, mix 1 tablespoon of the cream with the cornstarch to make a smooth paste.

Add the rest of the cream to the saucepan and bring to a simmer. Stir in the cornstarch mixture, bring to a boil, and simmer for 8 to 10 minutes, skimming any foam from the surface. Strain the sauce through a fine strainer into another saucepan. Add the cooked wild rice, pecans, and scallions and simmer for 2 to 3 minutes. Season to taste with salt and pepper. Remove from the heat and cover to keep warm.

Meanwhile, put the pearl onions, $1\frac{1}{2}$ cups water, the butter and sugar in a skillet large enough to hold the onions in a single layer. Bring to a boil over high heat and cook until the water has evaporated and the onions are beginning to caramelize. Lower the heat and cook for about 5 minutes longer, until the onions are evenly golden brown and caramelized. Using a slotted spoon, transfer the onions to a bowl and cover to keep warm.

Cut off the leg and thigh sections from the pheasants. Separate the legs from the thighs and remove the thigh bones. Cut the breasts away from the bone.

Put a breast and a thigh on each serving plate. (Pheasant legs contain a lot of cartilage and therefore are best left unserved.) Spoon the sauce over, and surround with the caramelized onions.

NOTE: To cook wild rice, rinse $\frac{1}{2}$ cup of wild rice under cold running water. Put the rice in a saucepan and add $1\frac{1}{2}$ cups of cold water. Add salt to taste. Bring to a boil, stir, and cover. Reduce the heat to low and cook for 35 to 40 minutes, until the rice is tender and the hulls open to expose the white interior. Let the rice stand off the heat for 10 minutes, then drain. This yields about 2 cups of cooked rice—reserve the leftover for another use.

ROAST PHEASANT WITH NATURAL PAN JUICES

SCALLOPED GINGER SUNCHOKES

SERVES 4

Two 2- to 2½-pound pheasants, livers and giblets discarded

About 2 tablespoons olive oil

Salt and freshly ground black pepper

½ carrot, peeled and chopped

½ onion, chopped

1 clove garlic, sliced

1½ cups Dark Poultry Stock (page 35) or Chicken Stock (page 33) or canned broth

1 tablespoon cornstarch

1 tablespoon unsalted butter, at room temperature

Scalloped Ginger Sunchokes (recipe follows)

THIS IS A SIMPLE ROAST BIRD served with a creamy gratin made with sunchokes. While I use pheasant, a flavorful chicken would work very well here too. Sunchokes, also called Jerusalem artichokes, are the tubers of a type of sunflower, native to the Americas. They are increasingly easy to find at greengrocers, supermarkets, and farm markets. Their thin skin often comes off with just a good scrubbing under running water. After they are peeled, treat them as you would any root vegetable, such as potatoes. Here I slice them, combine them with ginger and cream, top the casserole with bread crumbs, and bake it. The pheasant is served with its pan juices alongside the flavorful casserole.

Preheat the oven to 400°F.

Remove the wings and necks from the pheasants and chop into pieces. Spread the pieces in a lightly oiled roasting pan. Rub the pheasants with olive oil and season with salt and pepper. Set the pheasants breast side up on top of the chopped wings and necks, and roast for 20 minutes. Lower the oven temperature to 350°F. Add the carrot, onion, and garlic to the pan and continue to roast, basting the pheasants with the pan juices, for 35 to 40 minutes, until the juices run clear when the thighs are pierced with a fork.

Let the pheasants rest in the roasting pan for about 5 minutes, then transfer to a platter and cover loosely with foil to keep warm. Pour off any oil from the roasting pan, add the stock to the pan, stir to deglaze, scraping up any browned particles sticking to the bottom. Pour the contents of the pan into a medium saucepan and bring to a boil. Cook until reduced by half, skimming off any fat or foam from the surface.

Combine the cornstarch and butter to make a paste. Lower the heat under the sauce, whisk in the cornstarch paste, and simmer for 2 to 3 minutes. Strain the sauce through a fine sieve.

continued

Carve the pheasants and place on serving plates (see Note). Serve with the pan juices, with the scalloped sunchokes arranged around the meat.

NOTE: Pheasant legs contain a lot of cartilage and are best left unserved.

––––––

SCALLOPED GINGER SUNCHOKES

SERVES 4

2 cups sliced peeled sunchokes (Jerusalem artichokes; 7 to 10 sunchokes)

1 cup heavy cream

3 tablespoons grated fresh ginger

1½ teaspoons minced garlic

¾ teaspoon salt

¼ teaspoon freshly ground white pepper

1½ teaspoons cornstarch

1 cup dried bread crumbs

Preheat the oven to 400°F. Generously butter a 1-quart casserole or small gratin dish.

In a large saucepan, combine the sliced sunchokes, all but 2 tablespoons of the cream, the ginger, garlic, salt, and pepper and simmer over medium heat, stirring occasionally to prevent scorching. Mix the cornstarch with the remaining 2 tablespoons of cream to make a paste; stir into the sunchokes and simmer for another 5 minutes.

Spoon the sunchokes and cream into the prepared casserole dish and top evenly with the bread crumbs. Place the casserole in a larger baking pan and add enough water to come about halfway up the sides of the casserole. Bake for about 30 minutes or until the top is golden brown.

GRILLED QUAIL WITH GRILLED FOREST MUSHROOMS

GINGER DRESSING

■■

SERVES 4

8 to 12 forest (wild) mushrooms, such as shiitakes, oysters, cèpes, or chanterelles, trimmed and cleaned

Salt and freshly ground black pepper

8 boneless quail (see Note)

2 tablespoons extra-virgin olive oil

2 cups assorted lettuces, such as arugula, endive, watercress, and/or red oak, washed and dried

2 tablespoons chopped fresh chives

Ginger Dressing (recipe follows)

NOTE: Boneless quail can be ordered from a butcher or specialty market, or by mail order.

AN INCREASINGLY POPULAR way to cook thick-sliced cèpes or wild mushrooms is to grill them. The intense heat brings out their woodsy flavor. I serve them with grilled quail, tossed with greens and a creamy gingery dressing, as an appetizer or a main course for lunch or a light supper.

Prepare a medium-hot fire in a charcoal or gas grill or preheat the broiler.

Put the mushrooms in a bowl. Add 2 tablespoons of the ginger dressing and toss. Season to taste with salt and pepper.

Brush the quail with the olive oil and season with salt and pepper. Grill or broil the quail for 3 to 4 minutes on each side, until their juices run clear when the thighs are pricked with a fork. Set aside to keep warm.

Drain the mushrooms and grill or broil for 2 to 3 minutes on each side.

Place the lettuce in a medium bowl. Add 2 tablespoons of the ginger dressing, season with a little pepper, and toss. Arrange the lettuce on four serving plates. Place 2 or 3 grilled mushrooms and 2 grilled quail on each plate, sprinkle with the chives, and drizzle with a little ginger dressing.

———

GINGER DRESSING

¼ cup mayonnaise, preferably homemade

1 tablespoon prepared mustard

2 tablespoons finely grated fresh ginger

1 tablespoon soy sauce

1 tablespoon fresh lemon juice

1 tablespoon white wine vinegar

2 tablespoons olive oil

Salt and freshly ground black pepper

To make the dressing, combine the mayonnaise, mustard, and ginger in a small bowl. Whisk in the soy sauce, lemon juice, vinegar, and oil. Season to taste with salt and pepper.

GRILLED MARINATED QUAIL WITH CHESTNUTS AND WILD HUCKLEBERRIES
WILD RICE HARVEST CAKES

■■

SERVES 6

¼ cup pure maple syrup

2 tablespoons fresh lemon juice

1 tablespoon chopped fresh herbs, such as thyme or tarragon

1 tablespoon peanut oil

12 boneless quail (see Note)

Sauce

1½ cups wild huckleberries or wild blueberries

2 tablespoons cracked black pepper

1 tablespoon sugar

¼ cup red wine vinegar

2 cups Dark Poultry Stock (page 35) or canned broth

2 tablespoons unsalted butter, at room temperature

1 tablespoon cornstarch

1¼ pounds fresh chestnuts (about 24 nuts), peeled (see Note, page 185)

4 tablespoons unsalted butter

Olive oil for brushing

Salt and freshly ground black pepper

12 Wild Rice Harvest Cakes (recipe follows)

MY DESIRE TO CELEBRATE the bounty of the land really pays off in this marvelous amalgam of flavors and tastes. I made this dish for the hundredth anniversary of Children's Hospital in Pittsburgh, and I wanted to incorporate a number of the best ingredients found in America. The quail is marinated in a little lemon juice and pure maple syrup, grilled, and served on top of a wild rice and wild hickory nut cake. The sauce is made with chestnuts and wild huckleberries. Huckleberries, part of the blueberry family, are a native berry; because they may be hard to find, you can replace them with dried wild blueberries (they will reconstitute in the sauce—no need to soak them first), tiny fresh blueberries from Maine, or even wild currants, if you come across them.

Combine the maple syrup, lemon juice, herbs, and oil in a small bowl. Put the quail in a shallow nonreactive pan or dish and pour the marinade over. Refrigerate and marinate for 1 hour.

Prepare a medium-hot fire in a charcoal or gas grill or preheat the broiler.

To make the sauce, combine ¼ cup of the berries, the pepper, and sugar in a heavy-bottomed saucepan. Cook, stirring, over medium heat for about 5 minutes, until the berries begin to caramelize. Add the vinegar, stir to deglaze the pan, and cook for 1 to 2 minutes. Add the stock, bring to a simmer, and cook for 8 to 10 minutes. Mix the butter and cornstarch into a paste, stir into the sauce until dissolved, and bring to a simmer for 2 to 3 minutes to thicken. Strain the sauce into another saucepan and add the remaining 1¼ cups berries. Simmer just another minute. Remove from the heat and set aside in a warm place.

Combine the chestnuts, butter, and 2 tablespoons water in a large skillet and bring to a simmer over medium heat. Cook for about 5 minutes, until the water has evaporated and the chestnuts are well coated

NOTE: Boneless quail can be ordered from a butcher or specialty market, or by mail order.

To peel chestnuts, use a sharp knife to cut an X on the flat side of each nut. Put the chestnuts in a saucepan and cover with cold water. Bring to a boil and boil for about 4 minutes. Drain, cool, and peel.

with butter. Season to taste and remove from the heat. Set aside in a warm place.

Remove the quail from the marinade and pat dry. Brush lightly with olive oil and season with salt and pepper.

Grill or broil the quail for 2 to 3 minutes on each side, until the juices run clear when the thighs are pierced with a fork.

Arrange 2 quail and 2 harvest cakes on each serving plate. Reheat the sauce and spoon it over the quail. Place the chestnuts around and serve immediately.

———

WILD RICE HARVEST CAKES

MAKES 12 CAKES

6 tablespoons unsalted butter, plus more if needed

2 tablespoons minced onion

1 teaspoon minced garlic

2 tablespoons minced red bell pepper

2 tablespoons minced Anaheim pepper

¼ cup diced wild mushrooms, such as cèpes, chanterelles, or shiitakes

3 tablespoons chopped hickory nuts

3 tablespoons chopped pecans

¼ cup plus 2 tablespoons all-purpose flour, plus flour for dusting

¼ cup heavy cream

1 cup cooked wild rice (see Note, page 180)

Salt and freshly ground black pepper

¼ cup fresh bread crumbs

2 tablespoons chopped fresh chives

Melt 4 tablespoons of the butter in a heavy skillet over medium heat. Add the onions, garlic, and both peppers and cook, stirring, for 3 to 4 minutes, until tender. Add the mushrooms and nuts and cook, stirring, for 2 to 3 minutes, until softened. Sprinkle with the flour and cook, stirring, for another 2 to 3 minutes, being careful not to burn the flour. Stir in the cream and bring to a simmer. Stir in the wild rice and season to taste with salt and pepper. Reduce the heat to low and cook for 2 to 3 minutes, until most of the liquid is absorbed. Remove from the heat and stir in the bread crumbs and chives.

Scrape the mixture into a shallow glass or ceramic dish. Cover with parchment or waxed paper and let cool to room temperature. Refrigerate for at least 8 hours, or overnight.

Shape the chilled rice mixture into 12 oval cakes and dust each cake lightly with flour.

Melt the remaining 2 tablespoons butter in a nonstick skillet. Sauté the cakes, in batches, until lightly browned on both sides, adding more butter to the pan as necessary. Drain on paper towels and serve immediately.

PAN-ROASTED PARTRIDGE WITH OYSTERS

■■■■■■■■■■■■■■■■■■■■■■■■■■■■■■■■■■■

SERVES 4

4 partridges or squab

Salt and freshly ground black pepper

24 medium oysters, shucked and
    liquor reserved

2 tablespoons finely chopped scallions

Olive oil for roasting

1/2 cup white wine

6 tablespoons unsalted butter, at
    room temperature

1 teaspoon Worcestershire sauce

6 to 8 drops Tabasco

Juice of 1/2 lemon

2 tablespoons chopped fresh chives

THIS IS AN ADAPTATION of an old Virginia recipe for game birds roasted with oysters. The bird is stuffed with freshly shucked oysters, which are then removed from the cavity after roasting, mixed with the pan juices, butter, and seasoning, and served with the sliced partridge meat. All the recipes for game birds in this book are adaptable enough so that you can use any bird you want. Substitute pheasant for partridge, if you wish, or use a free-range chicken or squab.

Preheat the oven to 400°F.

Wipe out the cavity of each bird with a damp cloth. Lightly season the cavities with salt and pepper.

In a large bowl, toss the oysters and scallions together. Put 6 oysters into the cavity of each bird. Truss the birds, rub with olive oil, and season with salt and pepper.

Lightly oil a roasting pan and heat it in the oven. When it is hot, place the partridges on their sides in the pan and roast for 5 minutes. Turn the birds over onto their other sides and roast for 5 minutes. Turn them breast side up and roast for about 7 to 10 minutes longer, until their juices run clear when the thighs are pierced with a fork.

Let the birds rest for 5 to 10 minutes, then cut and discard the trussing string and pour the oysters and cooking juices into a bowl.

Strain the cooking liquid into a saucepan, and set the oysters aside. Add the reserved oyster liquor and the wine to the saucepan and bring to a boil over medium-high heat. Cook for 5 to 8 minutes, until reduced to approximately 1/4 cup.

Lower the heat and add the butter a tablespoon at a time, whisking continuously to emulsify the sauce. Do not add the next tablespoon of butter until the preceding one is thoroughly incorporated. Whisk in the Worcestershire, Tabasco, and lemon juice and season to taste with salt and pepper. Stir in the oysters and chives.

Carve the partridges and arrange them on four serving plates. Arrange the oysters around the partridges and spoon the sauce over the meat.

PAN-ROASTED VENISON WITH WILD MUSHROOMS AND BRUSSELS SPROUTS

■■

SERVES 4

1 tablespoon olive oil

Four 5- to 6-ounce venison loin steaks, trimmed of all fat and sinew

1 tablespoon minced shallots

2 tablespoons grain mustard

¼ cup dry vermouth

1½ cups Dark Poultry Stock (page 35) or Chicken Stock (page 33) or canned broth

1 teaspoon cornstarch

½ cup heavy cream

2 tablespoons finely chopped flat-leaf parsley

Salt and freshly ground black pepper

2 tablespoons lightly salted butter

1 cup sliced wild mushrooms, such as cèpes, chanterelles, or morels

¾ pound small Brussels sprouts (about 16), blanched in boiling water until al dente, cooled, and sliced

THE COMBINATION of wild mushrooms and Brussels sprouts is one of my favorites, especially when they are browned in foaming butter. Pairing these vegetables with venison is wonderful.

Heat the oil in a large skillet over medium heat until hot. Add the venison and sear for 2 to 3 minutes on each side, until browned. Transfer to a plate and keep warm. Pour off the oil from the skillet and let the pan cool slightly.

Set the skillet over medium heat and add the shallots, 1 tablespoon of the mustard, and the vermouth, scraping the bottom of the pan to dislodge any browned bits. Add the stock, raise the heat to medium-high, and bring to a boil. Cook for 6 to 8 minutes, until the liquid is reduced by one third.

Stir the cornstarch into the cream until smooth, and stir into the sauce. Bring to a boil, lower the heat, and simmer for 3 to 4 minutes, until thickened. Strain the sauce through a fine sieve into a second pan. Stir in the remaining 1 tablespoon mustard and the parsley. Season to taste with salt and pepper. Keep warm.

In a large skillet, heat the butter until it foams and begins to brown. Add the sliced mushrooms and Brussels sprouts and sauté for 3 to 5 minutes, until lightly colored. Season to taste with salt and pepper.

Spoon the mushrooms and Brussels sprouts into the centers of the serving plates. Set the venison on top and spoon the sauce over the venison. Serve immediately.

PAN-ROASTED VENISON WITH DRIED CRANBERRY SAUCE
MAPLE-WHIPPED SWEET POTATOES

■■■■■■■■■■■■■■■■■■■■■■■■■■■■■■■■■■■■■■

SERVES 4

Four 5- to 6-ounce venison loin steaks

Salt and freshly ground black pepper

2 tablespoons olive oil

¼ cup sliced shallots

½ cup port

2 cups Dark Poultry Stock (page 35) or
 Chicken Stock (page 33) or
 canned broth

2 tablespoons unsalted butter, at
 room temperature

1 tablespoon cornstarch

½ cup dried cranberries

Maple-Whipped Sweet Potatoes
 (recipe follows)

ALTHOUGH MOST FRUITS and vegetables are available all year long, I like to cook with seasonal produce whenever I can. This recipe is a hearty and welcome wintertime "log-cabin" dish, using traditional ingredients that have always been accessible in the dead of winter. Sweet potatoes develop their flavor during baking. I scoop the flesh from the jackets and mix it with sour cream, butter, and maple syrup for a little sweetness that goes nicely with the venison cooked in pan juices flavored with tart dried cranberries.

Season the venison steaks generously with salt and pepper.

Heat the oil in a large skillet over high heat until hot. Add the venison and sear for about 2 minutes on each side, until well browned. Transfer to a plate and keep warm. Pour off the oil from the skillet and let the pan cool slightly.

Add the shallots and port to the pan and bring to a boil over medium-high heat. Cook for about 5 minutes, until the port is reduced by half. Add the stock, raise the heat to high, and bring to a boil. Cook for about 10 minutes, until reduced by about half.

Combine the butter and cornstarch to make a paste, and whisk into the sauce. Lower the heat and simmer for 1 to 2 minutes, until thickened. Strain the sauce into another skillet. Add the cranberries and seared venison to the skillet and simmer for about 2 minutes, turning the venison after 1 minute.

Spoon the sweet potatoes onto the serving plates. Set the venison to the side of the potatoes and spoon the sauce over the venison. Serve immediately.

MAPLE-WHIPPED SWEET POTATOES

SERVES 4

4 large sweet potatoes

1 tablespoon unsalted butter, at room temperature

2 tablespoons sour cream

2 tablespoons pure maple syrup

Salt and freshly ground black pepper

Preheat the oven to 375°F.

Pierce the potatoes with a fork or knife. Bake for 45 to 50 minutes, until soft. Let cool slightly.

When the potatoes are cool enough to handle, cut them in half and scoop the potato pulp into a bowl. Add the butter, sour cream, and maple syrup. Using a potato masher or sturdy whisk, mash or beat the potatoes until smooth. Season to taste with salt and pepper. Transfer to a covered casserole and keep warm until ready to serve.

Beef, Pork, Lamb, and Veal

DESPITE ALL OF OUR PROTESTATIONS to the contrary, Americans love red meat. We are crazy about beef—sizzling steaks, juicy burgers, hearty steak sandwiches. And when we take a break from beef, we eat lamb, pork, ham, and veal. We are fortunate that our ranches and farms produce some of the best meat and poultry in the world. Improved farming techniques and more organic farming guarantee that what we're eating is leaner, juicier, and more flavorful.

Lots of the recipes in this chapter are my updates or interpretations of classic American favorites: baked country ham, roast leg of lamb, veal chops, T-bone steak. And many of these recipes call for grilling, the most quintessentially American way to prepare meat and a technique that goes back to the Navajos.

I sometimes think, however, that meat is just a good excuse to have all the really marvelous side dishes that go with it. How to improve a T-Bone steak? Serve it with a plate of fries. Not just any fries—a luscious mound of crisp, golden Missouri-Style Morel Fries. A loin of lamb cut into medallions and gently grilled is even more sublime when it's partnered with my version of Jim Beard's favorite creamy hash browns. It is difficult to imagine a more intensely flavorful combination than Charred Beef Fillets Smothered in Vidalia Onions served with rich Cabernet Whipped Potatoes. Country-Style Lima Beans with a crunchy cornmeal coating have just enough assertive taste and texture to complement a Baked Country Ham with Red-Eye Gravy.

There's no question that when a simple chop or basic roast is perfectly prepared, then imaginatively enhanced with the right side dish, gravy, or vinaigrette, the notion of America as a land of meat and potato eaters takes on a new meaning.

GRILLED T-BONE STEAK

MISSOURI-STYLE MOREL FRIES

SERVES 4

Sauce

1 teaspoon olive oil

1 onion, sliced

1 teaspoon minced garlic

2 tablespoons tomato puree

2 tablespoons cider vinegar

1 teaspoon sugar

2 cups Dark Poultry Stock (page 35)
   or Chicken Stock (page 33) or
   canned broth

2 tablespoons unsalted butter

Two 24-ounce T-bone steaks, about 2
   inches thick

2 tablespoons olive oil

Salt and freshly ground black pepper

Missouri-Style Morel Fries
   (recipe follows)

IF THE IDEA of deep-fried morels sounds exotic to us now, it was actually just the opposite fifty years ago. Shortly after the Second World War, when touring America became popular, it was commonplace to find deep-fried morels offered in diners and at roadside stands during the mushroom season. They were so plentiful in the surrounding woods no one thought of them as being anything special. Local cooks prepared them just as I have here, dipping them in cream and flour, then deep-frying them until crispy and golden. Often they were served with catsup, like French fries, which is the reason I have made a tomato-based sauce to serve with them and the T-bones. These would be great with any grilled beef or lamb.

To make the sauce, heat the oil in a heavy skillet over medium heat. Add the onion and cook, stirring, for 3 to 4 minutes, until lightly browned. Add the garlic and tomato puree and cook for 2 minutes. Stir in the vinegar and sugar and cook for 1 to 2 minutes. Add the stock and bring to a boil over high heat, skimming the surface of any fat or oil. Lower the heat and simmer, uncovered, for about 20 minutes, until the sauce has reduced by half and thickened. Remove from the heat and whisk in the butter. Strain the sauce through a fine strainer and keep warm.

Prepare a medium-hot fire in a charcoal or gas grill or preheat the broiler.

Rub the steaks with the oil and season with salt and pepper. Grill or broil for 4 to 5 minutes on each side for medium rare.

Slice the steaks and serve with the sauce and fried morels on the side.

MISSOURI-STYLE MOREL FRIES

SERVES 4

Peanut oil for deep-frying

$\frac{1}{2}$ pound morels, trimmed, cleaned, and cut in half lengthwise

1 cup light cream

1 cup all-purpose flour

$\frac{1}{2}$ cup stone-ground cornmeal

$\frac{1}{2}$ teaspoon cayenne pepper

Salt and freshly ground black pepper

In a deep-fryer or a deep heavy pan, heat the oil to 375°F.

Put the morels in a bowl, add the cream and toss.

Put the flour, cayenne, and cornmeal in a shallow bowl, season with salt and pepper, and stir to combine. Drain the morels and add them to the flour mixture, tossing until evenly coated.

Fry the morels a few at a time in the hot oil, taking care not to crowd them, for 2 to 3 minutes, until golden brown. Drain on paper towels and sprinkle lightly with salt. Serve immediately.

BARBECUED "FRANKS" IN A SOFT PRETZEL

■■■

MAKES 12 FRANKS

Twelve 6- to 8-inch buffalo sausages or other kielbasa-style sausages

¼ cup Barbecue Sauce (page 152) or American Spoon Foods or other prepared barbecue sauce

1 recipe pretzel dough (page 233)

Twelve ¼-inch-thick slices Crowley or white Cheddar cheese, approximately 3 by 5 inches

6 cups water

One 12-ounce bottle amber beer, such as Samuel Adams

2 tablespoons malt

3 tablespoons baking soda

1 large egg beaten with 2 tablespoons water for egg wash

Coarse sea salt

Spicy brown mustard for serving

YOU CAN TELL that I'm not a pretentious food snob—this recipe is my take on "Pigs in a Blanket," the quintessential 1950s cocktail food. It's just wonderful! The soft pretzel dough is wrapped around the sausage and cheese and the "franks" are poached briefly before being baked. The dough calls for malt, which is available at health food stores. Serve these right from the oven.

Combine the sausages and barbecue sauce in a large skillet, bring to a simmer over low heat, and cook for 2 to 3 minutes. Remove from the heat and let cool.

Make the pretzel dough as described. On a lightly floured surface, roll the pretzel dough out to an 18- by 16-inch rectangle. Cut the dough lengthwise into 4 strips, then cut each strip crosswise into 3 pieces to make twelve 6- by 4-inch rectangles. Lay a slice of cheese on each rectangle, leaving a ½-inch border around the cheese; trim the slices if necessary. Spread a little of the barbecue sauce from the sausages on each piece of cheese, and center a sausage lengthwise down each rectangle; the ends of the sausages will extend a little beyond the edges of the dough. Brush the long edges of each rectangle of dough with water and fold up over the sausage, pressing the seam to seal. Set the sausage rolls seam side down on a baking sheet or plate.

Preheat the oven to 350°F. Lightly oil a baking sheet.

Combine the water, beer, malt, and baking soda in a large saucepan and bring to a simmer over medium heat. Using a slotted spoon, lower the wrapped sausages, one at a time, into the liquid and poach for 30 seconds. Remove with the slotted spoon and place seam side down on the prepared baking sheet.

Lightly brush the pretzel dough with the egg wash and sprinkle with coarse sea salt. Bake for 10 minutes, or until golden brown.

Serve the franks hot, with spicy brown mustard.

PHILLY CHEESESTEAK

■■■■■■■■■■■■■■■■■■■■■■■■■■■■■■■■■■■■■■■

SERVES 6

6 hero loaves Pennsylvania Dutch Potato Bread (page 232) or soft potato rolls

Six 4- to 5-ounce boneless sirloin steaks, trimmed of all fat

Salt and freshly ground black pepper

2 tablespoons peanut oil

1 onion, chopped

1 red bell pepper, cored, seeded, and thinly sliced

1 green bell pepper, cored, seeded, and thinly sliced

1 jalapeño pepper, seeded and very finely chopped

Twelve ⅛-inch-thick slices aged Crowley or sharp white Cheddar cheese

1½ cups Dark Poultry Stock (page 35) or Chicken Stock (page 33) or canned broth

THIS EXTREMELY TASTY homage to Philadelphia is an upscale version of a classic cheesesteak. It has all the ingredients of the original, but I've upped the ante by using sirloin and Crowley cheese, or sharp cheddar, instead of minute steaks and processed American cheese. The soft Dutch potato rolls absorb all the delicious juices.

Preheat the broiler.

Cut the potato rolls in half lengthwise and set the bottoms on a baking sheet.

Using a mallet, flatten the steaks slightly. Season with salt and pepper.

Heat the oil in a large heavy skillet over high heat until hot. Add the steaks and cook for 2 minutes on each side for medium rare. Remove the steaks from the pan; add the onion and all the peppers to the skillet and cook, stirring, over medium heat for 3 to 4 minutes, until nicely softened. Slice the steaks and set them on the bottom halves of the rolls. Using a slotted spoon, spoon the onion-pepper mixture over the steaks, and set the skillet aside.

Put 2 slices of cheese on each steak. Broil for 1 to 2 minutes, until the cheese is completely melted.

Meanwhile, add the stock to the skillet and bring to a boil. Cook for 1 minute, then strain through a fine sieve.

Transfer the sandwiches to a cutting board. Drizzle a few tablespoons of the strained stock onto the cut side of each reserved top bread half, put the halves on top of the sandwiches, and cut in half. Serve with a small bowl of the remaining stock for dipping.

CHARRED MEDALLIONS OF BEEF WITH CABERNET SAUCE

PARSNIP HASH BROWNS

■■■■■■■■■■■■■■■■■■■■■■■■■■■■■■■■■■

SERVES 4

4 medium beets, scrubbed but not peeled

Olive oil

Four 7- to 8-ounce center-cut beef
    fillet steaks

Salt and freshly ground black pepper

1 tablespoon olive oil

1 tablespoon minced garlic

2 tablespoons red wine vinegar

1 cup cabernet sauvignon

1½ cups Dark Poultry Stock (page 35)
    or Chicken Stock (page 33) or
    canned broth

3 tablespoons unsalted butter, at room
    temperature

1 tablespoon cornstarch

2 teaspoons chopped fresh thyme

Parsnip Hash Browns (recipe follows)

I CAME UP WITH this rich, rewarding American beef recipe when I took An American Place on the road to Tokyo. It was a big hit! I made the sauce with a nice, rich California cabernet, which tastes great with the creamy parsnip hash browns.

Preheat the oven to 350°F.

Rub the beets lightly with oil. Roast for 20 to 25 minutes, until cooked but still slightly firm. Let cool.

Using a sharp knife, peel the beets. Cut the beets into ¼-inch slices and then cut the slices into julienne.

Season the steaks with salt and a generous amount of pepper.

Heat the olive oil in a large heavy skillet over high heat until smoking hot. Add the steaks and cook for 2 to 3 minutes on each side for medium rare. Transfer the steaks to a plate and keep warm.

Pour off the oil from the pan. Add the garlic and red wine vinegar to the pan and cook for 30 seconds. Stir in the wine, scraping up any browned particles from the bottom of the pan. Bring to a boil and cook for 5 to 6 minutes, until reduced to about ⅓ cup. Add the stock, bring to a boil, and cook for 4 to 5 minutes, until reduced by half. Mix the butter and cornstarch into a paste. Lower the heat and stir in the butter mixture. Let simmer for 2 to 3 minutes to thicken. Season with salt and pepper to taste. Strain the sauce through a fine sieve into a second pan, and add the julienned beets and the thyme.

Spoon the potatoes into the centers of the serving plates and nestle the beef medallions in the potatoes. Spoon the sauce and beets over the top and serve.

PARSNIP HASH BROWNS

SERVES 4

6 parsnips, peeled and cut into large
   pieces

$\frac{1}{4}$ cup olive oil

1$\frac{1}{2}$ teaspoons minced garlic

2 tablespoons minced onion

3 tablespoons cream sherry

$\frac{1}{2}$ cup heavy cream

Salt and freshly ground black pepper

Cook the parsnips in boiling salted water for 10 minutes, until cooked but still firm. Drain and let cool; cut into small cubes.

Heat the oil in a large nonstick skillet over high heat. Add the parsnips and sauté for about 4 to 5 minutes, until golden brown. Drain off the oil, and add the garlic and onion to the parsnips. Cook, stirring for 1 to 2 minutes. Add the sherry and cook another minute. Add the cream, season with salt and pepper, and bring to a simmer. Cook for 2 to 3 minutes, until the cream begins to thicken. Remove from the heat and serve.

CHARRED BEEF FILLETS SMOTHERED IN VIDALIA ONIONS
CABERNET WHIPPED POTATOES

<hr />

SERVES 4

Four 7- to 8-ounce center-cut beef fillet steaks

Salt and freshly ground black pepper

2 tablespoons olive oil

4 tablespoons chopped onions

1 tablespoon minced garlic

3 tablespoons pure chile powder

2 tablespoons red wine vinegar

2 cups Dark Poultry Stock (page 35) or Chicken Stock (page 33) or canned broth

2 tablespoons unsalted butter, at room temperature

1 tablespoon cornstarch

2 medium Vidalia onions, cut into ¼-inch-thick slices

Cabernet Whipped Potatoes (recipe follows)

1 tablespoon finely chopped fresh chives

THIS IS ANOTHER DISH I made for our stint in Tokyo several years ago. What makes it special is that the mashed potatoes are flavored with a reduction of red wine, shallots, and cream. These potatoes would taste good with any meat. The crunch of the stir-fried Vidalia onions gives the dish a nice balance. Vidalia onions are sweet and mellow, but you could use any onions you like.

Season the steaks with salt and a generous amount of pepper. Heat 1 tablespoon of the oil in a large heavy skillet over high heat until smoking hot. Add the steaks and cook for 2 to 3 minutes on each side for medium rare. Transfer the steaks to a plate and keep warm.

Pour off any oil from the pan. Add the onions, garlic, and chile powder to the pan and cook, stirring, for 1 to 2 minutes. Stir in the vinegar, scraping up any browned particles from the bottom of the pan. Bring to a boil. Add the stock, bring to a boil for 4 to 5 minutes, until reduced by half. Mix the butter and cornstarch into a paste and stir into the sauce. Lower the heat and let simmer for 3 to 4 minutes to thicken. Season with salt and pepper to taste. Strain the sauce through a fine sieve and keep warm until ready to serve.

Meanwhile, heat the remaining 1 tablespoon oil in a large skillet over high heat until smoking hot. Add the onions and cook, tossing or stirring, until lightly browned; the onions should remain crisp. Season lightly with salt, and remove from the heat.

Spoon the potatoes into the center of the serving plates and nestle the beef medallions in the potatoes. Spoon the sauce around the fillets and cover the steaks completely with the onions. Sprinkle with the chives and serve.

CABERNET WHIPPED POTATOES

2 pounds Yukon gold or baking potatoes, peeled and sliced

1½ cups cabernet sauvignon

2 tablespoons minced shallots

1 tablespoon minced garlic

4 tablespoons unsalted butter, at room temperature

½ cup heavy cream

Salt and freshly ground black pepper

2 tablespoons chopped chives

Put the potatoes in a large pot of lightly salted water and bring to a boil. Reduce the heat to a simmer and cook for 20 to 30 minutes, until the potatoes are tender.

Meanwhile, combine the wine, shallots, and garlic in a small non-corrosive saucepan and bring to a boil over high heat. Cook for 7 to 8 minutes, until the liquid is reduced to about ⅓ cup. Set aside.

Drain the potatoes and return them to the pan. Stir over medium-high heat for about 1 minute to dry them out.

Add the reduced red wine mixture, and mash the potatoes with a fork or potato masher, mixing in the wine. (Or press the potatoes through a potato ricer into a bowl, add the wine mixture, and blend well.)

Heat the cream in a saucepan over medium-high heat until scalded but not boiling. Add the butter and cream to the potatoes, and salt and pepper to taste, and mash with the fork or potato masher until smooth. Stir in the chives. Serve immediately, or keep warm until ready to serve.

CHARRED BEEF FILLET
CARPETBAGGER-STYLE

■■

SERVES 4

12 oysters, shucked and liquor reserved

1 teaspoon lightly salted butter

Four 7-ounce center-cut beef fillet steaks

Salt and freshly ground black pepper

2 tablespoons olive oil

1 tablespoon minced shallots

4 ounces shiitake mushrooms, trimmed,
  cleaned, and sliced

1 tablespoon red wine vinegar

½ cup red wine

1½ cups Dark Poultry Stock (page 35) or
  canned beef broth

2 tablespoons unsalted butter, at room
  temperature

1 tablespoon cornstarch

1 tablespoon chopped fresh chives

THIS IS A REMAKE of a classic dish that was served in San Francisco around the time of the Gold Rush. Back then, cooks would take a big fillet of beef, cut a pocket in it, and stuff the pocket with raw oysters. I think the idea is interesting, but I decided to sauté the oysters lightly in their own liquid before stuffing them into individual fillet steaks.

In a small sauté pan, combine the oysters, their liquor, and the lightly salted butter. Cook over medium heat for 1 to 2 minutes, until the edges of the oysters begin to curl. Transfer the oysters to a bowl, cover, and refrigerate until cold.

Using a thin-bladed sharp knife, carefully cut a small pocket in the side of each fillet, making as small an opening as possible. Stuff each one with 3 oysters and season with salt and pepper.

Heat the oil in a large cast-iron or other heavy skillet until very hot. Add the steaks to the pan and cook for 2 to 3 minutes to a side for medium rare, taking care the oysters do not fall from the pockets when turning the meat. Transfer the steaks to a plate and keep warm. Pour off all but 1 teaspoon of the fat from the pan.

Heat the pan over high heat. Add the shallots and mushrooms and cook, stirring, for about 2 to 3 minutes, until the mushrooms are lightly colored and the shallots soften. Add the vinegar and cook for 1 minute longer. Add the wine, bring to a boil, and cook for 4 to 5 minutes, until reduced by half. Add the stock, bring to a boil, and cook for 7 to 8 minutes, until reduced by half.

Meanwhile, in a small bowl, combine the unsalted butter and the cornstarch to make a paste. Reduce the heat so that the sauce is simmering and stir in the paste. Simmer gently for 2 to 3 minutes to thicken.

Put the fillets in the center of four serving plates. Spoon the sauce over the steaks and sprinkle with the chives.

CHARRED SIRLOIN STEAK WITH
BLUE CHEESE BAKED ONIONS

■■

SERVES 4

2 large Bermuda or red onions

Salt and freshly ground black pepper

2 tablespoons olive oil or vegetable oil

1 cup Dark Poultry Stock (page 35)
    or Chicken Stock (page 33) or
    canned broth

4 to 5 ounces blue cheese, such as
    Maytag, crumbled

1/4 cup fresh bread crumbs

Four 8- to 10-ounce sirloin steaks,
    trimmed

2 tablespoons port

4 tablespoons unsalted butter, at room
    temperature

2 tablespoons chopped flat-leaf parsley

THERE ARE A NUMBER of traditional American food combinations that seem to me a perfect match. I have always been intrigued by the teaming of beef with blue cheese. I included roasted onions for another dimension of flavor, as well, to add sweetness that complements the sharpness of the cheese.

Preheat the oven to 350°F.

Slice each onion into 4 thick slices, being careful not to separate the rings. Season with salt and pepper.

Heat 1 tablespoon of the oil in a large heavy skillet until very hot. Add the onion slices and brown on both sides, 1 to 2 minutes. Carefully transfer the slices to a shallow casserole or baking dish large enough to hold them in a single layer, and pour in the stock.

Cover the casserole loosely with foil. Bake for about 30 minutes, or until the onions are cooked but still firm.

Raise the oven temperature to 475°F. Top the onions with the crumbled cheese and then the bread crumbs. Return the casserole to the oven and bake, uncovered, for 3 to 4 minutes, or until the cheese is melted. Remove the casserole from the oven and preheat the broiler.

Place the casserole under the broiler to brown the bread crumbs lightly. Remove from the broiler and keep warm.

Meanwhile, heat the remaining 1 tablespoon oil in a heavy skillet over medium-high heat until very hot. Season the steaks with salt and pepper. Add the steaks to the pan and cook for 3 to 4 minutes on each side for medium rare.

Pour off the oil from the skillet, and add the port. Remove the skillet from the heat and stir in the butter and parsley until smooth.

Place a steak on each serving plate and spoon the sauce over. Serve with the onions.

CHARRED RIB-EYE STEAK
MIDWEST SMASHED NEW POTATOES

■■

SERVES 4

Four 10- to 12-ounce center-cut rib-eye
     steaks

Salt and freshly ground black pepper

Cayenne pepper

2 tablespoons lightly salted butter,
     softened

1 large red onion, halved and sliced

1 teaspoon minced garlic

1 tablespoon spicy brown mustard

1 tablespoon grain mustard

2 tablespoons brandy

¾ cup Dark Poultry Stock (page 35)
     or Chicken Stock (page 33) or
     canned broth

3 to 4 tablespoons unsalted butter,
     softened

Midwest Smashed New Potatoes
     (recipe follows)

MEAT AND POTATOES, as good as it gets. This hearty dish is redolent of America's heartland. Although you could cook any steak for this, I like the rib-eye, also called Delmonico cut. It's important not to overmash the potatoes for this dish–they should be chunky, which is why I call them smashed, not mashed. The Wisconsin havarti cheese adds the Midwest to the potatoes.

Season the steaks on both sides with salt, a generous amount of black pepper, and a little cayenne. Brush the steaks on both sides with the softened salted butter.

Heat a heavy skillet over medium-high heat until hot. Add the steaks and cook for 3 to 4 minutes on each side for medium rare. Set aside in a warm place.

Pour off the fat from the pan and return to the heat. Add the onions and cook for about 5 minutes, stirring occasionally, until lightly browned. Stir in the garlic and both mustards and cook, stirring, for 2 minutes. Add the brandy and bring to a boil. Add the stock and bring to a boil. Skim the surface of any fat or foam and cook for 3 to 4 minutes, until reduced by half. Lower the heat and stir in the unsalted butter, a tablespoon at a time. Remove from the heat.

Place a spoonful of the potatoes slightly off-center on each serving plate. Lean the steaks against the potatoes and spoon the sauce over the steaks. Pass any remaining potatoes and sauce separately.

MIDWEST SMASHED NEW POTATOES

SERVES 4

16 to 20 red-skinned new potatoes,
   scrubbed and halved

Salt

1/2 cup milk

2/3 cup sour cream, at room temperature

4 tablespoons lightly salted butter,
   at room temperature

Pinch of freshly grated nutmeg

Freshly ground black pepper

3 to 4 ounces havarti cheese, grated

Put the potatoes in a large pan, cover with cold water, and season with salt. Bring to a boil over high heat, lower the heat to simmer, and cook the potatoes for about 15 to 20 minutes, until tender. Drain the potatoes and return them to the pan.

Set the pan over medium-high heat for about 2 minutes, shaking the pan occasionally, to dry the potatoes. Add the milk, sour cream, and butter. With a fork or potato masher, gently blend the ingredients, leaving lots of potato chunks. Season to taste with the nutmeg, salt, and pepper. Stir in the grated cheese and serve.

Sautéed Beef Fillets Heaped with Roasted Root Vegetables

■■■

Serves 4

8 baby red or golden beets, peeled

12 baby carrots, peeled

8 baby turnips, peeled

Olive oil

Salt and freshly ground black pepper

Four 6-ounce beef fillet steaks

2 tablespoons olive oil

¼ cup dry sherry

2 cups Dark Poultry Stock (page 35) or
    Chicken Stock (page 33) or
    canned broth

3 tablespoons unsalted butter, at room
    temperature

1 tablespoon cornstarch

1 tablespoon chopped fresh thyme

1 carrot, peeled and cut into julienne

I ORIGINALLY MADE this dish with buffalo—and of course you still can if you have access to buffalo meat. I char the meat in a hot skillet, then pile on roasted root vegetables that have been mixed with the sauce at the last minute and topped with a julienne of blanched carrots.

Preheat the oven to 400°F.

In lightly salted boiling water, separately blanch the baby beets, carrots, and turnips for about 5 minutes; drain. Toss with a little olive oil, season to taste with salt and pepper, and place on a baking sheet in the oven; cook until tender, about 10 to 15 minutes. Set the vegetables aside.

Season the steaks on both sides with salt and pepper.

Heat the olive oil in a large heavy skillet over medium-high heat until hot. Cook the steaks for 3 to 4 minutes to a side for medium rare. Transfer to a plate and keep warm.

Pour off the fat from the skillet. Add the sherry and scrape the bottom and sides of the pan to loosen any browned particles. Add the stock, bring to a boil, and cook for 5 to 7 minutes, until reduced by half.

Mix 2 tablespoons of the butter with the cornstarch to make a paste. Stir into the sauce and let simmer for 3 to 4 minutes to thicken. Strain into a second pan.

Cut the beets and turnips in half through the tops and add to the sauce. Add the baby carrots and thyme and simmer another minute.

Combine the remaining 1 tablespoon butter and 1 tablespoon water in a small saucepan and heat over medium heat until the butter is melted. Add the julienne of carrot and cook gently for about 1 minute, until crisp-tender. Drain and season to taste with salt.

Place a steak in the center of each serving plate. Mound the root vegetables over the meat, spoon the sauce around, and scatter the carrots over the top.

BAKED GOAT CHEESE IN COUNTRY HAM WITH RAMPS AND MORELS

░░░░░░░░░░░░░░░░░░░░░░░░░░░░░░░░░░

SERVES 4

One 6-ounce log fresh goat cheese, at room temperature

8 very thin slices country ham or prosciutto

1 tablespoon olive oil

Freshly ground black pepper

1 tablespoon lightly salted butter

4 ounces fresh morels, trimmed, cleaned, and halved

2 cups sliced, washed, and dried ramp (wild leek) leaves

2 tablespoons Chicken Stock (page 33) or canned broth

2 tablespoons cream sherry

¼ cup heavy cream

Salt

THIS REALLY IS A LOVELY AMALGAM of American ingredients, old and new and rediscovered. It uses mild fresh goat cheese (a new product at the time I first made it), wrapped in paper-thin slices of Smithfield ham, so aged it is almost a prosciutto. The mildness of the cheese and the saltiness of the ham go together very well, set off by a bed of morels and ramps.

Ramps, which are wild leeks, have a wonderfully aromatic garlicky aroma and distinctive flavor. Ten years ago you couldn't buy them except regionally, but now you can get them at nearly any farmers' market on the East Coast in the spring. They don't grow out West, but you can substitute roasted garlic and scallions combined in approximately equal measures. Or use the garlic chives that seem to grow everywhere.

Preheat the oven to 275°F.

Cut the goat cheese into 4 pieces. Lay 4 slices of the ham well apart on a work surface and lay the remaining 4 slices across them, forming 4 crosses. Put a piece of cheese in the center of each cross and fold the ends of the ham up over it to make a round package.

Brush a baking sheet with half the olive oil. Place the cheese packages seam side down on the baking sheet. Brush them with the remaining olive oil and sprinkle generously with pepper. Bake for 3 to 5 minutes, until the cheese is just heated through.

Meanwhile, heat the butter in a sauté pan over high heat until it starts to foam. Add the morels and cook, stirring, for 1 minute. Add the ramp leaves and stir for 30 seconds. Add the chicken stock and sherry, bring to a boil, and cook for 2 to 3 minutes, until most of it has evaporated.

Add the heavy cream and simmer for about 2 to 3 minutes. Season with salt and pepper.

Spoon the ramps and morels onto four serving plates and top with the cheese bundles. Serve immediately.

BAKED COUNTRY HAM WITH RED-EYE GRAVY
COUNTRY-STYLE LIMA BEANS

■■■■■■■■■■■■■■■■■■■■■■■■■■■■■■■■■■■■■

SERVES 6 TO 8

One 12-pound country ham, aged 6 to
   9 months

2 cups honey

½ cup packed light brown sugar

½ cup spicy brown mustard

1½ cups dried bread crumbs

Gravy

1 cup reserved ham trimmings
   (see method)

1 onion, sliced

1 tablespoon minced garlic

⅓ cup grenadine

2 cups strong coffee

3 cups Dark Poultry Stock (page 35) or
   canned chicken broth

2 tablespoons cornstarch

3 tablespoons unsalted butter, at
   room temperature

Freshly ground black pepper

Country-Style Lima Beans (recipe follows)

IF YOU WEREN'T QUITE SURE how to go about cooking the perfect country ham, this is just about guaranteed to get you rave reviews. The success of this recipe relies on a great ham. Buy a country ham, such as a Smithfield or Ozark, that is aged at least four to six months. These hams must be boiled for several hours before baking. After boiling, I lather with honey, sugar, and mustard and coat with bread crumbs.

Country ham has a wonderful taste and is not like the more familiar baked ham. Slice it thin and eat. The classic gravy got its name because of the grenadine syrup that is added to the coffee-based sauce. When it is poured into the brown sauce, it pools in the center and almost looks like a red eye. It's important to use *real* grenadine, made with pomegranates, not the sort made with corn syrup and red coloring.

The lima beans are great with the ham, or with any meat. Fresh lima beans are best, but you can use frozen. After the beans are sautéed in butter, they're mixed with cornmeal to soak up the butter and give them a nice crunchy coating.

Scrub the ham with a brush under warm running water until thoroughly clean. Put the ham in a large pot, cover with warm water, and let soak overnight at room temperature.

Drain the ham, return it to the pot, and cover with cold water. Add all but 3 tablespoons of the honey and bring just to a simmer. Lower the heat so that the water barely bubbles and cook for 4½ to 5 hours, until the ham is tender when pierced with a skewer and the small bone next to the shank bone pulls out easily with a twist. Carefully remove the ham from the pot and set aside to cool. Discard the water, or save for another use (such as split-pea soup or braised black-eyed peas).

Preheat the oven to 350°F.

When the ham is cool enough to handle, split and peel off the skin. Trim off the excess fat, leaving a covering about ¼ inch thick. Reserve 1 cup of the scraps for the gravy.

Put the ham on a rack in a roasting pan with the rounded side facing up. Rub the ham all over with the remaining 3 tablespoons honey. Combine the brown sugar and mustard in a small bowl, and rub over the ham. Coat the ham evenly with the bread crumbs. Bake for 25 to 35 minutes, until the bread crumbs are golden.

Meanwhile, to make the gravy, put the ham trimmings and the onion in a large heavy skillet or saucepan and cook over medium heat, stirring often, for 3 to 4 minutes until the meat is browned and the fat is rendered. Add the garlic and cook, stirring, for 1 minute. Add the grenadine and coffee. Bring to a boil and skim off any fat from the surface. Cook for 10 minutes, or until reduced by half, skimming the surface if necessary. Add the stock and continue to boil another 7 to 8 minutes, until reduced by a third.

Mix the cornstarch with the butter to make a smooth paste. Stir the paste into the gravy, return the gravy to a simmer, and cook for 5 to 6 minutes; season to taste with pepper. Strain the gravy through a fine strainer, and pour into a sauce boat.

Put the ham on a platter and carve it at the table. Serve with the gravy and lima beans and some of our country-style biscuits (pages 236–237).

———

COUNTRY-STYLE LIMA BEANS

SERVES 6 TO 8

1 pound shelled fresh young lima beans (about 2 pounds in the shell) or frozen lima beans

4 tablespoons lightly salted butter

1 teaspoon minced garlic

Salt and freshly ground black pepper

¼ cup plus 2 tablespoons stone-ground cornmeal

¼ cup chopped flat-leaf parsley

Cook the lima beans in salted boiling water until tender, 4 to 5 minutes. Drain.

In a sauté pan, heat the butter over medium heat until it foams and turns a light nutty brown. Add the limas and garlic, season to taste with salt and pepper, and cook for 2 minutes. Add the cornmeal and parsley and stir until the beans are evenly coated with the cornmeal. Serve.

ASPARAGUS IN AMBUSH

PARSLEY SAUCE

■■■

SERVES 4

Four 8- to 10-inch flour tortillas

4 large thin slices baked country ham
(slightly smaller than the tortillas)

4 large thin slices Crowley cheese or
white Cheddar cheese (slightly smaller
than the tortillas)

20 asparagus stalks, peeled, trimmed, and
cooked in boiling salted water until
al dente

1 tablespoon unsalted butter, melted

Parsley Sauce (recipe follows)

THE ONLY NAME BETTER than "Pigs in a Blanket" is "Asparagus in Ambush," another popular 1950s cocktail hors d'oeuvre. The original was made with sliced deli ham and Swiss cheese rolled up around asparagus spears and held together with a toothpick.

I use tender spring asparagus or baby white asparagus, Ozark country ham, and Vermont Crowley cheese and have some fun with a little-known dish from America's past.

Preheat the oven to 325°F.

Spread the tortillas on a work surface. Lay a slice of ham in the center of each and top with a slice of cheese. Arrange 5 asparagus stalks in a bundle on each tortilla, with the tips extending over the edge. Roll the tortillas tightly up around the asparagus. Moisten the edges of each tortilla with a little water and press to seal the seam.

Brush a baking sheet with half the melted butter. Put the tortillas seam sides down on the baking sheet and brush with the remaining butter. Bake for 3 to 4 minutes, until heated through.

Place each asparagus roll in the center of a plate, spoon the parsley sauce over, and serve.

PARSLEY SAUCE

MAKES ABOUT $\frac{2}{3}$ CUP

$\frac{1}{2}$ teaspoon minced garlic

$1\frac{1}{2}$ teaspoons minced scallions

$\frac{1}{4}$ cup heavy cream

$\frac{1}{4}$ cup unsalted butter, at
room temperature

2 tablespoons fresh lemon juice

$\frac{1}{4}$ cup chopped flat-leaf parsley

$\frac{1}{2}$ cup chopped, peeled, and seeded
tomatoes

Salt and freshly ground black pepper

In a small saucepan, combine the garlic, scallions, and heavy cream and bring to a simmer over medium-high heat. Cook for 1 to 2 minutes, until reduced by half.

Remove from the heat and whisk in the butter a tablespoon at a time; do not add the next tablespoon until the one before is completely incorporated. Stir in the lemon juice. Stir in the parsley and tomato and season with salt and pepper. Use immediately or keep warm over warm water until ready to use.

Pork with New Potatoes and Half-Sours

Four 4- to 5-ounce pork medallions (cut from a boneless loin of pork)

Salt and freshly ground black pepper

2 tablespoons olive oil

1 onion, sliced

1/4 teaspoon minced garlic

2 tablespoons spicy brown mustard

1/2 cup dry white vermouth or white wine

1 cup Dark Poultry Stock (page 35) or Chicken Stock (page 33) or canned broth

1 tablespoon cornstarch

3/4 cup heavy cream

4 tablespoons lightly salted butter

8 small new potatoes, cooked in boiling salted water until al dente, drained, and sliced

1 medium to large half-sour pickle, quartered and sliced

1 tablespoon chopped fresh herbs, such as parsley, chervil, tarragon, basil, or oregano

I LOVE FLAVORS that both contrast and complement—this dish succeeds on both counts. Mixing sautéed sliced new potatoes with half-sours is a way to turn sautéed potatoes into a kind of warm potato salad. The pickle juices infuse the potatoes and butter with a vinegary flavor that goes very well with the pork. Half-sours are crisp, tangy, pickle-barrel cucumber pickles that have not been completely cured. They are sold in the refrigerated section of most supermarkets and in delis. If you cannot get them, substitute dill pickles.

Season the pork medallions with salt and pepper.

Heat the oil in a deep medium sauté pan over medium heat. Add the pork and cook for 3 to 4 minutes on each side, until lightly browned and cooked. Remove the pork from the pan and put on a plate. Set aside to keep warm.

Add the onion to the pan and cook, stirring, for 3 to 4 minutes, until softened and lightly browned. Stir in the garlic and mustard and cook for 1 minute. Stir in the vermouth or wine, scraping the sides and bottom of the pan to loosen any browned particles. Bring to a simmer and cook for 2 to 3 minutes, until the liquid is reduced by about half.

Add the stock, raise the heat to high, and bring to a boil, skimming off any foam from the surface. Cook for about 10 minutes, until the stock is syrupy and reduced to about 1/4 cup.

Stir the cornstarch into the cream until smooth and add to the pan. Reduce the heat to medium and simmer for 3 to 4 minutes. Stir briefly and cook for another 1 to 2 minutes, until thickened. Strain the sauce through a sieve and keep warm.

Heat the butter in a large sauté pan over medium-high heat until it begins to foam and turn a light nutty brown. Add the sliced potatoes and sauté until they are golden brown. Remove the pan from the heat and stir in the pickle and herbs. Season to taste with salt and pepper.

With a slotted spoon, transfer the potatoes to the centers of four serving plates. Place the pork medallions on top, spoon over the sauce, and serve.

PORK WITH PEPPERED APPLES AND ONIONS

■■

SERVES 4

Four 4- to 5-ounce pork medallions (cut from a boneless loin of pork)

Salt and freshly ground black pepper

2 tablespoons olive oil

1 onion, thinly sliced

¼ teaspoon minced garlic

½ cup port

2 cups Dark Poultry Stock (page 35) or Chicken Stock (page 33) or canned broth

2 tablespoons unsalted butter

Apples and Onions

2 tablespoons salted butter

1 onion, halved and thinly sliced

2 tart apples, peeled, cored, and thinly sliced

1½ teaspoons coarsely ground black pepper

2 tablespoons cider vinegar

THE COMBINATION of pork and apples is a classic. In this recipe I count on the apples for both sweetness and tartness—just as I do with the onions. Coarsely ground pepper finishes the dish with a little bit of heat and spice.

Season the pork medallions with salt and pepper.

Heat the oil in a medium sauté pan over medium heat. Add the pork and sauté for 3 to 4 minutes on each side, until lightly browned and cooked. Remove the medallions from the pan and put on a plate. Cover loosely with foil and set aside to keep warm.

Add the onion to the pan and cook for about 5 minutes, stirring, until softened and lightly browned. Add the garlic and cook for 1 minute. Stir in the port, scraping the sides and bottom of the pan to loosen any browned particles. Bring to a simmer and cook for 2 to 3 minutes, until the port is reduced by about half. Add the stock, raise the heat to high, and bring to a boil, skimming off any foam from the surface. Cook for 7 to 8 minutes, until the stock is reduced by half.

Remove the pan from the heat and stir in the unsalted butter a tablespoon at a time. Strain the sauce through a fine strainer and keep warm.

To prepare the apples and onions, in another sauté pan, heat the lightly salted butter over medium heat until it begins to foam and turn a light nutty brown. Add the onion and apples, season with pepper, and sauté for 2 to 3 minutes, until the apples are lightly browned. Add the vinegar and scrape the bottom and sides of the pan to loosen any browned particles. Stir well and cook for 1 minute. Remove from the heat.

Arrange the medallions in the centers of the serving plates and spoon the sauce around them. Spoon the apples and onions over the pork and serve.

CENTER-CUT PORK CHOPS WITH BEER AND CABBAGE

■■

SERVES 4

4 center-cut pork chops, about 1¼ inches thick

Salt and freshly ground black pepper

1 tablespoon vegetable oil

1 small red onion, thinly sliced

1 tablespoon prepared mustard

½ head savoy cabbage, cored and thinly sliced

1 tart apple, peeled, cored, and thinly sliced

1 cup beer or ale

1 sprig fresh thyme or ½ teaspoon dried thyme

½ cup Dark Poultry Stock (page 35) or Chicken Stock (page 33) or canned broth

THIS DISH IS BASED on the traditional combination of pork and sauerkraut. I decided to make it with cabbage, which I prefer, and to use beer as a braising liquid to add yet another dimension. I use savoy cabbage, but you could also use the big round heads of garden-variety cabbage.

Season the pork chops on both sides with salt and pepper.

Heat the oil in a large heavy skillet until hot. Add the chops and cook for 4 to 5 minutes on each side, until well browned. Transfer the chops to a plate and set aside.

Add the onions to the pan and cook, stirring, for 2 to 3 minutes, until lightly browned. Stir in the mustard and 1 teaspoon pepper. Add the cabbage and apple, season lightly with salt, and cook, stirring, for 1 minute. Add the beer, bring to a boil, and cook for 3 to 4 minutes.

Return the chops to the skillet, burying them in the cabbage mixture. Add the thyme and stock, cover the pan, and simmer for 40 to 50 minutes, until the pork is cooked through and tender. Arrange the pork on serving plates, topped with the cabbage.

GRILLED VEAL CHOPS WITH GRILLED
BEEFSTEAK TOMATOES AND RED ONIONS

■■■

SERVES 4

4 veal rib chops, 1½ to 2 inches thick, plus trimming and bones (from the butcher)

1½ cups Dark Poultry Stock (page 35) or Chicken Stock (page 33) or canned broth

¼ cup plus 2 tablespoons chopped fresh basil

2 tablespoons chopped flat-leaf parsley

Salt and freshly ground black pepper

¼ cup olive oil

1 large red onion, cut into 4 thick slices

2 large ripe beefsteak tomatoes, cut into 8 thick slices

THIS IS REALLY A SUMMER DISH, because it should be made only with tomatoes that are at their best and onions that are fresh and sweet. I suggest red onions because they tend to be milder than yellow onions, but if you can buy fresh onions from a farmstand, they will be sweet, as onions develop their strong taste as they age. Vidalia onions are great too. Cut the onion and tomatoes into thick slices so they will hold up on the grill. Serve them with other grilled meats too, particularly steak and skewered cubes of beef or lamb. When making the sauce, you will get the best flavor if you grill or broil the bones and trimmings, but you could certainly oven-roast them as well.

Prepare a medium-hot fire in a charcoal or gas grill or preheat the broiler.

Grill or broil the veal trimmings and bones for 5 to 8 minutes, until evenly browned.

Put the trimmings and bones in a large saucepan, add the stock, and bring to a simmer. Cook for 10 to 15 minutes, until the stock is reduced by half. Strain the stock into another saucepan, stir in the basil and parsley, and season with salt and pepper. Cover and keep warm.

Brush a baking sheet with about half of the olive oil. Lay the onion and tomato slices on the pan and season with pepper. Carefully turn the slices over and season with more pepper.

Rub the veal chops with the remaining olive oil. Season with salt and pepper. Grill or broil for 4 to 5 minutes on each side, until browned and medium rare.

While the chops are cooking, place the onion slices directly on the grill or under the broiler and cook for 2 to 3 minutes, until they begin to caramelize slightly. Using a spatula, taking care not to break them, gently turn the slices, and cook for 2 to 3 minutes longer. Place the tomato slices on the grill or under the broiler and cook for 2 to 3 minutes on each side.

Arrange the tomatoes and onions around the edges of the plates and place a veal chop in the center. Spoon the sauce over the meat and serve.

GRILLED VEAL CHOPS

LADIES' CABBAGE

■■

SERVES 4

4 veal rib chops, about 1¼ inches thick

Olive oil

Salt and freshly ground black pepper

4 tablespoons unsalted butter, at room
   temperature

2 tablespoons chopped flat-leaf parsley

Ladies' Cabbage (recipe follows)

HERE'S A CASE where an old-fashioned philosophy resulted in a really delicious recipe. Ladies' Cabbage is a dish that dates from the late 1800s. Because garden cabbage on its own was considered "too strong" for ladies, someone came up with the idea of mixing the blanched leaves with custard and baking it to rid the cabbage of its acidity. I like to make the cabbage in individual ramekins, which unmold nicely onto the serving plates to accompany the veal chops, but it tastes just as good made in a casserole.

Prepare a hot fire in a charcoal or gas grill or preheat the broiler.

Rub the chops with a little oil and season on both sides with salt and pepper.

Grill or broil the chops for 2 to 3 minutes on each side for rare, 3 to 5 minutes for medium rare.

Put the chops on serving plates, brush generously with the butter, and sprinkle with the parsley. Serve with the cabbage.

———

LADIES' CABBAGE

SERVES 4

3 cups chopped green cabbage

2 tablespoons unsalted butter

¼ cup finely chopped onion

Salt and freshly ground black pepper

1 cup heavy cream

1 large egg

4 large egg yolks

A few dashes of Tabasco

Preheat the oven to 325°F. Lightly butter four 4-ounce custard cups or ramekins or a ½-quart casserole.

Bring a large pot of water to a boil over high heat. Add the cabbage and blanch for 2 to 3 minutes; drain. Repeat the process once more to remove all bitterness.

Melt the butter in a large skillet over medium heat. Add the onions and sauté for about 5 minutes, until softened. Add the cabbage and cook for 2 to 3 minutes. Season to taste with salt and pepper. Transfer to a bowl and let cool slightly.

In a medium bowl, combine the cream, egg, egg yolks, and Tabasco. Pour over the cabbage and stir until evenly mixed.

Ladle the custard into the prepared custard cups or casserole. Cover with buttered waxed paper. Put the custard cups or casserole in a roasting pan and add enough hot water to the pan to come halfway up the sides of the cups or casserole. Bake for 30 to 35 minutes, until the custard is set.

Remove the custard from the water bath and let set at room temperature for 5 to 6 minutes.

If using in custard cups, invert a plate over each one and invert again. Gently shake to unmold the custard. (If necessary, loosen the custard with a knife.) If using in a casserole, simply spoon the custard onto the plates.

VEAL STEAK WITH ROASTED CORN AND BLACK PEPPER SAUCE
POTATO AND CÈPE CASSEROLE

<hr />

SERVES 4

2 ears fresh corn (in their husks)

Four 5-ounce boneless veal steaks, cut from the loin

Salt and freshly ground black pepper

2 tablespoons olive oil

2 tablespoons finely chopped onion

1 tablespoon coarsely ground black pepper

1½ cups Dark Poultry Stock (page 35) or Chicken Stock (page 33) or canned broth

2 tablespoons white wine vinegar

½ teaspoon cornstarch

½ cup heavy cream

4 tablespoons unsalted butter

1 tablespoon chopped flat-leaf parsley

1 tablespoon chopped cilantro (fresh coriander)

Potato and Cèpe Casserole (recipe follows)

A SPICY ROASTED CORN SOUP I tasted in a small Native American restaurant in northern Michigan gave me the idea for this sauce. Roasting the corn in the husks intensifies its sweetness, which is nicely counterbalanced by the black pepper.

Preheat the oven to 375°F.

Put the unhusked corn on a baking sheet and roast, turning several times, for about 20 minutes, until browned. Let cool.

Remove the husks and cornsilk from the corn. Using a sharp knife, scrape the kernels from the cobs into a bowl.

Season the veal with salt and pepper. Heat the oil in a sauté pan over medium-high heat until very hot. Add the veal and cook for 2 to 3 minutes on each side, until browned and medium rare. Transfer the veal to a plate and keep warm.

Pour off the oil from the pan. Add the onion and coarsely ground pepper and sauté over medium heat for 1 minute. Add the stock and vinegar, raise the heat to high, and bring to a boil. Cook, skimming off any fat or foam from the surface, for 8 to 10 minutes, until the liquid is reduced by two-thirds.

Stir the cornstarch into the cream until smooth, and add to the sauce. Bring to a boil, reduce the heat to low, and simmer, stirring occasionally, for 2 to 3 minutes, until the sauce begins to thicken. Remove the pan from the heat and stir in the corn. Stir in the butter a tablespoon at a time, then stir in the parsley and cilantro.

Place the veal in the center of the serving plates and spoon the sauce over the meat. Serve with the potato casserole.

POTATO AND CÈPE CASSEROLE

SERVES 4

3 tablespoons unsalted butter

¼ pound cèpes, trimmed, cleaned, and sliced

Salt and freshly ground black pepper

1½ pounds all-purpose potatoes, peeled and cut into chunks

1 clove garlic

1 large egg yolk

¼ cup heavy cream

2 tablespoons chopped flat-leaf parsley

Preheat the oven to 350°F.

In a small skillet, melt 1 tablespoon of the butter over medium heat. Add the mushrooms, season to taste with salt and pepper, and cook, stirring, for 4 to 5 minutes, until softened. Remove from the heat and set aside.

Put the potatoes and garlic in a large saucepan and add water to cover; lightly salt the water. Bring to a boil over high heat, reduce the heat to a simmer, and cook for 15 to 20 minutes, until the potatoes are tender. Drain and return the potatoes and garlic to the pan.

Add the remaining 2 tablespoons butter to the pan and mash the potatoes with a potato masher or fork until smooth. Whisk the egg yolk into the cream and stir into the potatoes until blended. Stir in the mushrooms and parsley and adjust seasoning. Scrape the potatoes into a small casserole and bake, uncovered, for about 20 minutes, until the top is lightly browned.

GRILLED LAMB CHOPS, NEW POTATOES, AND ASPARAGUS

MINT AND BLACK PEPPER VINAIGRETTE

■ ■

SERVES 4

8 new potatoes, scrubbed but not peeled

16 medium asparagus spears, trimmed

Mint and Black Pepper Vinaigrette
    (recipe follows)

8 rib lamb chops

Salt

4 cups assorted lettuces, washed
    and dried

LIGHT AND FLAVORFUL, this is a lovely spring dish. The vinaigrette is made with just enough oil to make it a dressing and so is best when allowed to mingle with the lamb juices on the plate.

Prepare a hot fire in a charcoal or gas grill, or preheat the broiler.

Cook the potatoes in lightly salted boiling water for about 15 minutes, until tender but still firm. Drain and set aside to cool.

Blanch the asparagus in lightly salted boiling water for 2 to 3 minutes. Immediately plunge into ice water. When chilled, drain and set aside.

Cut the potatoes in half. Put in a bowl and toss with a little of the mint vinaigrette. Put the asparagus on a plate and brush lightly with the vinaigrette.

Season the lamb chops with salt and brush with a little vinaigrette.

Grill or broil the potatoes for 3 to 4 minutes, turning occasionally, until lightly browned, and grill or broil the asparagus for 2 to 3 minutes. Set aside to keep warm.

Grill or broil the lamb chops for 3 to 4 minutes on each side for medium rare. Arrange the lamb chops, potatoes, and asparagus on serving plates lined with a bed of lettuce and drizzle with the remaining vinaigrette.

———

MINT AND BLACK PEPPER VINAIGRETTE

2 tablespoons chopped fresh mint

1 teaspoon sugar

1 teaspoon prepared mustard

2 teaspoons coarsely ground black pepper

2 tablespoons cider vinegar

1/4 cup olive oil

Put the mint in a bowl and sprinkle with the sugar. Stir in the mustard, pepper, and vinegar. Slowly whisk in the olive oil.

GRILLED LOIN OF LAMB WITH CREAMED HASH BROWNS

■■

SERVES 4

Tomato Relish

2 large ripe tomatoes, seeded and diced

½ red bell pepper, cored, seeded
    and chopped

1 small jalapeño pepper, seeded
    and chopped

1 teaspoon fresh lime juice

1 tablespoon olive oil

½ teaspoon freshly ground black pepper

¼ cup assorted chopped fresh herbs,
    such as parsley, basil, and/or tarragon

Hash Browns

2 baking potatoes, scrubbed but
    not peeled

¼ cup vegetable oil

2 tablespoons unsalted butter

½ cup heavy cream

Salt and freshly ground black pepper

Lamb

1 boneless loin of lamb, trimmed of all fat
    and sliced into 8 medallions
    (see Note)

Olive oil for brushing

Salt and freshly ground black pepper

I'M ALWAYS DELIGHTED to cook for people who love potatoes as much as I do. I made this dish one night when Jim Beard came into the restaurant. He had told me once that he especially liked creamed hash browns, made by adding cream to the potatoes so that they are crusty on the outside and creamy on the inside. After that evening, this became one of our most popular dishes. The hash browns are good with almost anything.

Prepare a hot fire in a charcoal or gas grill or preheat the broiler.

To make the tomato relish, combine the tomatoes, bell pepper, jalapeño, lime juice, olive oil, pepper, and herbs in a small bowl. Set aside.

To make the hash browns, cook the potatoes in boiling salted water for 15 to 20 minutes, until tender but still firm. Drain and allow to cool. Peel the potatoes and cut into 1-inch cubes.

Heat the oil in a large heavy skillet. Add the potatoes and sauté for about 10 minutes, until golden brown. Drain off the oil and add the butter and heavy cream to the pan. Season with salt and pepper and bring to a simmer. Cook for about 10 minutes, until the cream begins to thicken the potatoes. Press gently to brown the bottoms. Turn and continue to brown.

Lightly brush the lamb medallions with olive oil and season with salt and pepper. Grill or broil for 2 to 3 minutes on each side for medium rare.

Onto the center of each serving plate, spoon the hash browns. Arrange 2 medallions on the potatoes and spoon the tomato relish over the lamb.

NOTE: Ask the butcher to trim and cut the lamb.

DOUBLE LOIN LAMB CHOPS WITH SAUTÉ OF SPRING VEGETABLES

1 pound thin asparagus spears, trimmed and cut into 1½ to 2-inch lengths

24 fiddlehead ferns, washed and trimmed

8 double loin lamb chops, about 1 inch thick

Salt and freshly ground black pepper

Olive oil

4 tablespoons lightly salted butter

6 ounces wild mushrooms, preferably morels, trimmed, cleaned, and sliced

8 ramps, with their leaves, or 8 scallions, sliced into ½-inch pieces

Juice of 1 lemon

½ cup Dark Poultry Stock (page 35) or canned broth

THIS DISH INCORPORATES all the fresh, exuberant flavor of spring—native ramps, wild asparagus, green fiddleheads. Ramps are wild leeks, with a garlicky flavor. Fiddleheads, which are available in many markets and greengrocers in the early spring, are furled young ferns with a mild flavor. They are a favorite of foragers in the northern woodlands. If you can find wild asparagus, by all means use it, but the flavor of cultivated asparagus is just the same.

Prepare a hot fire in a charcoal or gas grill or preheat the broiler.

Blanch the asparagus and fiddleheads separately for 1 minute in boiling salted water, and remove with a skimmer. Plunge each vegetable into cold water to refresh it. Drain and pat dry.

Season the lamb chops with salt and pepper and rub with a little oil. Grill or broil, about 5 to 6 inches from the heat, for 3 to 4 minutes on each side for medium rare. Transfer to a platter and cover to keep warm.

Heat 2 tablespoons of the butter in a large sauté pan until foamy. Add the mushrooms, asparagus, and fiddleheads and cook, tossing, for 1 to 2 minutes. Add the ramps and cook for 1 minute longer. Season with salt and pepper, remove from the heat, and keep warm.

Heat the remaining 2 tablespoons butter in a small saucepan over medium heat until foamy and a nutty brown. Add the lemon juice and stock, bring to a boil, and cook for 1 minute. Season lightly with salt and pepper and remove from the heat.

Place 2 chops on each plate and arrange the vegetables around them. Spoon the sauce over all, and serve.

GRILLED SPRING LAMB WITH RHUBARB AND DANDELION

██

SERVES 4 TO 6

Marinade

½ cup Dark Poultry Stock (page 35) or canned broth

¼ cup soy sauce

2 tablespoons fresh lemon juice

¼ cup spicy brown mustard

Few dashes of Tabasco

2 tablespoons chopped fresh thyme

4 scallions, white and green parts, finely chopped

1 teaspoon minced garlic

One 4¼-pound baby lamb shoulder, trimmed, boned, and slightly flattened (2½ to 3 pounds trimmed and boned weight; see Note)

1 pound rhubarb, trimmed, peeled, and washed

¼ cup sugar

Salt and freshly ground black pepper

Olive oil for grilling

2 tablespoons red wine vinegar

¼ cup olive oil

2 bunches tender dandelion greens, arugula, or other bitter greens, washed and dried

2 tablespoons sliced toasted almonds

THIS IS A DISH I think of as truly a spring celebration. I started making it when we began serving baby lamb and needed a way to serve the shoulder. I decided to marinate a boned shoulder, grill it, and serve it with a salad of rhubarb and dandelion greens—two other sure signs of spring.

Baby lamb is sold only in the spring, and you will probably have to ask the butcher to order it. You can, however, substitute steaks from a boned leg of lamb, or any other tender cut. The rhubarb is blanched in a sugar water to sweeten it a little so that it blends nicely with the bitter greens, although if picked before they flower, dandelion greens are not nearly as bitter as some people think. They are increasingly available in farmers' markets and greengrocers in the spring. Or substitute arugula or another slightly bitter green.

To make the marinade, combine all the ingredients in a noncorrosive pan or dish large enough to hold the lamb. Add the lamb, turn to coat, cover, and marinate for 2 to 3 hours in the refrigerator, turning several times.

Prepare a medium-hot fire in a charcoal or gas grill, or preheat the broiler.

Cut the rhubarb into 2-inch lengths. Cut each length into strips.

Combine the sugar and 2 cups water in a medium saucepan and bring to a boil over medium-high heat. Add the rhubarb, lower the heat, and simmer for about 2 minutes. Remove from the heat and let the rhubarb cool in the liquid.

Remove the lamb from the marinade, reserving the marinade. Rub with a little oil and season with salt and pepper. Grill or broil for 6 to 8 minutes to a side for medium rare. Transfer to a cutting board.

Meanwhile, pour the marinade into a noncorrosive saucepan and bring to a boil over medium-high heat. Cook for 3 to 4 minutes, until reduced by half. Skim off any foam from the surface, and whisk in the vinegar and oil. Remove from the heat and keep warm.

continued

Toss the greens with a few tablespoons of the warm dressing and arrange on individual plates or a serving platter. Drain the rhubarb and arrange the greens.

Slice the lamb, arrange the slices on the greens, and season lightly with pepper. Drizzle a little dressing over the meat and greens and sprinkle with the toasted almonds. Pass the remaining dressing separately.

NOTE: Ask the butcher to prepare the lamb.

ROAST LEG OF LAMB WITH NATURAL PAN JUICES
ARTICHOKE AND POTATO PANCAKES

SERVES 6 TO 8

One 7- to 7½-pound leg of lamb, boned and tied (bones reserved and roughly chopped; see Note)

¼ cup olive oil

Salt and freshly ground black pepper

1 onion, sliced

1 carrot, peeled and sliced

4 cloves garlic, minced

3 to 4 sprigs fresh thyme

¼ cup dry white wine

3 cups Dark Poultry Stock (page 35) or canned broth

1 tablespoon cornstarch

Artichoke and Potato Pancakes (recipe follows)

EVERYONE MAKES his or her culinary associations. For some reason I always think of artichokes when I think of lamb, probably because both evoke the fresh appeal of springtime. In this recipe, I pair a boned leg of lamb with potato pancakes that contain grated fresh artichokes. If you don't want to go through the trouble of trimming the bottoms of fresh artichokes, use finely chopped artichoke hearts; use about one-half cup for every artichoke bottom.

Preheat the oven to 450°F.

Rub the lamb with 2 tablespoons of the olive oil and season with salt and pepper.

Brush a large roasting pan with the remaining 2 tablespoons olive oil and place in the oven to heat for 5 minutes.

Add the lamb to the pan, seam side down, and scatter the chopped bones around it. Roast for 25 to 30 minutes.

Turn the lamb over and add the onion, carrot, garlic, and thyme to the pan. Stir the vegetables and the bones together and roast for 1 hour longer.

Remove the lamb to a platter or carving board and let it rest for 10 to 15 minutes before carving.

Meanwhile, drain the contents of the roasting pan in a strainer to remove the fat. Return the vegetables and bones to the roasting pan and add the wine, scraping the sides and bottom of the pan to loosen any browned particles. Pour the contents of the pan into a medium saucepan and add the stock. Bring to a boil over medium-high heat, skimming off any fat or foam that rises to the surface. Cook for 8 to 10 minutes, until reduced by half. Dissolve the cornstarch in a little water and stir into the sauce. Let simmer for 2 to 3 minutes. Season with salt and pepper to taste and strain through a fine strainer into a saucepan.

Carve the lamb and arrange the slices on serving plates with the artichoke pancakes. Spoon the sauce over and around the meat and serve.

NOTE: Ask the butcher to bone the lamb for you and give you the bones separately.

_____

ARTICHOKE AND POTATO PANCAKES

SERVES 6 TO 8 (MAKES 18 TO 24 PANCAKES)

2 large cooked artichoke bottoms (see page 146)

2 baking potatoes, peeled

1 tablespoon finely chopped onion

½ teaspoon fresh lemon juice

2 tablespoons fresh bread crumbs

1 large egg, lightly beaten

Salt and freshly ground black pepper

Preheat the oven to 200°F.

Using a cheese grater or food processor, coarsely grate the artichoke bottoms and potatoes and place in a bowl. Add the onion and lemon juice and toss well. Stir in the bread crumbs and egg. Season to taste with salt and pepper and stir until well blended.

Lightly oil a griddle or skillet and heat over medium heat until very hot but not smoking. Spoon about 2 tablespoons of batter for each pancake onto the griddle and cook, for 3 to 4 minutes on each side, until browned and crisp. Drain the pancakes on paper towels and keep warm in the oven until ready to serve; do not cover the pancakes.

From America's Bakeshops

IF YOU'VE EVER HAD a flaky Southern-style biscuit, slathered with wildflower honey, served so fresh and hot that you are torn between burning your fingers and having to wait one minute longer to eat it, you understand the sheer pleasure home baking can give. There might be something more inviting than a homemade Chocolate Walnut Fudge Cake, a Blackberry and Apple Crisp, a batch of moist Fudge Brownies, or a loaf of Granny's Irish Soda Bread, but I'm not sure what it would be. The difference between homemade and store-bought is night and day. Store-bought is convenient, predictable, easy, often a safe solution if you're in a hurry. But something that comes from your oven has the possibility of being supernal—warm and warming, fragrant, flaky, tender, rich, fully ripened, bursting with flavors that melt on your tongue and keep you from stopping at just one bite or one piece or one bowlful. In an age of speed and convenience and instant gratification, it is reassuring to note that the old-fashioned American bakeshop is alive and thriving.

Breads

I HAVE TO ADMIT that bread making, with its endless kneading, rising, proofing, and waiting is not my favorite way to spend time in the kitchen. What I really enjoy is making simple breads, biscuits, scones, and rolls. So, with a few exceptions, every recipe in this chapter gives you the unmitigated delight of warm, flavorful, undeniably homemade breads without the long, labor-intensive work of classic bread making.

If there is one recipe that proves what rewarding results you can get from very minimal effort, it's Southern-style biscuits. They have all the airy delicacy of traditional Southern beaten biscuits—without having to be beaten. Equally effortless and delightful are the tangy Cheddar Cheese Biscuits and my version of the classic Parker House Roll. Each Country Ham, Cheese, and Scallion Biscuit is a mouthful of color, flavor, and crunch. They've been a staple in the bread basket at An American Place since the day we opened, and every time I try to freshen the selection by substituting a different biscuit, I get so many complaints I put it right back!

One of the reasons that the breads in this chapter are so user-friendly is that they're not all traditional yeast breads. The spicy Chile Corn Bread is a batter bread you can cook in a cast-iron skillet and serve directly from the stove. The Fresh Corn Spoonbread is really more a soufflé than a bread. It's lovely as a side dish with an entrée like Deviled Crab Cakes. And with the addition of some chopped cooked broccoli or diced asparagus, it easily turns into a more substantial offering.

Whether it means serving your own corn crackers with a rich clam chowder or enveloping your juicy steak sandwich in a still-warm Pennsylvania Dutch Potato Bread, home baking adds so much to whatever you're making that I think it's worth doing when you can. It is also the single best way I know to pamper your family, spoil your guests, and reward yourself. How could you have anything but a good day if you start it off with a plateful of plump, creamy homemade scones studded with dried sour cherries? Especially if you didn't have to get up at 6:00 A.M. to start baking.

AN AMERICAN PLACE PEPPER BREAD

MAKES THREE 9- BY 5-INCH LOAVES

¼ cup milk

1 package (¼ ounce) active dry yeast

⅓ cup sugar

¾ pound unsalted butter, at room temperature

1½ teaspoons salt

5 to 6 cups unbleached all-purpose flour

8 large eggs, lightly beaten

2 tablespoons red wine vinegar

2 tablespoons cracked black pepper

WE HAVE BEEN MAKING this bread since I was the chef at The River Café in Brooklyn in the late 1970s and early 1980s. When I first started there, a friend who was an Italian baker used to bring by peppery croutons made from his leftover loaves of Italian bread. I loved the burst of black pepper flavor and so developed this quick brioche and added pepper to the dough.

In the bowl of an electric mixer fitted with a bread hook, combine the milk, yeast, and sugar. Stir and let stand for about 10 minutes, until the mixture bubbles and swells.

With the mixer on low speed, beat in the butter, salt, and 3 cups of flour. Beat in the eggs, vinegar, and pepper. Add 2 cups more flour, ½ cup at a time, and continue to mix until the dough pulls away from the sides of the bowl, adding up to 1 cup additional flour if necessary.

Gather the dough into a ball and put it into a lightly oiled bowl. Turn several times to coat the dough with oil. Cover and refrigerate overnight.

Lightly dust three 9- by 5-inch bread pans with flour.

Turn the dough out onto a lightly floured surface and divide it in thirds. Form each piece into a loaf and fit the loaves into the bread pans. Cover and set aside in a warm place for 1½ to 2 hours, or until doubled in volume.

Preheat the oven to 350°F.

Bake the loaves for 35 to 40 minutes, or until the crust is lightly browned and the loaves sound hollow when tapped on the bottom. Cool completely on wire racks.

WILD RICE BREAD

MAKES 1 LARGE LOAF

1 tablespoon bacon fat

1 cup cooked wild rice (see Note, page 180)

1 tablespoon chopped fresh rosemary

Salt and freshly ground black pepper

2 packages (¼ ounce each) active dry yeast

½ cup warm water

1 cup milk, at room temperature

1 cup water

3 tablespoons olive oil

2 tablespoons honey

1 teaspoon salt

3 cups whole wheat flour

1 cup rice flour

About 2 cups unbleached all-purpose flour

BEFORE IT IS ADDED to the dough, the wild rice in this bread is sautéed in bacon fat and seasoned with fresh rosemary to give it a rich flavor. I love the way the smokiness of the bacon and the earthiness of the wild rice make this American-style bread taste.

In a frying pan, heat the bacon fat over medium-high heat. Add the wild rice and cook for about 1 minutes, stirring, until well coated. Stir in the rosemary and season to taste with salt and pepper. Set aside to cool to room temperature.

In the bowl of an electric mixer fitted with a dough hook, sprinkle the yeast over the warm water. Let stand for about 10 minutes, until the mixture bubbles and swells. Add the milk, water, olive oil, honey, and salt.

With the mixer on low speed, add the rice flour and whole wheat flour and mix just until incorporated. Add the wild rice and mix well. Add all-purpose flour ½ cup at a time, mixing on low until the dough pulls from the sides of the bowl. Then continue to mix for 3 to 4 minutes until the dough is smooth and elastic. Turn out onto a lightly floured surface and knead 3 to 4 times.

Gather the dough into a ball and put in a lightly oiled bowl. Turn to coat with oil. Cover and let stand in a warm place for about 1 hour, or until doubled in volume.

Lightly oil a baking sheet.

Punch down the dough and turn out onto a lightly floured surface. Shape the dough into a 10-inch round or oval loaf and put on the baking sheet or in the baking pan. Cover and set aside in a warm place for about 45 minutes, or until almost doubled in volume.

Preheat the oven to 375°F.

Using a plant mister, spray the loaf with water and bake for 5 minutes. Spray again, without removing from the oven, and bake for 1 hour longer, or until the crust is lightly browned and the loaf sounds hollow when tapped on the bottom. Cool completely on a wire rack.

YEAST-RAISED CORN BREAD

■■■■■■■■■■■■■■■■■■■■■■■■■■■■■■■■■■■■■■■

1 cup water

1 cup yellow or white stone-ground
    cornmeal

1 tablespoon salt

1 package (¼ ounce) active dry yeast

½ cup warm water

1 tablespoon sugar

1 cup warm milk

¼ cup packed light brown sugar

About 4 cups unbleached all-purpose flour

THIS RECIPE WAS INSPIRED by Jim Beard's yeast-raised corn bread—an unusual bread with a slightly sweet flavor. Heed the warning about not cutting it while it's still hot (I didn't the first time I made it)—it will turn mushy. If you want to eat it warm, cut it in substantial pieces and warm them briefly on the grill. This bread, by the way, works wonders on any kind of grilled sandwich, even a simple grilled cheese.

In a small saucepan, bring the water to a boil over high heat. Whisk in the cornmeal and 1 teaspoon of the salt, reduce the heat to low, and cook for about 1 minute, until thickened to mush. Transfer to the bowl of an electric mixer and set aside to cool to room temperature.

In a small bowl, sprinkle the yeast over the warm water. Stir in the sugar and let stand for about 10 minutes, until the mixture bubbles and swells.

Add the yeast to the cornmeal mush. Using the dough hook on low speed, mix in the milk, the remaining 2 teaspoons salt, and the brown sugar. Add flour a cup at a time, mixing until the dough pulls away from the sides of the bowl, then mix for a few minutes longer, until the dough is smooth. Turn out a lightly floured surface and knead 3 or 4 times.

Gather the dough into a ball and put it in a lightly buttered bowl. Turn to coat with butter. Cover and let stand in a warm place for about 2 hours, or until doubled in volume.

Butter two 9- by 5-inch bread pans.

Punch down the dough and turn out onto a surface lightly dusted with cornmeal. Divide the dough in half and shape into loaves. Press into the bread pans, cover, and set aside for about 45 minutes, or until nearly doubled in volume.

Preheat the oven to 425°F.

Bake for 10 minutes. Reduce the oven temperature to 350°F and bake for another 20 to 25 minutes, or until the loaves are lightly browned on top and sound hollow when tapped on the bottom. Cool to room temperature on wire racks before slicing.

PENNSYLVANIA DUTCH POTATO BREAD

■■■■■■■■■■■■■■■■■■■■■■■■■■■■■■■■■■■■■

**MAKES 6 CLUB
LOAVES OR 1 LARGE
ROUND LOAF**

1 large potato, peeled and diced

1 package (¼ ounce) active dry yeast

¼ teaspoon sugar

½ cup buttermilk

1½ teaspoons salt

3 to 4 cups unbleached all-purpose flour

1 egg yolk beaten with 2 tablespoons
   water for egg wash

WHEN WE BEGAN serving our version of Philadelphia cheese-steak (see page 195), we started making this bread, which is similar to the potato breads made by the Pennsylvania Dutch.

Put potato in a saucepan, with 1½ cups water and bring to a boil over high heat. Cook for 15 to 20 minutes, or until tender. Drain the potato, reserving the liquid. Put the potato in a large bowl and mash with a fork or potato masher until smooth. Set aside.

Measure ½ cup of the reserved potato liquid into a small bowl and let cool to 110° to 115°F. Add the yeast and sugar and stir to dissolve. Let stand for about 10 minutes, until the mixture foams and swells.

In a saucepan, warm the buttermilk until lukewarm, not hot, over medium-low heat. Add to the mashed potatoes along with the salt and stir until smooth. Add the yeast mixture and 1½ cups flour. Stir vigorously with a wooden spoon until a soft dough forms. If the mixture is too wet, add another ½ cup of flour.

Turn out the dough onto a lightly floured surface and knead for 7 to 8 minutes, adding a little more flour if necessary. The dough should be soft and moist, not dry.

Transfer the dough to a lightly oiled bowl and turn once or twice to coat. Cover and let rise in a warm place for about 1 hour, or until doubled in volume.

Punch down the dough and turn out onto a lightly floured surface. Divide the dough into 6 pieces and form each into a hero-shaped loaf (an elongated oval 5 to 6 inches long). Alternatively, form the dough into a single round loaf. Put the loaves (loaf) on an ungreased baking sheet, or two sheets if necessary. Cover and let rise for about 30 minutes, or until nearly doubled in volume.

Preheat the oven to 375°F.

Brush the loaves (loaf) with the egg wash. Bake individual loaves for 25 to 30 minutes, or until the crust is golden brown and crisp and the loaves sound hollow when tapped on the bottom. Bake the single loaf for 45 to 50 minutes, until the crust is golden brown and the loaf sounds hollow when tapped. Cool completely on a wire rack.

SOFT PRETZELS

■■

MAKES ABOUT 15 PRETZELS

Pretzel Dough

2 teaspoons sugar

1 package (¼ ounce) active dry yeast

2 cups warm water

2 teaspoons salt

2 tablespoons peanut oil

1½ cups whole wheat flour

1¾ cups bread flour

Poaching Liquid

6 cups water

One 12-ounce bottle amber beer, such as Samuel Adams, at room temperature

3 tablespoons baking soda

2 tablespoons malt (see Note)

1 large egg beaten with 2 tablespoons water for egg wash

Kosher or coarse sea salt

Spicy brown mustard for serving

NOTHING IS MORE NEW YORK than a warm soft pretzel. Being an innovative New Yorker, I once came up with the idea of wrapping the pretzel dough around a barbecued country sausage to make a new portable food. Everyone loved the idea! (See page 194 for the recipe.) With or without the sausage, these pretzels are great!

Preheat the oven to 350°F. Lightly oil a baking sheet.

In a large bowl, combine the sugar, yeast, and warm water. Let stand for about 10 minutes, until the mixture foams and swells. Add the salt and oil.

In the bowl of an electric mixer fitted with a dough hook, combine the flours. Add the yeast mixture 1 cup at a time, mixing well after each addition. With the mixer on low, knead the dough until it pulls away from the sides of the bowl and is smooth and elastic.

Turn the dough out onto a lightly floured surface. Roll into an 8- × 15-inch rectangle about ¼ inch thick. Cut into fifteen 6- to 8-inch-long strips about 1 inch wide and twist each into a pretzel shape.

In a large pot, combine the water, beer, baking soda, and malt, and bring to a simmer over medium heat. Using a slotted spoon, lower the pretzels into the liquid, without crowding. Poach for 30 seconds, then remove from the liquid with the slotted spoon and put seam side down on the baking sheet.

Lightly brush each pretzel with the egg wash and sprinkle with kosher or coarse salt. Bake for about 10 minutes, or until golden brown. Serve the pretzels hot with spicy brown mustard

NOTE: Malt is available at health food stores.

CUMIN BEER BREAD ROLLS

■■■

**MAKES ABOUT
30 ROLLS**

1 tablespoon cumin seed

2 teaspoons caraway seed

1 cup diced onions

One 12-ounce bottle amber beer, such as
    Samuel Adams, at room temperature

2 cups warm water

1 package (¼ ounce) active dry yeast

¾ teaspoon sugar

3 to 4 cups unbleached all-purpose flour

1 tablespoon plus 1½ teaspoons salt

Kosher or coarse sea salt

THESE GOLDEN, FULL-FLAVORED dinner rolls are served in the bread basket at An American Place. They are crispy on the outside, soft on the inside. To give them more flavor, we sprinkle them with a little kosher salt before baking.

Preheat the oven to 275°F.

Spread the cumin and caraway seeds on a baking sheet and toast in the oven for 6 to 8 minutes, or until lightly browned and fragrant.

In a nonstick skillet, cook the onions over medium heat for 8 to 10 minutes, or until lightly browned. Stir in the toasted seeds, and set aside to cool to room temperature.

In the bowl of an electric mixer fitted with a dough hook, combine the beer, water, yeast, and sugar. Stir and let stand for about 10 minutes, until the mixture bubbles and swells.

Add the onions, 3½ cups flour, and salt. Mix on low speed until the dough comes together in a smooth mass, adding ½ cup additional flour if necessary.

Turn the dough out onto a lightly floured surface and knead for 7 to 8 minutes, until smooth and elastic. Gather the dough into a ball and place in a lightly oiled bowl. Turn to coat the dough. Cover and let stand in a warm place for about 2 hours, or until tripled in volume.

Punch down the dough and pinch off 3-ounce, roll-sized pieces. Using cupped hands, on a lightly floured surface, roll the dough into rounds and place on ungreased baking sheets about 2 inches apart. Cover and let stand in a warm place for about 45 minutes, or until almost doubled in size.

Preheat the oven to 450°F.

Make a 1-inch-long slit in the top of each roll with a razor blade or sharp knife and brush the rolls lightly with water. Sprinkle each roll with a pinch of kosher or sea salt. Bake for 10 to 12 minutes, or until lightly browned. Cool slightly, and serve warm or at room temperature.

NOTE: Alternatively, form the dough into 3 loaves and bake in 9- × 5-inch pans. Bake for 25 to 30 minutes, or until the crust is lightly browned and the bottoms sound hollow when tapped. Cool on wire racks.

PARKER HOUSE ROLLS

■■■ ■ ■■ ■ ■■ ■ ■ ■■ ■ ■■ ■ ■■ ■ ■■ ■ ■ ■■ ■ ■■ ■ ■■ ■ ■ ■■ ■ ■ ■■■

**MAKES ABOUT
12 ROLLS**

1 package (¹⁄₄ ounce) active dry yeast

¹⁄₄ cup sugar

¹⁄₄ cup warm water

8 tablespoons unsalted butter, melted

1 cup milk, at room temperature

1 large egg, lightly beaten

3 to 4 cups unbleached all-purpose flour

1¹⁄₂ teaspoons salt

BEWARE OF IMITATIONS: When correctly made, nothing beats a soft, slightly sweet, classic Parker House roll warm from the oven.

In the bowl of an electric mixer fitted with a dough hook, dissolve the yeast and sugar in the water. Let stand for about 10 minutes, until the mixture bubbles and swells.

Add ¹⁄₄ cup of the melted butter, the milk, and egg and stir to blend. Add 3¹⁄₂ cups flour and the salt and mix on low speed for about 5 minutes, until the dough comes together in a smooth mass, adding ¹⁄₂ cup additional flour if necessary.

Transfer the dough to a large bowl, cover and let stand in a warm place for about 2 hours, or until doubled in volume.

Butter 1 baking sheet.

Punch down the dough and turn it out onto a lightly floured surface. Roll the dough into an 8- × 12-inch rectangle about ¹⁄₄ inch thick. Cut into pieces about 4 inches long and 2 inches wide. Brush with the remaining ¹⁄₄ cup melted butter. Fold the pieces in half so that the end of the top half extends about ¹⁄₂ inch beyond the bottom half.

Place the rolls, folded side down, in rows side by side on the baking sheets so that each roll touches the next. Refrigerate for 30 minutes.

Preheat the oven to 350°F.

Bake for 15 to 20 minutes, or until golden brown. Serve warm.

BUTTERMILK-YEAST BISCUITS

■■

**MAKES ABOUT
30 BISCUITS**

½ cup heavy cream

½ cup buttermilk

1 package (¼ ounce) active dry yeast

2½ cups unbleached all-purpose flour

2 tablespoons sugar

½ teaspoon baking soda

1 teaspoon salt

½ cup lard, cut into pieces

8 tablespoons unsalted butter, melted and
   kept warm

THESE ARE MY RENDITION of old-fashioned beaten biscuits—without the beating. The recipe is adapted from those served along Maryland's Eastern Shore. Unlike most yeast doughs, this does not need two risings.

In a small saucepan, combine the cream and buttermilk and heat over medium heat until warm, but not hot. Pour into a small bowl. Add the yeast and let stand for about 10 minutes, until the mixture bubbles and swells.

Sift the flour, sugar, baking soda, and salt into a large bowl, Add the lard and blend with a pastry blender or your fingertips until the mixture resembles coarse meal. Add the cream mixture and stir until the dough holds together.

Turn out onto a lightly floured surface and knead only until smooth and elastic. With a floured rolling pin, roll out to a thickness of about ½ inch. Using a 2-inch biscuit cutter or glass, stamp out biscuits. Dip each biscuit in the melted butter and place about 2 inches apart on ungreased baking sheets. Gather up the scraps, reroll, and make more biscuits until all the dough is used.

Cover the biscuits and set aside in a warm place for about 1 hour, or until nearly doubled in volume.

Preheat the oven to 400°F.

Bake for 12 to 15 minutes, or until lightly browned. Serve hot.

CHEDDAR CHEESE BISCUITS

■■

MAKES ABOUT 24 BISCUITS

3 cups unbleached all-purpose flour

1 tablespoon plus 1½ teaspoons
　　baking powder

1 tablespoon sugar

2¼ teaspoons salt

2½ cups heavy cream

½ cup grated sharp Cheddar cheese

3 tablespoons unsalted butter, melted

THESE ARE OUR SIGNATURE BISCUITS from The Beekman Tavern. They are typical New England–style cheese biscuits, flaky and favorful, rich with sharp Cheddar and heavy cream.

Preheat the oven to 350°F.

In a large bowl, combine the flour, baking powder, sugar, and salt. Whisk to mix. Add the cream and cheese and blend with a wooden spoon or your fingers until the dough comes together.

Turn the dough out onto a lightly floured surface and knead 6 to 8 times. Using a lightly floured rolling pin, roll the dough to a thickness of ½ inch. Or pat out the dough with floured hands.

Using a 2-inch biscuit cutter or glass, stamp out biscuits and place about 2 inches apart on ungreased baking sheets. Gather the scraps together and continue to make biscuits. Brush each one with melted butter.

Bake for 18 to 20 minutes, or until golden brown. Serve hot.

COUNTRY HAM, CHEESE, AND SCALLION BISCUITS

■■

MAKES ABOUT TWELVE 2-INCH BISCUITS

2 cups unbleached all-purpose flour

1 tablespoon baking powder

2 teaspoons sugar

1 teaspoon salt

3 tablespoons finely grated sharp
　　Cheddar cheese

3 tablespoons finely chopped country ham

2 tablespoons minced scallions

¾ cup heavy cream

3 tablespoons unsalted butter, softened

THESE SIMPLE COUNTRY BISCUITS are made in the classic style of American baking powder biscuits and they're what you find in every bread basket at An American Place. Hint: Make a lot!

Preheat the oven to 375°F.

In a large bowl, whisk together the flour, baking powder, sugar, and salt. Add the cheese, ham, scallions, and cream and mix gently with a wooden spoon and then your fingertips to make a soft, moist dough.

Turn the dough out onto a lightly floured surface and knead for 1 to 2 minutes just until cohesive. Do not overknead. Pat the dough out to a thickness of about 1 inch. Using a 2-inch biscuit cutter, cut out 12 biscuits. Brush each biscuit with the butter and lay the biscuits on ungreased baking sheets, leaving about 1 inch between them.

Bake for 18 to 20 minutes, or until golden brown. Serve hot.

CHILE CORN BREAD

■■

**MAKES ONE 9-INCH
SQUARE BREAD**

1¼ cups yellow or white stone-ground cornmeal

1 cup unbleached all-purpose flour

2 tablespoons sugar

1 tablespoon baking powder

2 large eggs

1¼ cups milk

6 tablespoons unsalted butter

½ cup finely chopped onion

1 poblano chile, seeded and finely chopped

2 tablespoons pure chile powder

1 teaspoon salt

YOU CAN MAKE this tangy batter corn bread in a baking pan or a cast-iron skillet. No matter how you make it, serve directly from the oven—the sooner the better!

Preheat the oven to 425°F. Lightly butter a nonstick 9-inch square baking pan, or melt about a tablespoon of butter in a 10-inch cast-iron skillet, tilting the skillet to distribute the butter evenly.

In a large bowl, combine the cornmeal, flour, sugar, and baking powder.

In another bowl, beat the eggs with the milk. Add to the dry ingredients all at once and stir just until the batter is free of lumps.

In a small skillet, melt the butter over medium-high heat. Add the onions, poblano chile, and chile powder and cook for 2 to 3 minutes, until the vegetables begin to soften. Add to the batter along with the salt and stir to mix.

Pour the batter into the prepared pan or skillet. Bake for 20 to 25 minutes, or until the cornbread is slightly risen and feels firm to the touch. A toothpick inserted in the middle should come out clean. Serve hot with soft butter.

FRESH CORN SPOONBREAD

SERVES 6 TO 8

1½ cups milk

1 cup yellow or white stone-ground
  cornmeal

1½ cups fresh corn kernels (from 1
  to 2 ears)

1 teaspoon salt

4 large eggs, separated

2 tablespoons chopped flat-leaf parsley

½ teaspoon baking powder

SPOONBREAD IS MORE than a bread—it is a wonderful side dish. This is a classic version baked in a casserole; it is based on old recipes from the southern Atlantic seaboard states. Spoonbreads are similar to soufflés in that they are light and airy, but they are not as fragile.

Preheat the oven to 375°F. Butter a shallow 2-quart casserole.

In a large saucepan, bring the milk to a simmer over medium-high heat. Add the cornmeal, corn kernels, and salt, and cook, stirring, for about 5 minutes, or until thickened to mush. Remove from the heat.

In a small bowl, lightly beat the egg yolks. Add the cornmeal mixture along with the parsley and baking powder. Whisk well to blend.

In a large bowl, using an electric mixer set on medium-high speed, beat the egg whites to soft peaks. Fold the whites into the cornmeal mixture.

Pour into the casserole and bake for 35 to 40 minutes, or until the spoonbread is set in the center. Serve immediately.

DRIED SOUR CHERRY SCONES

■■■■■■■■■■■■■■■■■■■■■■■■■■■■■■■■■

**MAKES ABOUT
15 SCONES**

2 cups unbleached all-purpose flour

¼ cup sugar

1 tablespoon baking powder

¼ cup unsalted butter, cut into pieces
    and chilled

⅓ cup milk

1 small egg, lightly beaten

⅓ cup dried sour cherries,
    roughly chopped

UNLIKE THE OTHER BISCUITS we serve at the restaurants (and scones are essentially biscuits), these are not enriched with heavy cream, but instead call for milk and eggs and butter. I developed these for American Spoon Foods when we first marketed dried cherries—their sweet-sour taste shines through.

Preheat the oven to 350°F. Butter 2 baking sheets.

In a large bowl, combine the flour, sugar, and baking powder and whisk until mixed. Add the butter. Using a pastry blender or your fingers, blend until the mixture resembles coarse crumbs. Add the milk and egg and stir until smooth. Add the cherries and stir just until combined.

Turn the dough out onto a lightly floured surface and roll or pat to a thickness of ½ inch. Using a 2½-inch biscuit cutter or glass, stamp out scones. Place the scones on the baking sheets, leaving about 1 inch between them.

Bake for about 20 minutes, or until lightly browned. Serve warm.

OLD-FASHIONED CORN CRACKERS

■■■

**MAKES ABOUT
36 CRACKERS**

½ cup white stone-ground cornmeal

½ cup unbleached all-purpose flour

1½ teaspoons sugar

1½ teaspoons baking powder

¼ teaspoon salt

1 large egg

¾ cup milk

4 tablespoons unsalted butter, melted

YOU *COULD MAKE* a rich seafood stew or chowder and serve it without corn crackers, but why would you? This old New England recipe produces cornmeal crackers with wonderful corn flavor (be sure to use the best stone-ground cornmeal you can find). The melted butter brushed on after they come out of the oven gives them a rich finish.

Preheat the oven to 425°F. Line 3 baking sheets with parchment paper and butter the parchment.

Sift the cornmeal, flour, baking powder, sugar, and salt, into a large bowl.

In another bowl, beat the egg with the milk. Add to the dry ingredients all at once and mix with a wooden spoon just until the batter is free of lumps. Add 3 tablespoons of the melted butter and stir to incorporate.

Drop the batter by tablespoonfuls onto the buttered parchment, leaving about 3 inches between them. Using the spoon, spread the batter as thin as possible to make circles that are 3 to 3½ inches in diameter.

Bake for 15 to 20 minutes, or until lightly browned. Remove from the oven and brush the crackers with the remaining 1 tablespoon melted butter. Cool on wire racks. When cool, store in an airtight container.

GRANNY'S IRISH SODA BREAD

■■■■■■■■■■■■■■■■■■■■■■■■■■■■■■■■■■■■■■

MAKES 1 ROUND LOAF

4 cups unbleached all-purpose flour

¼ cup sugar

1 teaspoon baking powder

1 teaspoon salt

4 tablespoons unsalted butter, cut into pieces and chilled

1 cup raisins

1½ cups buttermilk

1 large egg

1 teaspoon baking soda

MY IRISH GRANDMOTHER, Granny Lu, loved to bake. And bake and bake! It wasn't unusual for us to be offered five or six desserts after Sunday dinner. This soda bread was just a simple recipe my grandmother baked for an afternoon snack. I remember eating it right from the oven with lots of butter and jam.

Preheat the oven to 375°F. Butter a shallow 2- to 2½-quart casserole.

Sift the flour, sugar, baking powder, and salt into a large bowl. Add the butter and, using a pastry blender or your fingers, blend until the mixture resembles coarse crumbs. Stir in the raisins.

In another bowl, whisk together the buttermilk, egg, and baking soda. Add to the dry ingredients all at once and stir just until moistened. Scrape into the casserole.

Bake for 45 to 50 minutes, or until golden brown and firm to the touch. Turn out onto a wire rack and cool for about 10 minutes. Serve hot with soft butter.

Old-Fashioned Desserts

DESSERT FALLS INTO the same contemporary American myth as red meat—everyone thinks that nobody is eating it anymore. Having cooked for more than twenty years in restaurants, I am here to state categorically that people love desserts. Many of our regular diners at An American Place start talking about what they are going to have for dessert as soon as they sit down, planning the rest of their meal around their Old-Fashioned Double Chocolate Pudding or warm Old-Fashioned Strawberry Shortcake.

Like soup, dessert has a powerful emotional component, not just a taste component. It feels good, welcoming, embracing, loving. It conjures up memories of childhood, home, comfortable kitchens filled with the heady smells of cinnamon, nutmeg, stewing fruits, bubbling brown sugar, warm chocolate, toasting coconut.

As inventive, clever, or complex as a modern dinner might be, I believe that dessert should bring us back to basics. It is somehow a reminder of our roots, a celebration of native ingredients, conceived with an eye for intensifying flavor, balancing sweetness and tartness, understanding the delicate synergy between sugars, spices, fruits, nuts, and sauces. So the desserts in this chapter are homey, traditional, nostalgic, and they are truly American. And while some are entirely the result of my tinkering—like a Banana Betty or a Pumpkin Cheesecake—most are pretty accurate facsimiles of original recipes.

There are luscious fruit desserts—Apple Pandowdy, Quince and Raspberry Tart, Rhubarb and Strawberry Crisp, Peach and Strawberry Cobbler with Spiced Topping, and Maple-Stewed Summer Fruits—that will make you long for a farm stand in August. There are cakes and pies that would take the blue ribbon at any country fair: Granny's Chocolate Cake and Pennsylvania Dutch Chocolate Nut Pie. And there is my absolute favorite—the ultimate Bread Pudding. With help from Jim Beard, I developed a recipe that starts with a homemade brown-sugar corn bread that's soaked in a heavenly mixture of eggs, vanilla, cinnamon, nutmeg, and milk. It's brushed with butter, topped with brown sugar and spices, baked until it's all puffy and golden, and served warm with a vanilla-infused Sour Cherry Bourbon Sauce. Needless to say, this bread pudding became a favorite at An American Place the day we put it on the menu.

More than any other category, American desserts demonstrate how a few simple ingredients can ultimately be transformed into the most miraculous results.

OLD-FASHIONED DOUBLE
CHOCOLATE PUDDING

SERVES 4

2¼ cups milk

½ cup sugar

1 large egg

2 large egg yolks

3 tablespoons cornstarch

2 tablespoons unsweetened cocoa
   powder, sifted

¼ teaspoon salt

3½ ounces semisweet chocolate,
   finely chopped

2 tablespoons unsalted butter, cut into
   small pieces

1½ teaspoons dark rum

1½ teaspoons vanilla extract

Sweetened whipped cream for
   serving (optional)

CHOCOLATE PUDDING is the quintessential childhood dessert. Who could ever outgrow a love for something so simple, so dense, so smooth, so wildly satisfying, so full of pleasure, so rich in memories? Certainly, no one *I* know. Which are all of the reasons that chocolate pudding has been on our menu from Day One. This version is very rich and very creamy. We make it with both cocoa and chocolate, and that makes it taste intense.

Put 2 cups of the milk and ¼ cup of the sugar in a large saucepan and heat over medium-high heat until scalded. Remove from the heat and set aside.

Put the egg and egg yolks in a medium bowl and whisk until blended. Add the remaining ¼ cup milk, ¼ cup sugar, the cornstarch, cocoa, and salt, and whisk until well blended.

Whisk the cocoa mixture into the scalded milk. Set over low heat and cook, stirring with a wooden spoon, for 4 to 6 minutes, until the mixture thickens and comes to a low boil, causing large bubbles to form.

Immediately remove from the heat, add the chopped chocolate, butter, rum, and vanilla, and stir until the butter and chocolate are completely melted. (The pudding will continue to thicken as it cools.)

Pour the pudding into four individual dishes or glasses and let cool for about 10 minutes. Cover tightly with plastic wrap and refrigerate. The pudding will keep in the refrigerator for 3 to 5 days.

If desired, top with a dollop of lightly whipped cream before serving.

BANANA BETTY

SERVES 4

Crumb Mixture

1 cup coarse gingersnap crumbs (about 6 ounces cookies)

2 tablespoons sugar

2 tablespoons unsalted butter, melted

5 to 6 ripe but firm medium bananas, cut into ¼-inch-thick slices

Custard

1 cup heavy cream

3 large egg yolks, at room temperature

3 tablespoons sugar

1 tablespoon dark rum

½ teaspoon vanilla extract

NOTE: The dessert can also be made in a 1-quart casserole or baking dish. Sprinkle half the crumbs over the bottom of the dish and the remainder on top of the custard. Bake for 20 to 30 minutes.

BACK IN THE DAYS of the clipper ships, there was a trade triangle connecting the Caribbean with Boston and England, which is how ginger, rum, and other tropical ingredients made their way into so many old-time recipes in New (and old) England. This dessert combines a classic English custard with a tropical fruit and ginger. When most people think of brown Betty, they think of apple Betty, but you can make Bettys with nearly any fruit. We use gingersnaps for the crumb topping.

We make the Bettys individually so that they are easy to serve and somewhat unusual; over the years they have become one of our most requested desserts. They can be assembled hours or even a day ahead of time and refrigerated; let them come to room temperature before baking.

Combine the gingersnap crumbs and sugar in a bowl. Gradually add the melted butter and work the mixture with your fingertips until it holds together when pressed between your fingers.

Preheat the oven to 350°F.

Sprinkle about 1 tablespoon of the crumb mixture each over the bottom of four 8-ounce ramekins or soufflé molds. Fill the ramekins with the banana slices to about ½ inch from the top.

To make the custard, pour the cream into a large saucepan and bring just to a simmer over medium heat. Remove from the heat.

Whisk the egg yolks and sugar together in a medium bowl. Gradually whisk in about ¼ cup of the hot cream to temper the yolks. Then whisk the yolk mixture into the hot cream in the saucepan. Cook over medium-low heat, stirring constantly with a wooden spoon, for about 5 minutes, until the custard thickens enough to coat the back of the spoon (it should register no more than 180°F on a candy thermometer); do not let it boil. Remove from the heat and strain through a fine strainer into a bowl. Stir in the rum and vanilla.

Pour the hot custard into the molds and give each mold a little shake so that the custard spreads evenly through the banana slices. Refrigerate for 20 to 30 minutes, or until the custard sets.

Sprinkle the remaining crumb mixture over the custards, completely covering the tops, put the ramekins in a large roasting pan and add hot water to the pan to come halfway up the sides of the molds. Bake for 15 to 20 minutes, until the topping is crisp and golden brown. Serve hot or at room temperature.

Old-Fashioned Apple and Quince Duff

■■

Serves 6 to 8

Fruit

1½ cups apple cider

¾ cup sugar

2 tablespoons quick-cooking tapioca

3 quinces (about 1½ pounds), peeled, cored, and sliced

4 crisp apples, such as Macoun or Northern Spy, peeled, cored, and sliced

2 tablespoons applejack

1 tablespoon grated fresh ginger

Grated zest of 1 lemon

Batter

⅔ cup sugar

4 large eggs, separated

2 teaspoons vanilla extract

½ cup all-purpose flour, sifted

Confectioners' sugar for dusting

HERE'S ANOTHER EXAMPLE of creating something that seems to be both incredibly old-fashioned and completely modern. When I developed it, I was looking for a dessert that was extremely American, with Colonial New England as a frame of reference. Quinces are related to apples and they work well together in this dessert, made by pouring batter over the fruit and baking it. *Duff* is one of those regional terms like *crisp*, *cobbler*, and *buckle* that seem to vary in meaning but always refer to some sort of baked fruit dessert.

Preheat the oven to 350°F. Butter a shallow 2½-quart casserole.

Put the cider, sugar, and tapioca in a large, noncorrosive saucepan and bring to a boil. Stir in the quinces, apples, applejack, ginger, and lemon zest and bring to a boil over high heat. Cover the pan, lower the heat, and simmer gently for 6 to 7 minutes, until the fruit has softened slightly. Spoon the mixture into the casserole and set aside.

To make the batter, combine the egg yolks and sugar in a large bowl and beat with an electric mixer until pale in color and thick, 3 to 4 minutes. Beat in the vanilla.

In another bowl using clean beaters, beat the egg whites until soft peaks form. Using a rubber spatula, fold the flour into the whites, then fold this mixture into the beaten egg yolks. Pour the batter over the fruit in the casserole and smooth the top.

Bake for 30 to 40 minutes, until the cake topping is golden brown and begins to pull away from the side of the casserole. Sprinkle with confectioners' sugar and serve warm.

APPLE PANDOWDY

■■ ■

SERVES 4

8 thin slices firm white or whole
    wheat bread

6 tablespoons unsalted butter, at room
    temperature

Granulated sugar for sprinkling

Apples

4 large baking apples, such as Jonathan or
    Rome, peeled, cored, and cut into 4-
    inch-thick slices

2 tablespoons molasses

¼ cup plus 2 tablespoons packed light
    brown sugar

½ teaspoon cinnamon

¼ teaspoon freshly grated nutmeg

¼ teaspoon ground cloves

2 tablespoons dark rum

2 tablespoons fresh lemon juice

1 tablespoon vanilla extract

5 tablespoons unsalted butter, chilled and
    cut into small pieces

Sweetened whipped cream for
    serving (optional)

ONCE I FIGURE OUT how something was made, I can start figuring out how I think it should be made. Jim Beard was every bit as obsessional as I am. Once, he and I were exploring the evolution of pandowdy; the farther back our research took us, the more convinced we became that bread was often used as the "crust." Firm homemade bread would always have been around because every household made its own, so all that would be needed were good apples. This pandowdy is simply buttered bread sprinkled with sugar and topped with a spiced apple mixture. When baked, the bread turns crispy and brown but the inside of the bottom slices stay soft, for an interesting contrast in texture. Be sure to use good-quality firm bread.

Preheat the oven to 375°F. Butter four 8-ounce ramekins or soufflé dishes.

Using a 3¼-inch cutter, cut the bread into rounds that fit neatly into the ramekins. Spread the softened butter on both sides of the bread rounds. Sprinkle one side of each round with a little sugar. Place a bread round in each ramekin, sugared side down. Set the remaining rounds aside.

Put the apple slices in a large bowl and add the molasses, brown sugar, cinnamon, nutmeg, cloves, rum, lemon juice, vanilla, and chilled butter. Toss well. Spoon the apple mixture into the prepared ramekins, filling them almost full, and spoon any juices over the fruit. Top each pandowdy with a second bread round, sugared side up.

Put the ramekins on a baking sheet and bake on the bottom rack of the oven for 25 minutes, until the bread is golden brown. Transfer the ramekins to a rack to cool slightly.

Serve the warm dowdys in the baking dishes. Pass whipped cream separately if desired.

APPLE CRISP WITH OATMEAL
CRUMB TOPPING

■■■■■■■■■■■■■■■■■■■■■■■■■■■■■■■■■■■■■

5 to 6 crisp, tart apples, such as Granny Smith or Winesap (about 1¾ pounds), peeled, cored, and cut into ¾-inch-thick slices

2 tablespoons granulated sugar

2 tablespoons lightly packed brown sugar

1½ teaspoons cinnamon

¼ teaspoon freshly grated nutmeg

2 tablespoons unsalted butter, melted

Oatmeal Crumb Topping

¾ cup plus 2 tablespoons all-purpose flour

¼ cup plus 2 tablespoons old-fashioned oatmeal

¼ plus 3 tablespoons granulated sugar

¼ cup plus 3 tablespoons lightly packed brown sugar

12 tablespoons unsalted butter, cut into small pieces and slightly softened

Sweetened whipped cream or ice cream for serving

PLAIN AND SIMPLE doesn't mean boring or uninteresting. This crisp is a case in point. Using oatmeal in the topping makes this like an oatmeal cookie, a nice variation on the traditional crumb mixture. Choose tart apples, such as Granny Smiths, Winesaps, or Gravensteins, all of which have firm, crunchy flesh.

Preheat the oven to 375°F.

In a large bowl, toss the apple slices with both sugars and the spices. Let sit for 20 minutes, or until the apples release some juice and the sugar is moist.

Meanwhile, combine the flour, oatmeal, and both sugars for the topping in a bowl and mix well with your fingertips, crumbling any lumps. Add the butter and work the mixture gently until it resembles coarse crumbs. Cover and refrigerate until ready to use.

Transfer the apples, with their juices, to a 1½-quart casserole. Pour the melted butter over the apples. Sprinkle the topping evenly over them.

Bake for 30 to 40 minutes, until the topping is golden brown and the filling is bubbling. Serve warm, with whipped cream or ice cream.

RHUBARB AND STRAWBERRY CRISP

■■

SERVES 4 TO 6

2¼ pounds rhubarb, trimmed, washed, and dried

1 cup plus 2 tablespoons sugar

2 pints strawberries, rinsed and hulled

3½ tablespoons all-purpose flour

Crumb Topping (page 251)

ALTHOUGH YOU COULD use this filling for a traditional pie, I prefer fruit desserts with crumb toppings. They are easy to make and easy to serve right from the oven; if you try to slice a just-baked traditional pie, it falls apart. Many Early American desserts had only a top crust or a crumbly topping, because, if allowed to sit around for more than a day, bottom crusts turn doughy. Early American cooks, who as a rule made four, five, or six pies at a time, knew to make bottom crusts only for the ones that would be eaten the same day they were baked.

Preheat the oven to 375°F.

If the rhubarb stalks are more than 1 inch thick, split them in half lengthwise. Using a sharp knife, cut the stalks into 1-inch pieces. Place in a bowl, add 1 cup of the sugar, and toss well. Let sit for about 20 minutes, or until the rhubarb starts to release some liquid and the sugar is moist.

Depending on the size of the strawberries, cut them in half or quarters. Toss with the remaining 2 tablespoons sugar and add to the rhubarb. Add the flour and toss gently.

Spoon the fruit mixture into a 1½-quart casserole. Sprinkle the crumb topping evenly over the fruit. Bake for 50 to 60 minutes, until the topping is golden and the filling is bubbling. Serve warm or at room temperature.

The crisp can be prepared up to 8 hours in advance and refrigerated. Bring to room temperature before serving.

BLACKBERRY AND APPLE CRISP
CRUMB TOPPING

■■

SERVES 6 TO 8

3 cups blackberries, preferably wild

4 baking apples, peeled, cored, and sliced

3 tablespoons fresh lemon juice

½ cup sugar

4 tablespoons unsalted butter, cut into pieces

Crumb Topping (recipe follows)

Sweetened whipped cream or vanilla ice cream for serving

APPLES AND BLACKBERRIES go together beautifully—tart, sweet, and ripe all mixed up in one mouthful. Wild berries do not require much sugar for sweetness, as do some cultivated fruits that are sometimes so overirrigated their flavor is lost. Berries grown on huge farms may be big and look plump, but often they are filled with water. Wild berries and those allowed to ripen naturally develop perfect sweetness. But if you cannot find wild blackberries, the dessert is still delicious made with cultivated ones.

Preheat the oven to 350°F.

Put the berries in a bowl, discarding any that are damaged or underripe. Add the apples, lemon juice, sugar, and butter and toss until well combined. Transfer to a 1½- to 2-quart baking dish or shallow casserole. Sprinkle the topping evenly over the fruit.

Bake in the center of the oven for 30 to 35 minutes, or until the topping is crisp and golden and the filling is bubbling. Let cool on a wire rack for 20 to 25 minutes.

Serve the crisp warm with sweetened whipped cream or vanilla ice cream.

_____

CRUMB TOPPING
MAKES ABOUT 1½ CUPS

¾ cup all-purpose flour

¾ cup packed brown sugar

1 teaspoon ground ginger

6 tablespoons unsalted butter, cut into small pieces and slightly softened

Combine all the ingredients in a bowl and mix well with your fingertips, crumbling any lumps. Work the mixture gently until it resembles coarse crumbs. Use immediately or cover and refrigerate until ready to use.

PEACH AND STRAWBERRY COBBLER
WITH SPICED TOPPING

■■■

SERVES 8 TO 10

Topping

1 cup all-purpose flour

¾ cup sugar

1 teaspoon cinnamon

1 teaspoon baking powder

½ teaspoon salt

1 large egg, beaten

5 tablespoons unsalted butter, melted

Filling

2 cups sliced ripe strawberries (1 pint)

6 ripe but firm peaches, peeled, pitted,
    and sliced

2 tablespoons unsalted butter

1 teaspoon quick-working tapioca

1 teaspoon cinnamon

Pinch of freshly grated nutmeg

2 tablespoons packed light brown sugar

Sweetened whipped cream, for serving

THE ONLY PROBLEM with summer fruits is that there are so many and so many ways of showing them off. Every summer I get a little overwhelmed. I particularly like the combination of peaches and strawberries, but just peaches would also be great with the cinnamon crust. It tastes like a cross between a cinnamon cookie and a spiced pie dough, with a crisper texture. We've also made this with peaches and raspberries.

To make the topping, sift all the dry ingredients together into a bowl. Add the egg and stir until smooth. Add the melted butter and stir until smooth. Gather the dough into a ball, flatten it into a dish, and wrap in plastic wrap. Refrigerate for at least 4 hours, or overnight.

Preheat the oven to 350°F.

To make the filling, put the sliced strawberries in a bowl.

Melt the butter in a medium frying pan over low heat. Add the peaches, toss, and cook for 2 minutes. Stir in the tapioca, then stir in the cinnamon and nutmeg.

Add the peach mixture to the strawberries. Gently stir in the brown sugar. Spoon the mixture into a shallow 1½-quart casserole. Let the filling cool slightly.

Roll out the chilled dough between two pieces of waxed paper to a ¼-inch thickness. Using a 2½- to 3-inch cutter, cut the dough into rounds. Layer them over the fruit, covering it completely by overlapping the rounds.

Bake for 35 to 40 minutes, until the crust is lightly browned and the filling is bubbling.

Serve warm, with whipped cream.

QUINCE AND RASPBERRY TART

4 quinces (about 2 pounds), cored and cut into 1-inch chunks

1½ cups sugar

½ cup water

¼ cup fresh lemon juice

1 prebaked Basic Pie Shell (page 271)

1 pint raspberries

Topping

½ cup all-purpose flour

½ cup packed light brown sugar

8 tablespoons unsalted butter, chilled and cut into small pieces

QUINCES USED TO BE something of an endangered species. They still aren't a very well known fruit, so they're fun to try. Quince and raspberry is a wonderful combination. For this tart the quinces, which have a lot of pectin, are cooked down to a thick sauce, spooned into a pie shell, and studded with raspberries.

Quinces are extremely tart and tannic when underripe, but because they bruise easily, they often are shipped before they ripen. Let them ripen before using, or buy them ripe and ignore the bruises.

Put the quinces, sugar, water, and lemon juice in a heavy noncorrosive saucepan and bring to a simmer. Cover, reduce the heat to low, and simmer for 20 to 30 minutes, until the quinces are tender, stirring occasionally to prevent sticking. (The cooking time depends on the ripeness of the quinces.) Remove from the heat.

Preheat the oven to 350°F.

Remove the quinces from the syrup with a slotted spoon, reserving the syrup, and press through a fine stainer into a bowl, or puree in a food processor or blender. Return the puree to the syrup and cook gently, uncovered, for 6 to 8 minutes, until the puree thickens to the consistency of thick apple butter or applesauce.

Spoon the puree into the prebaked pie shell. Stud the tart with the raspberries, pressing the berries lightly into the puree.

To make the topping, sift the flour into a bowl and add the sugar. Add the butter and work into the dry ingredients with your fingertips until the mixture resembles coarse crumbs.

Sprinkle the topping over the quince puree and raspberries. Bake the tart for 45 to 50 minutes, until the topping is golden brown. Transfer to a rack and let cool before serving.

BREAD PUDDING

SOUR CHERRY BOURBON SAUCE

■■

SERVES 6 TO 8

6 cups trimmed and cubed (1-inch cubes) Yeast-Raised Corn Bread (page 231) or any good-quality firm bread

½ cup dried sour cherries

⅓ cup toasted pecans, coarsely chopped

6 large eggs

1 cup plus 3 tablespoons sugar

1 quart milk

1 tablespoon vanilla extract

2 teaspoons cinnamon

1 teaspoon freshly grated nutmeg

8 tablespoons unsalted butter, melted

Topping

⅔ cup packed brown sugar

1 tablespoon cinnamon

1 tablespoon freshly grated nutmeg

2 tablespoons unsalted butter at room temperature

Sour Cherry Bourbon Sauce (recipe follows), warmed

THE SIMPLE IS TRANSPORTED to the sublime in this recipe. If I sound a little hyperbolic, just wait till *you* try this bread pudding. It has been one of our most popular desserts ever since we opened. It uses Yeast-Raised Corn Bread as its base. I have always liked bread pudding, but so often it turns out to be more pudding than bread. Jim Beard's suggestion was to be sure to soak the stale bread in the uncooked custard for as long as it needs to absorb all the liquid it can. Break a bread cube open after twenty minutes or so to see if the custard has reached its center; if it has, it's time to cook the pudding. You always get a nice, firm bread pudding this way, never one that is too soupy or too dry.

Although the corn bread adds a nice texture, you can substitute any firm bread. Just don't use soft store-bought bread.

Spread the bread cubes on a baking sheet and set aside in a dry place for 3 to 4 hours, or overnight, to dry out. Soak the dried cherries in water to cover for 2 to 3 hours, or overnight, to soften; drain.

Combine the cherries, pecans, and bread cubes in a large bowl.

In a large bowl, using an electric mixer or whisk, beat the eggs and sugar for 3 to 4 minutes, until thick and lemon-colored. Reduce the speed to low and gradually add the milk. Beat in the vanilla, cinnamon, nutmeg, and melted butter. Pour the mixture over the bread cubes and let stand, stirring occasionally, for 45 to 60 minutes, until most of the liquid has been absorbed. If you break apart a bread cube, it should be soaked through.

Preheat the oven to 375°F. Lightly butter a 2½-quart casserole.

To make the topping, combine the sugar, cinnamon, and nutmeg and toss well. Sprinkle half the topping over the bottom of the prepared casserole.

Spoon the bread mixture, with any liquid, into the casserole. Cover with buttered foil and set the dish in a roasting pan. Add hot water to the pan to come halfway up the sides of the casserole.

Bake for 1 hour. Remove the foil, brush the top of the pudding with the butter, and sprinkle with the remaining topping.

Bake, uncovered, for 15 minutes longer, or until the top is brown and crispy. (The pudding will puff up slightly during baking and fall a little when removed from the oven.) Serve warm with the warm sour cherry sauce.

———

SOUR CHERRY BOURBON SAUCE

MAKES ABOUT 3½ CUPS

1 cup dried sour cherries	6 large egg yolks
¼ cup plus 2 tablespoons bourbon	½ cup sugar
2 cups light cream	1½ teaspoons cornstarch
½ vanilla bean, split lengthwise	¼ cup heavy cream

Combine the cherries and bourbon in a bowl and let soak for 2 to 3 hours, or overnight.

Put the light cream and vanilla bean in a large saucepan and bring just to a boil. Remove from the heat and set aside to infuse for about 10 minutes.

Remove the vanilla bean from the cream and scrape any remaining seeds into the cream. Discard the bean.

In a large bowl, whisk together the egg yolks, sugar, and cornstarch. Whisk in about ½ cup of the infused cream, then whisk the mixture into the cream in the saucepan. Cook over low heat, stirring, for 5 to 8 minutes, until the sauce is slightly thickened and coats the back of a spoon. Remove from the heat and set aside.

Put the soaked cherries and bourbon in a small saucepan and heat until hot. Remove from the heat and carefully ignite.

When the flames subside, stir the heavy cream into the cherries. Bring the mixture to a boil over medium-high heat, lower the heat, and simmer for 1 minute.

Add the sour cherry mixture to the custard sauce and stir until well mixed. Serve immediately or store tightly covered in the refrigerator for up to 2 days. Reheat the sauce gently over low heat, stirring constantly, before serving.

BAKED PERSIMMON AND
BUTTERMILK PUDDING
FOAMY SAUCE

■■■

SERVES 6 TO 8

1½ cups all-purpose flour

1½ teaspoons baking soda

1½ teaspoons baking powder

½ teaspoon cinnamon

½ teaspoon freshly grated nutmeg

½ teaspoon salt

1½ cups unsweetened persimmon pulp, fresh, canned, or frozen and thawed (see Note)

2½ cups buttermilk

1½ cups sugar

4 tablespoons unsalted butter, melted

4 large eggs, beaten

About 1 tablespoon unsalted butter, melted

Sugar for sprinkling

Foamy Sauce (recipe follows)

NOTE: If you cannot find persimmon puree, substitute canned unsweetened pumpkin puree.

WE ALL GET STUCK in a rut, making the same things over and over. This warm, festive pudding is worth trying if you want to do something different. I make it with wild persimmons—not the big imported Japanese fruit. Persimmon trees are indigenous to the Midwest, where the only way to gather them is to wait for the ripe fruit to drop from the trees. People spread large sheets under the trees and wait for the fruit to fall—and then hurry to get to the fruit before the birds do. When you split a ripe persimmon open, the pulp is pudding-like and gooey. You can use Japanese persimmons for this recipe, but their flavor is not nearly as intense; be sure that they are ripe. Pumpkin puree works, too, although the flavor is quite different.

The pudding puffs up and then falls a little, and, like a soufflé, should be served as close to coming from the oven as possible. Don't worry: It doesn't require the same careful handling as a soufflé—it's sturdier.

Preheat the oven to 400°F. Butter a 2-quart soufflé dish or deep 2-quart baking dish.

Sift together the flour, baking soda, baking powder, cinnamon, nutmeg, and salt. Put the persimmon pulp in a large bowl. Add the buttermilk and beat with a wooden spoon until smooth. Beat in the sugar and melted butter. Beat in the eggs. Add the dry ingredients a little at a time, beating well after each addition.

Pour the pudding into the prepared baking dish. Put the dish in a roasting pan and add enough hot water to the pan to come halfway up the sides of the dish. Bake in the center of the oven for 45 to 55 minutes, until a toothpick inserted in the center of the pudding comes out clean.

Brush the pudding with the melted butter and sprinkle with sugar. Serve immediately with the sauce, spooning it over the top of the pudding or passing it separately.

FOAMY SAUCE

MAKES ABOUT 1 CUP

4 large egg whites, at room temperature   ¼ cup milk

⅔ cup confectioners' sugar   1 teaspoon vanilla extract

In a large bowl, using an electric mixer, beat the whites on medium speed until soft peaks form. Gradually add the sugar, and continue beating until the whites are stiff and shiny.

Combine the milk and vanilla in a small saucepan and heat until very hot but not simmering. With the mixer on low speed, gradually add the hot milk to the egg whites.

Serve immediately.

COCONUT CRÈME CARAMEL
TROPICAL FRUIT AMBROSIA

■■■

SERVES 4

2 cups sweetened shredded coconut

1 cup plus 3 tablespoons sugar

⅓ cup water

1½ cups milk

1½ cups heavy cream

1 large egg

5 large egg yolks

1¼ teaspoons vanilla extract

Tropical Fruit Ambrosia (recipe follows)

SOMETIMES, IF YOU'RE LUCKY, things get better and better. We had a classic crème caramel on the menu, and we were working on a recipe for coconut cream pie. We decided to combine the crème caramel with the coconut flavor and serve it with a tropical fruit salad, an "ambrosia" that derives its coconut from the custard.

Preheat the oven to 325°F.

To make the crème caramel, spread the coconut on a baking sheet. Toast in the oven, stirring from time to time, for 8 to 10 minutes, until lightly browned. Remove from the oven and set aside.

Put 1 cup of the sugar in a medium frying pan and shake the pan to spread the sugar evenly. Slowly pour the water into the pan, directing it down the side of the pan. Cook over medium-low heat for 2 to 3 minutes, until the sugar has dissolved. Using a wet pastry brush, wash down the sides of the pan. Increase the heat to high and cook without stirring, for 5 to 6 minutes, until the syrup turns a light golden brown. Immediately remove from the heat.

Carefully pour the caramelized sugar into four 6-ounce ramekins or custard cups, turning each as you pour so that the caramel swirls most of the way up the sides; use oven mitts or other protection, as the caramel is very hot. Work quickly but carefully so that the caramel does not harden before it coats the sides of the cups. Set the cups aside.

Combine the milk and cream in a large saucepan and heat over medium-high heat for 4 to 5 minutes, until steam appears and small bubbles form around the sides of the pan. Remove from the heat and add all but 2 tablespoons of the toasted coconut. Cover the pan and let the mixture steep for 30 minutes.

Preheat the oven to 325°F.

Using a fine-meshed strainer, strain the coconut milk into a bowl, pressing as much milk out of the coconut as possible. Discard the coconut.

In a medium bowl, combine the egg, egg yolks, and the remaining 3 tablespoons sugar and whisk until well blended. Gently whisk in the strained coconut milk. Stir in the vanilla.

Pour the custard into the prepared custard cups. Set the cups in a roasting pan and add enough hot water to the pan to come halfway up the sides of the custard cups. Cover the pan with aluminum foil and pierce a few small holes in the foil to release steam.

Bake in the center of the oven for 1 hour. Remove the foil and bake for 5 to 10 minutes more, until a knife inserted in the center of the custards comes out clean. Transfer the custards to a wire rack and let cool to room temperature. Cover the custards with foil or plastic wrap and refrigerate for at least 4 hours. (The custards will keep in the refrigerator for up to 4 days.)

To unmold the custards, gently press each one around the edges, or run a knife around the edges, and invert the cup onto the center of a dessert plate. Tap to loosen the mold and remove it, making sure to pour all the liquid caramel over the custard.

Spoon the ambrosia around the custards and sprinkle with the remaining 2 tablespoons toasted coconut.

———

TROPICAL FRUIT AMBROSIA

MAKES ABOUT 2 CUPS

1 orange

¼ pineapple, cut into small cubes
   (about ½ cup)

¼ papaya, cut into small cubes
   (about ¼ cup)

½ mango, cut into small cubes
   (about ¼ cup)

2 tablespoons fresh lime juice

1 tablespoon sugar

Using a sharp knife, peel the orange, removing all the bitter white pith. Working over a bowl to catch the juices, cut between the membranes to release the orange segments. Add the pineapple, papaya, mango, lime juice, and sugar to the bowl and let stand for at least 20 minutes before serving. (The ambrosia can be prepared up to 6 hours before serving and refrigerated.)

NOTE: The ambrosia makes a light and refreshing dessert on its own. Sprinkle it with toasted coconut just before serving.

MAPLE-STEWED SUMMER FRUITS

■■■■■■■■■■■■■■■■■■■■■■■■■■■■■■■■■■■■■

1 cup pure maple syrup

1 cup water

½ cup maple sugar or brown sugar

1 cinnamon stick

⅛ teaspoon freshly grated nutmeg

Grated zest of 1 lemon

Juice of 1 lemon

2 medium Bosc pears

3 ripe but firm peaches or nectarines or
     a combination

2 ripe but firm apricots

1 cup fresh sweet cherries, pitted

¼ cup dried sour cherries

½ cup coarsely chopped black walnuts,
     English walnuts, or pecans

1 pint ripe strawberries, hulled and
     cut in half

THIS IS A RECIPE I developed when asked for a summer dessert that was made without white sugar and stayed within organic guidelines. Sweetening the fruit with syrup made with maple and sugar works really well. Maple sugar is sold in specialty food stores and at stands that sell maple syrup and other maple products.

Combine the maple syrup, water, sugar, cinnamon stick, nutmeg, lemon zest, and lemon juice in a heavy noncorrosive saucepan. Cook over low heat for 2 to 3 minutes, stirring, until the sugar has dissolved. Set aside.

Halve the pears and core them. Halve the peaches or nectarines and the apricots and remove the pits. Cut each fruit half into three wedges.

Put the fruit in a large, noncorrosive saucepan and add the fresh cherries, dried cherries, and nuts. Pour the syrup over the fruit, and cover the fruit with a circle of parchment paper. Bring to a boil over medium heat. Immediately remove the pan from the heat, remove the parchment paper, and let the fruit cool completely in the syrup.

Add the strawberries to the cooled stewed fruits. Serve at room temperature or chilled.

GRANNY'S CHOCOLATE CAKE

■■■

Cake

2½ cups all-purpose flour

1 teaspoon baking soda

½ teaspoon baking powder

½ teaspoon salt

1¼ cups buttermilk

1 teaspoon vanilla extract

11 tablespoons unsalted butter, at room
    temperature

1½ cups sugar

2 large eggs

4 ounces unsweetened chocolate, melted

Frosting

6 ounces semisweet chocolate,
    coarsely chopped

½ cup plus 2 tablespoons water

1½ teaspoons vanilla extract

Pinch of salt

10 tablespoons unsalted butter, melted

7 large egg yolks

5 cups confectioners' sugar

WHEN I WAS GROWING UP, this was one of my favorite cakes. We began serving it when we opened An American Place, and everyone loved it. Of course we modified the recipe from the days when my Irish grandmother made a similar cake for my birthday every year. When Granny made the cake, she put an inch of fudge frosting between every layer; there was as much fudge as cake. Store any leftover cake under a cake dome; if you refrigerate it, it will dry out.

Preheat the oven to 350°F. Butter three 9-inch round cake pans and line the bottoms with waxed or parchment paper. Lightly butter the paper. Dust the pans with flour and shake out the excess.

Sift together the flour, baking soda, baking powder, and salt.

Combine the buttermilk and vanilla in a small bowl.

In a large bowl, using an electric mixer set at medium-high speed, cream the butter. Slowly add the sugar and continue beating until well blended and light colored. Add the eggs one a time, beating well after each addition. Add the dry ingredients alternately with the buttermilk mixture in 2 or 3 additions, beating well after each addition. Beat in the melted chocolate until well blended. Spoon the batter into the prepared pans and smooth the tops with a rubber spatula.

Bake for 30 to 35 minutes, or until a toothpick inserted in the center of a cake layer comes out clean. Let the cake layers cool in the pans on wire racks for 10 minutes, then invert onto other racks and peel off the paper. Invert again and let cool completely on the racks.

To make the frosting, combine the chocolate, water, vanilla extract, and salt in the top of a double boiler. Stir the mixture over hot, not simmering, water until the chocolate is almost completely melted. Remove the top of the double boiler from the heat, add the melted butter and stir until smooth. Let cool slightly.

Transfer the chocolate mixture to a large bowl. Using an electric mixer set on low speed, add the egg yolks one at a time, beating well after each addition, gradually add the sugar, beating well. (Do not be tempted to beat at high speed, as the frosting may curdle.) Make sure the frosting is at room temperature before spreading it on the cake.

continued

Place a cake layer on a cardboard cake round or flat serving plate. Using a metal spatula, spread about ¹/₂ cup of the frosting over the layer. Position another layer on top and spread with another ¹/₂ cup of frosting. Place the third layer on top. Smooth any filling that may have seeped from between the layers, and refrigerate for 15 to 20 minutes, until the filling has set.

Brush any crumbs from the sides and top of the cake. Frost the cake with half of the remaining frosting. Refrigerate the cake for 15 to 20 minutes, until the frosting has set. Then frost it with the remaining frosting. (The chilled frosting acts as a coating and makes the final application of frosting easy and smooth. For an extra-silky finish, smooth the frosting with a metal spatula warmed in hot water and wiped dry.) Serve the cake at room temperature. Store under a cake dome or upside-down bowl.

Chocolate Walnut Fudge Cake

Serves 10 to 12

13 ounces semisweet chocolate, coarsely chopped

3 ounces unsweetened chocolate, coarsely chopped

¹/₂ pound unsalted butter

1 cup unsweetened cocoa powder

7 large eggs

1¹/₂ cups sugar

1 cup walnuts or pecans, coarsely chopped

Confectioners' sugar for dusting

This is a rich, fudgy, flourless cake that goes well with ice cream or fruit and is delicious on its own. At my house, it is the cake I always make for birthdays.

Preheat the oven to 350°F. Lightly butter and flour a 10- by 3-inch spring-form pan. Using a large piece of aluminum foil, wrap the bottom and sides of the pan. Or lightly butter and flour a 10- by 2¹/₂-inch cake pan.

Combine both chocolates and the butter in the top of a double boiler and stir over hot, not simmering, water until melted. Remove from the heat and stir in the cocoa.

Combine the eggs and sugar in a large bowl. Set the bowl over a saucepan of hot water and beat with an electric mixer on low speed, or whisk, for 2 to 3 minutes, until the mixture is warm. Remove from the heat and beat with an electric mixer on medium speed until the mixture triples in volume and becomes pale-colored. Fold in the chocolate mixture and then the walnuts.

Pour the batter into the prepared pan. Put the springform or cake pan in a roasting pan and add enough hot water to come halfway up the side of the cake pan (be sure the water does not come to the top of the foil if using a springform pan). Bake for 30 to 35 minutes, or until a toothpick inserted in the center of the cake comes out clean.

Allow the cake to cool completely on a rack. Release the sides of the springform pan and set the cake on a plate, or invert the cake pan onto a plate and unmold the cake. Dust with confectioners' sugar before serving.

ANGEL FOOD CAKE

SERVES 8 TO 10

2 cups egg whites (about 14 large egg whites)

1 cup cake flour

2 cups superfine granulated sugar

1½ teaspoons cream of tartar

2 teaspoons vanilla extract

1 teaspoon fresh lemon juice

ALTHOUGH ANGEL FOOD CAKE probably derives from an English recipe, we think of it as purely American, a classic like strawberry shortcake. Serve the cake on its own or with ice cream, fresh fruit, or a fresh fruit puree.

Preheat the oven to 350°F.

Warm the egg whites to room temperature.

Sift together the flour and half the sugar.

In a large, grease-free bowl, using an electric mixer set at high speed, beat the egg whites until soft peaks form. Whisk in the cream of tartar, vanilla, and lemon juice. Add the remaining sugar a little at a time, and beat until the egg whites form stiff peaks. Using a rubber spatula, fold the dry ingredients into the egg whites a little at a time, being careful not to overmix.

Pour the batter into an ungreased 10-inch angel food cake pan with a removable bottom or a loaf pan. Bake for 40 minutes, until lightly browned on top and the cake pulls away from the sides of the pan.

Invert the cake pan onto a wire rack and let the cake cool completely in the pan, for about 1 hour.

Run a knife around the edge of the cake and remove from the pan. Serve with fresh fruit or ice cream, or lightly toast under the broiler.

KEY LIME CHIFFON ANGEL FOOD CAKE
TROPICAL FRUIT SAUCE

██

SERVES 10 TO 12

1 package unflavored gelatin (about 2¾ teaspoons)

3 tablespoons tepid water

Grated zest of 4 Key limes

²/₃ cup fresh Key lime juice

1 cup granulated sugar

4 large eggs, separated

¹/₂ teaspoon cream of tartar

1 teaspoon vanilla extract

1 cup heavy cream

5 cups small cubes Angel Food Cake (page 263), lightly packed

Confectioners' sugar

Tropical Fruit Sauce (recipe follows)

I ASSOCIATE ANGEL FOOD CAKE with Southern cooking and imagine people sitting on their porches eating it at teatime. My thoughts then just naturally turn to charlottes and chiffon pies, so I came up with the idea of combining the three. This cake is soft and tender; the chiffon adds a refreshing crispness of real southern Key limes.

Combine the gelatin and water in a small bowl and let the gelatin soften for 2 to 3 minutes.

Set the bowl of softened gelatin over a saucepan of warm water until the gelatin dissolves completely. Set aside in a warm place.

Combine the lime zest, lime juice, and half the sugar in the top of a double boiler or a large heatproof bowl. Set over hot water. Stir until the sugar dissolves completely.

Place the egg yolks in a small bowl. Whisk in about one third of the hot lime juice mixture to temper, then stir the yolks into the remaining lime juice.

Over hot water, cook over medium-high heat, stirring constantly for 4 to 5 minutes, until the mixture thickens and coats the back of a spoon. Immediately remove the curd from the heat and stir in the dissolved gelatin.

Set the curd over a bowl of ice water and stir for a few minutes, until cooled to room temperature. Remove from the ice water and set aside.

Beat the egg whites with the cream of tartar until soft peaks form. Gradually add the remaining ¹/₂ cup sugar and the vanilla, and beat until firm peaks form. Gently but thoroughly fold the egg whites into the lime curd.

In a medium bowl, beat the heavy cream until soft peaks form. Fold the cream into the lime mixture.

Put the cake cubes in a large bowl. Add the Key lime chiffon and fold gently together until the cubes are evenly distributed. Scrape the mixture into a 10-inch by 3-inch springform pan, cover, and refrigerate for at least 4 hours, or until set.

To unmold, dip the pan briefly in warm water and run a thin-blade knife around the edges. Release the sides of the pan and remove. With a clean, hot knife, cut the cake into 10 or 12 wedges.

Serve on a plate dusted with confectioners' sugar and spoon a little sauce around.

———

TROPICAL FRUIT SAUCE

MAKES ABOUT 1 CUP

1 cup fresh mango pulp

1 cup fresh papaya pulp

¼ cup superfine granulated sugar

2 tablespoons fresh Key lime juice

Place all the ingredients in a food processor and puree until smooth. Strain into a bowl and set aside or refrigerate until ready to serve.

PUMPKIN CHEESECAKE

■■■

SERVES 8 TO 10

Crust

1½ cups fine gingersnaps crumbs (about 8
   ounces cookies)

¾ cup chopped pecans or walnuts

6 tablespoons unsalted butter, melted

Filling

1¼ pounds cream cheese, at room
   temperature

½ cup granulated sugar

½ cup lightly packed brown sugar

1 teaspoon cinnamon

¾ teaspoon ground ginger

½ teaspoon ground cloves

½ teaspoon freshly grated nutmeg

2 cups fresh or solid-pack unsweetened
   pumpkin puree

5 large eggs

½ cup heavy cream

THIS VERSION OF A DENSE, New York–style cheesecake quickly became our most popular Thanksgiving dessert.

Lightly butter a 10- by 2-inch round cake pan or springform pan. (If using a springform pan, wrap the bottom and sides with foil.) To make the crust, combine the gingersnap crumbs, nuts, and butter in a bowl and mix well. Press the mixture firmly into the bottom of the prepared pan. Refrigerate for at least 30 minutes.

Preheat the oven to 350°F.

To make the filling, put the cream cheese in a large bowl. Using an electric mixer, beat until it is smooth. Beat in both sugars and the spices, and continue to beat for 3 to 4 minutes, until light in texture. Beat in the pumpkin puree. Beat in the eggs one at at time, scraping down the sides of the bowl after each addition. Beat in the cream.

Scrape the batter into the prepared pan. Put the cake pan in a roasting pan and add enough hot water to come halfway up the sides of the cake pan. Bake in the center of the oven for 45 to 60 minutes, until the cheesecake is firm to the touch and slightly puffed.

Transfer the cheesecake to a wire rack and let cool, then cover and refrigerate for at least 4 hours.

When the cheesecake is completely chilled, if baked in a cake pan, dip the pan into a large bowl of hot water for 2 to 3 minutes to loosen the crust. Invert a large flat plate on top of the cheesecake and invert the cake onto the plate. Put a second plate on the bottom of the cheesecake and turn it right side up. If baked in a springform pan, no need to invert the cake. Release the sides of the springform pan, transfer the cake to a serving plate, and serve. Cut into slices with a knife dipped into hot water and wiped dry.

The cheesecake can be refrigerated for 4 to 5 days or frozen, well wrapped, for up to 2 weeks.

OLD-FASHIONED
STRAWBERRY SHORTCAKE

■■■■■■■■■■■■■■■■■■■■■■■■■■■■■■■■■

SERVES 6

Shortcake

2 cups all-purpose flour

1/4 cup plus 1 tablespoon sugar

1 tablespoon plus 1/2 teaspoon
baking powder

6 tablespoons unsalted butter, chilled
and cut into small pieces

3/4 cup heavy cream

2 mashed hard-cooked large egg yolks

2 tablespoons unsalted butter, melted

Filling

3 pints strawberries, washed, hulled,
and halved (or quartered, depending
on size)

2 tablespoons sugar

1 cup heavy cream

STRAWBERRY SHORTCAKE is our "signature" dessert. What sets this shortcake apart from others is that the biscuit contains mashed hard-cooked eggs, an idea suggested by James Beard. The eggs add incredible moistness to the biscuits so they never are dry or cakey, but you don't taste them at all.

When strawberries are not in season, we use other berries such as blackberries and huckleberries or ripe, seasonal fruit such as apricots or peaches. But when strawberries are juicy and ripe, there is no comparison.

Preheat the oven to 375°F. Lightly butter a baking sheet.

Sift the flour, 1/4 cup of the sugar, and the baking powder into a bowl. Add the butter pieces. Using your fingertips, work the butter quickly and lightly into the flour until the mixture is the consistency of very fine crumbs or sand. Add the cream and egg yolks and stir with a fork until the dough just holds together.

Turn the dough out onto a floured work surface and knead briefly, just until it forms a smooth dough. Do not overwork. Pat or roll out the dough to a thickness of 3/4 inch. Using a floured 2 1/2- or 3-inch cookie cutter, cut out 4 rounds of dough. Gather up the dough scraps, reroll, and cut out 2 more rounds.

Put the rounds on the prepared baking sheet. Brush with the melted butter and sprinkle with the remaining 1 tablespoon sugar. Bake on the middle rack of the oven for 12 to 15 minutes, until the biscuits are golden brown and firm to the touch.

Meanwhile, put the strawberries in a bowl and toss them with the sugar.

In a medium bowl, whip the cream until soft peaks form. Cover and refrigerate.

Transfer the biscuits to a rack and let cool for 2 to 3 minutes.

Carefully split the biscuits in half and set the tops aside. Place the bottoms on dessert plates and heap the strawberries onto them. Generously spoon whipped cream over the strawberries, and replace the biscuit tops. Serve immediately, with any remaining whipped cream on the side.

PECAN PIE

■■■■■■■■■■■■■■■■■■■■■■■■■■■■■■■■■■■■■■

SERVES 6 TO 8

5½ cups pecan halves

3 tablespoons all-purpose flour

12 tablespoons lightly salted butter, at
 room temperature

1 cup packed light brown sugar

¾ cup plus 2 tablespoons light corn syrup

4 large eggs, lightly beaten

2 teaspoons vanilla extract

1 prebaked Basic Pie Shell (page 271)

THIS PIE IS MADE with an abundance of pecans, browned butter, and nut paste—all of which make this American classic better than ever.

Preheat the oven to 350°F.

Spread ½ cup of the pecans on a baking sheet and toast them in the oven for 8 to 10 minutes, until lightly browned and fragrant. Let cool. (Do not turn the oven off.)

Put the cooled nuts in a food processor or blender and process until smooth and buttery. Scrape the nut paste into a large bowl. Add the flour and work it in with a fork until completely incorporated. Set aside.

Heat the butter in a small saucepan over medium-high heat until it starts to foam and turns a light nutty brown. Pour into a small bowl.

Add the brown sugar, corn syrup, eggs, vanilla, and browned butter to the nut paste and stir until well blended. Fold in the remaining 5 cups pecans.

Pour the filling into the prebaked pie shell. Bake for 30 to 40 minutes, until the filling is slightly puffed and the crust is golden brown. Transfer to a rack to cool. Serve warm or at room temperature.

CHILLED RHUBARB-STRAWBERRY PIE

SERVES 6 TO 8

2 pints strawberries washed, hulled, and halved or quartered, depending on size

¾ cup plus 2 tablespoons sugar

2 pounds rhubarb, trimmed, washed, and dried

3 tablespoons all-purpose flour

1 tablespoon fresh lemon juice

1 prebaked Basic Pie Shell (page 271)

1 cup heavy cream

THE PALE PINKS and ripe crimsons complement each other beautifully; their varying sweetnesses balance perfectly. No wonder rhubarb and strawberries are a springtime classic. Because this is a refrigerated pie, you can make it ahead of time. Bake the pie shell ahead, but do not make the filling until you plan to serve the pie. Pour it into the pie shell while the fruit mixture is still warm so that it will adhere to the pastry; if you pour cold filling into a cool pie shell, the filling may slip off the crust when you slice it.

In a large bowl, toss the strawberries with ¼ cup of the sugar.

If the rhubarb stalks are more than 1 inch thick, split them in half lengthwise. Using a sharp knife, cut the rhubarb into 1-inch pieces.

Put the rhubarb in a large noncorrosive saucepan, and toss with the flour and ½ cup of the sugar.

Cook, covered, over medium heat for 4 to 5 minutes, until the rhubarb is tender. Add any liquid that has accumulated from the strawberries and cook until the rhubarb is soft and falling apart, with a few chunks still remaining. Add the lemon juice and strawberries and cook for 1 minute more. Cool slightly.

Pour the warm fruit mixture into the pie shell and let cool to room temperature. Cover and refrigerate for at least 1 hour.

In a medium bowl, whip the cream with the remaining 2 tablespoons sugar until soft peaks form.

Spoon the whipped cream onto the chilled pie and serve.

PENNSYLVANIA DUTCH
CHOCOLATE NUT PIE

SERVES 6 TO 8

¾ cup sugar, plus additional for sprinkling

¼ cup water

2 large eggs

¼ cup unsweetened cocoa powder

1 tablespoon plus 2 teaspoons flour

½ cup coarsely chopped walnuts or pecans

3 ounces semisweet chocolate, grated

½ cup plus 2 tablespoons dark corn syrup

1 prebaked Basic Pie Shell (page 271)

I ATE A SIMILAR PIE ONCE when I traveled through eastern and central Pennsylvania, where many Dutch people settled and where so much good American cooking took root. This pie, which was inspired by that trip, is rather like a chocolate pecan pie, very basic and very good.

Preheat the oven to 350°F.

Combine the sugar and water in a heavy saucepan and bring to a boil. Brush down the sides of the pan with a wet pastry brush and cook, without stirring until the syrup reaches 234° to 236°F on a candy thermometer. (A little of the syrup dropped in cold water will form a soft ball.) Immediately remove from the heat.

Meanwhile, using an electric mixer, beat the eggs in a heatproof bowl until foamy.

Beating at medium speed, gradually add the hot sugar syrup to the eggs. Beat until the mixture is cool, about 10 minutes.

Sift together the flour and cocoa. Gently but thoroughly fold the mixture into the cooled egg mixture a tablespoon at a time. Fold in the nuts and chocolate, and then stir in the corn syrup.

Pour the filling into the prebaked pie shell. Bake for 30 to 40 minutes, until the filling is puffed and slightly cracked on top. Transfer the pie to a rack and sprinkle with a little sugar. Let cool slightly before serving (the pie will fall slightly).

BASIC PIE SHELL

■■

**MAKES ONE 9-INCH
PIE SHELL**

1¼ cups all-purpose flour

1 teaspoon sugar

½ teaspoon salt

¼ cup lard, chilled and cut into small
   pieces

4 tablespoons unsalted butter, chilled and
   cut into small pieces

3 to 4 tablespoons cold water

PERFECT TASTE. Perfect results. Because this dough includes lard, it is much flakier than pastry made with all butter. In days gone by, American cooks would never even have considered making pie crust with butter—it was much too expensive and precious. But lard was never in short supply. You can use this pastry for both sweet and savory dishes, omitting the sugar for savory preparations.

Sift the flour, sugar, and salt into a bowl. Using your fingertips, work in the lard and butter until the mixture resembles coarse crumbs.

Sprinkle 2 tablespoons water over the mixture and blend lightly with a fork. Add another tablespoon of water and then, if necessary, a fourth. Use only enough water so that the dough holds together when pressed between your fingertips.

Gather the dough into a ball. With the heel of your hand, flatten it into a 2-inch-thick disk. Wrap the dough in waxed paper or plastic wrap and refrigerate for at least 30 minutes, or overnight. (If the chilled dough is very firm, let it sit at room temperature for about 15 minutes before rolling out.)

Lightly dust a work surface and rolling pin with flour. Flatten the pastry dish slightly and roll it into a circle about 10 ½ inches in diameter, turning the pastry by quarter-turns as you roll. Do not overwork the dough, or it will be tough.

Fit the pastry into a 9-inch pie plate. Trim and crimp the edges. Refrigerate for at least 30 minutes before baking.

To prebake the pie shell, preheat the oven to 375°F.

Line the pastry shell with parchment paper or aluminum foil and fill with dried beans or pie weights. Bake for 10 to 15 minutes. Carefully remove the weights and paper, and bake for 10 to 15 minutes more, until golden brown. Cool the pie shell on a rack before filling.

FUDGE BROWNIES

¹⁄₂ cup cake flour

¹⁄₂ teaspoon baking powder

¹⁄₂ teaspoon salt

2 ounces unsweetened chocolate, coarsely chopped

6 tablespoons unsalted butter, at room temperature

2 cups confectioners' sugar, sifted

2 large eggs

³⁄₄ teaspoon vanilla extract

³⁄₄ teaspoon dark rum

3 ounces semisweet chocolate, grated or finely chopped (about ¹⁄₂ cup)

¹⁄₂ cup chopped walnuts or pecans

BROWNIE LOVERS have strong opinions. These are for lovers of gooey brownies. To make them as chocolaty as possible, the batter contains both melted unsweetened chocolate and grated or finely chopped semisweet chocolate, which melts as the brownies bake. These brownies seem almost under-baked—just as a brownie should be. They are good warm or at room temperature, but don't serve chilled.

Preheat the oven to 350°F. Line an 8-inch square baking pan with parchment or waxed paper. Lightly butter the paper and the sides of the pan.

Sift together the flour, baking powder, and salt.

Put the unsweetened chocolate in the top of a double boiler over hot, not simmering, water. When the chocolate is almost completely melted, remove it from the heat, stir, and set aside to cool slightly. (It will melt completely during this cooling time.)

In a large bowl, using an electric mixer on medium-high speed, cream the butter and sugar. With the mixer on medium speed, beat in the eggs one at a time. Beat in the vanilla and rum. Stir in the melted chocolate just until blended. With the mixer on low speed, add the dry ingredients, being careful not to overmix. Using a wooden spoon, stir in the semisweet chocolate and nuts.

Scrape the batter into the prepared pan. Bake for 30 to 40 minutes, until a toothpick inserted in the center comes out with a few moist crumbs clinging to it; do not overbake. Transfer the pan to a wire rack and let cool before cutting into squares.

OATMEAL COOKIES

■■■

MAKES 24 TO 30 COOKIES

2½ cups all-purpose flour

1 teaspoon baking powder

1 teaspoon baking soda

½ teaspoon cinnamon

¼ teaspoon salt

½ pound unsalted butter, at room temperature

½ cup granulated sugar

1 cup packed light brown sugar

½ teaspoon vanilla extract

2 large eggs

1 cup quick-cooking rolled oats

1 cup sweetened shredded coconut

½ cup raisins

THESE ARE CLASSIC OATMEAL COOKIES with coconut, making them both crisp and chewy.

Preheat the oven to 350°F. Butter two baking sheets.

Sift together the flour, baking powder, baking soda, cinnamon, and salt. In a large bowl, using an electric mixer, cream the butter until light and fluffy. Beat in both sugars and the vanilla. Add the eggs one at a time, beating well after each addition. Gradually beat in the dry ingredients. Using a wooden spoon, stir in the oats, coconut, and raisins.

Drop the dough by heaping tablespoonfuls about 3 inches apart onto the prepared baking sheets. Bake for 15 minutes, or until lightly browned. Transfer the cookies to wire racks to cool.

CHOCOLATE CHIP COOKIES

■■■

MAKES 24 TO 30 COOKIES

2¼ cups all-purpose flour

½ teaspoon baking powder

½ teaspoon baking soda

½ teaspoon salt

½ pound unsalted butter, at room temperature

1 cup packed light brown sugar

¼ cup granulated sugar

2 large eggs

12 ounces semisweet chocolate, coarsely chopped

¾ cup chopped walnuts

EVERYONE THINKS his or her chocolate chip cookie recipe is the very best. I'm no exception! These chunky cookies are studded with chopped semisweet chocolate, not packaged chocolate chips.

Preheat the oven to 350°F. Butter two baking sheets.

Sift together the flour, baking powder, baking soda, and salt.

In a large bowl, using an electric mixer, cream the butter until light and fluffy. Beat in both sugars. Add the eggs one at a time, beating well after each addition. Gradually beat in the dry ingredients. Using a wooden spoon, stir in the chocolate and walnuts.

Drop the batter by heaping tablespoonfuls about 3 inches apart onto the prepared baking sheets. Bake for 8 to 10 minutes, until lightly browned. Transfer the cookies to wire racks to cool.

SUGAR COOKIES

■■■■■■■■■■■■■■■■■■■■■■■■■■■■■■■■■■■■■

MAKES 24 TO 30 COOKIES

2⅓ cups all-purpose flour

1½ teaspoons baking powder

½ teaspoon salt

1 large egg

3 tablespoons milk

1 teaspoon vanilla extract

½ pound unsalted butter, at room temperature

1 cup sugar, plus additional for sprinkling

WE SERVE ALL our ice cream desserts with these cookies, which are reminiscent of the big sugar cookies from the old Schrafft's restaurants in New York City.

Sift together the flour, baking powder, and salt.

Combine the egg, milk, and vanilla extract in a small bowl and mix lightly with a fork.

In a large bowl, using an electric mixer set on medium-high speed, beat the butter until smooth and cream. Add the sugar and beat until light and fluffy. Beat in the egg mixture, in two additions, scraping down the sides of the bowl after each addition. Beat in the dry ingredients just until combined.

Divide the dough in half and shape into 2 balls. Wrap each ball in plastic wrap and refrigerate for 1 to 2 hours, until firm enough to roll.

Preheat the oven to 350°F.

On a floured work surface, roll the chilled dough out to a thickness of ⅛ inch for crisp cookies or ¼ inch for soft cookies. Cut the dough with 3-inch round cookie cutters, or cookie cutters of your choice, and carefully place the cookies about 3 inches apart on ungreased baking sheets.

Bake for 8 to 10 minutes, or until lightly browned around the edges. Transfer the cookies to wire racks, sprinkle with sugar, and let cool.

Ice Creams, Sorbets, and Sauces

WE'RE A COUNTRY that has always loved frozen desserts—and in this chapter I offer recipes that speak to every craving. For the purist, there are unbeatable versions of vanilla ice cream, chocolate ice cream, warm butterscotch sauce, and hot fudge sauce. For others, there is a creamy amber caramel sauce spiked with a shot of rum that would deify a humble bowl of vanilla ice cream. There's a robust Spiced Ginger Ice Cream, a Baked Banana and Honey Ice Cream. And for all of us who will always be ten years old at heart, I offer homemade Peanut Butter Ice Cream Sandwiches that are good enough to rival any banana split or root beer float.

PINEAPPLE-LIME SORBET

■■■■■■■■■■■■■■■■■■■■■■■■■■■■■■■■■■■■

**MAKES ABOUT
1 QUART**

1 pineapple

¾ cup plus 1 tablespoon sugar

⅓ cup water

¾ cup fresh lime juice (7 to 8 limes)

Cut the top and bottom off the pineapple. Cut it into quarters and peel with a sharp knife. Remove and discard the tough core. Roughly chop three of the pineapple quarters and puree in a food processor blender. Finely chop the remaining quarter, cover, and refrigerate.

Measure 2¼ cups of pineapple puree. Combine it with ¼ cup plus 3 tablespoons of the sugar in a noncorrosive saucepan. Heat over low heat, stirring, until the sugar dissolves. Transfer the puree to a metal bowl, cover, and refrigerate until cold.

Combine the remaining ¼ cup plus 2 tablespoons sugar with the water in a small saucepan and bring to a boil over medium heat, stirring until the sugar dissolves. Let the syrup cool.

Stir the sugar syrup into the pineapple puree. Stir in the finely chopped pineapple and lime juice. Refrigerate until thoroughly chilled.

Pour into the chilled canister of an ice cream maker and freeze according to the manufacturer's instructions.

STRAWBERRY-LIME SORBET

■■■■■■■■■■■■■■■■■■■■■■■■■■■■■■■■■■■■

**MAKES ABOUT
1 QUART**

½ cup plus 2 tablespoons sugar

½ cup plus 2 tablespoons water

1 pint strawberries, washed, hulled, and quartered

½ cup fresh lime juice (5 to 6 limes)

Combine the sugar and water in a small saucepan and bring to a boil over medium heat, stirring until the sugar dissolves. Let the syrup cool.

Puree the strawberries in a food processor or blender. Pour the puree into a large bowl and stir in the lime juice and the sugar syrup. Cover and refrigerate until cold.

Pour into the chilled canister of an ice cream maker and freeze according to the manufacturer's instructions.

VANILLA ICE CREAM

**MAKES ABOUT
1 QUART**

2 cups heavy cream

²/₃ cup milk

1 vanilla bean, split lengthwise

6 large egg yolks

½ cup sugar

Combine the cream and milk in a large saucepan. Scrape the seeds from the vanilla bean into the cream mixture (discard the bean). Bring to a boil over medium-high heat. Remove from the heat, cover, and let steep for 15 to 20 minutes.

In a medium bowl, whisk the egg yolks with the sugar until light in color. Gradually whisk about a third of the cream mixture into the eggs, then add the egg mixture to the saucepan. Cook over medium-low heat, stirring constantly with a wooden spoon, for about 5 minutes, until the custard thickens enough to coat the back of the spoon (it should register 180°F on a candy thermometer); do not allow to boil.

Strain the custard through a fine-meshed strainer into a metal bowl, cover, and refrigerate, stirring occasionally, until cold.

Pour into the chilled canister of an ice cream maker and freeze according to the manufacturer's instructions.

CHOCOLATE ICE CREAM

**MAKES ABOUT
1 QUART**

5 ounces semisweet chocolate, coarsely chopped

1 ounce unsweetened chocolate, coarsely chopped

2 cups heavy cream

²/₃ cup milk

6 large egg yolks

½ cup sugar

1 teaspoon vanilla extract

Put both chocolates and ½ cup of the cream in the top of a double boiler and heat over barely simmering water until the chocolate is almost completely melted. Remove from the heat, stir with a rubber spatula until smooth, and set aside.

Combine the remaining 1½ cups of cream and the milk in a large saucepan and bring just to a boil. Remove from the heat.

In a medium bowl, whisk the eggs with the sugar until they start to lighten in color. Gradually whisk in one third of the hot cream to temper the eggs. Then add the egg mixture to the pan. Cook over medium-low heat, stirring constantly with a wooden spoon, for about 5 minutes, until the custard thickens enough to coat the back of the spoon (it will register 180°F on a candy thermometer); do not allow to boil. Strain the custard through a fine-meshed strainer into the melted chocolate, add the vanilla, and whisk to blend.

Pour the chocolate custard into a metal bowl, cover, and refrigerate, stirring occasionally, until cold.

Pour into the chilled canister of an ice cream maker and freeze according to the manufacturer's instructions.

continued

Mint Chocolate Ice Cream

Add 1½ cups coarsely chopped fresh mint (leaves and stems) to the chocolate custard before it cools and let steep for 15 minutes. Then strain through a fine-meshed strainer and chill.

Chocolate Chocolate Chip Ice Cream

Melt 3 ounces coarsely chopped semisweet chocolate in the top of a double boiler set over barely simmering water. Spread the melted chocolate as thin as possible on a parchment- or waxed paper–lined baking sheet. Refrigerate until the chocolate hardens.

Break the chocolate into rough chips and stir into the chilled chocolate custard before freezing. (Homemade chocolate chips are better in ice cream because they can be made thinner than the store-bought kind. Chunky chocolate chips tend to taste waxy when frozen.)

Toasted Almond, Walnut, or Pecan Ice Cream

Add ⅓ cup lightly toasted nuts to the chilled custard before freezing.

COCONUT ICE CREAM

MAKES ABOUT 1 QUART

6 ounces sweetened shredded coconut

1¼ cups heavy cream

½ cups milk

6 large egg yolks

½ cup sugar

Preheat the oven to 325°F.

Spread the coconut on a baking sheet and toast in the oven, stirring from time to time, for 8 to 10 minutes, until lightly browned.

Meanwhile, combine the cream and milk in a large saucepan and bring to a simmer. Remove from the heat.

Add the toasted coconut to the cream mixture, cover, and let steep for 20 to 25 minutes.

Strain the coconut milk through a fine-meshed strainer into another saucepan, pressing out as much liquid as possible from the coconut. Discard the coconut. Bring the coconut milk to a simmer, and remove from the heat.

In a medium bowl, beat the egg yolks with the sugar until they start to lighten in color. Gradually whisk in about one third of the hot coconut milk to temper the eggs, then add the egg mixture to the pan. Cook over medium-low heat, stirring constantly with a wooden spoon, for about 5 minutes, until the custard thickens enough to coat the back of the spoon (180°F on a candy thermometer); do not allow to boil.

Strain the custard into a metal bowl, cover, and refrigerate until cold.

Pour into the chilled canister of an ice cream maker and freeze according to the manufacturer's instructions.

BAKED BANANA AND HONEY ICE CREAM

**MAKES ABOUT
1 QUART**

3 bananas

½ cup sour cream

¼ cup dark rum

3 tablespoons honey

1½ cups heavy cream

⅔ cup milk

1 vanilla bean, split lengthwise

6 large egg yolks

½ cup sugar

Preheat the oven to 350°F.

Put the unpeeled bananas on a baking sheet and bake for 10 to 12 minutes, until the skins turn black and split. Let cool.

When the bananas are cool enough to handle, peel them and put them in a blender or food processor. Add the sour cream, rum, and honey, and process until smooth. Set aside.

Combine the cream and milk in a large saucepan. Scrape the seeds from the vanilla bean into the cream mixture (discard the bean) and bring to a boil over medium-high heat. Remove from the heat, cover, and let steep for 15 to 20 minutes.

In a medium bowl, whisk the egg yolks with the sugar until light in color. Gradually whisk in about one third of the cream into the eggs, then add the egg mixture to the saucepan. Cook over medium-low heat, stirring constantly with a wooden spoon, for about 5 minutes, until the custard thickens enough to coat the back of the spoon (it will register 180°F on a candy thermometer); do not allow the custard to boil.

Strain the custard through a fine-meshed strainer into a metal bowl. Stir in the banana mixture, cover, and refrigerate until cold.

Pour into the chilled canister of an ice cream maker and freeze according to the manufacturer's instructions.

SPICED GINGER ICE CREAM

**MAKES ABOUT
1 QUART**

2 cups heavy cream

1 cup milk

1 cinnamon stick

6 large egg yolks

⅓ cup lightly packed brown sugar

¼ cup molasses

½ teaspoon ground ginger

Put the cream, milk, and cinnamon stick in a large saucepan and bring just to a boil over high heat. Remove from the heat, cover, and let steep for 15 to 20 minutes.

In a medium bowl, whisk the egg yolks with the sugar, molasses, and ginger. Gradually whisk about one third of the cream into the egg mixture, then add the egg mixture to the pan. Cook over medium-low heat, stirring constantly with a wooden spoon, for about 5 minutes, until the custard thickens enough to coat the back of the spoon (it will register 180°F on a candy thermometer); do not let the custard boil.

Strain the custard through a fine-meshed strainer into a metal bowl, cover, and refrigerate, stirring occasionally, until cold.

Pour into the chilled canister of an ice cream maker and freeze according to the manufacturer's instructions.

STRAWBERRY ICE CREAM

**MAKES ABOUT
1 QUART**

1 pint strawberries, cut into small pieces

¾ to 1 cup sugar

2 cups heavy cream

⅔ cup milk

1 vanilla bean, split lengthwise

6 large egg yolks

Combine the strawberries and ¼ cup sugar in a bowl; if the strawberries are not very sweet, increase the sugar to ½ cup. Let the berries sit for at least 1 hour, until they have produced plenty of juice.

Combine the cream and milk in a large saucepan. Scrape the seeds from the vanilla bean into the cream mixture and bring to a boil over medium-high heat (discard the bean). Remove from the heat, cover, and let steep for 15 to 20 minutes.

In a medium bowl, whisk the egg yolks with ½ cup sugar until light in color. Gradually whisk about one third of the cream into the eggs, then add the egg mixture to the saucepan. Cook over medium-low heat, stirring constantly with a wooden spoon, for about 5 minutes, until the custard thickens enough to coat the back of the spoon (it will register 180°F on a candy thermometer); do not allow the custard to boil.

Strain the custard through a fine-meshed strainer into a metal bowl, cover, and refrigerate, stirring occasionally, until cold.

Stir the berries and juice into the custard and chill until very cold.

Pour into the chilled canister of an ice cream maker and freeze according to the manufacturer's instructions.

PEANUT BUTTER ICE CREAM SANDWICHES

COOKIE CHIPS

MAKES 4
(ABOUT 1½ PINTS ICE CREAM)

Ice Cream

1½ cups heavy cream

1 cup milk

4 large egg yolks

½ cup sugar

½ cup chunky peanut butter

1 teaspoon vanilla extract

Cookies

2½ ounces semisweet chocolate, coarsely chopped

1½ ounces unsweetened chocolate, coarsely chopped

3 tablespoons unsalted butter

1 large egg

⅓ cup sugar

¾ teaspoon vanilla extract

1 tablespoon plus 2 teaspoons flour

⅛ teaspoon baking powder

⅛ teaspoon salt

Cookie Chips (recipe follows)

To make the ice cream, combine 1¼ cups of the heavy cream and the milk in a large saucepan and bring just barely to a simmer. Remove from the heat.

In a medium bowl, whisk the egg yolks with the sugar until light in color. Gradually whisk in about one third of the cream mixture to temper the eggs, then add the egg mixture to the saucepan. Cook over medium-high heat, stirring constantly with a wooden spoon, for about 5 minutes, until the custard thickens enough to coat the back of the spoon (it will register 180°F on a candy thermometer); do not allow the custard to boil.

Strain the custard into a metal bowl and stir in the peanut butter. Cover and refrigerate, stirring occasionally, until cold.

Stir the remaining ¼ cup cream and the vanilla into the custard. Pour into the chilled canister of an ice cream maker and freeze according to the manufacturer's instructions. Transfer to a freezer container and freeze until ready to assemble the sandwiches.

Preheat the oven to 350°F. Lightly butter two large baking sheets.

To make the cookies, combine both chocolates and the butter in the top of a double boiler and stir over hot, not simmering, water until melted. Remove from the heat.

Combine the egg, sugar, and vanilla in a large bowl and beat with an electric mixer set on medium until thickened and pale yellow. Beat in the warm melted chocolate. Combine the dry ingredients and then beat into the batter.

Drop heaping tablespoonfuls of the cookie batter onto the prepared baking sheets, leaving 6 inches between each. (You will need a total of 8 cookies.) Using a small spatula, spread the batter into even 4-inch rounds.

Bake for 5 minutes, rotate the baking sheets, and bake for about 6 minutes longer. The cookies will puff up as they bake and then sink; when they sink, they are done. Let cool on the baking sheets on wire racks. Store the cooled cookies in an airtight container until ready to assemble the sandwiches.

To assemble, put 4 of the cookies upside down on serving plates. Scoop the ice cream onto the cookies. Top with the remaining cookies and gently press together. Serve with the cookie chips.

continued

COOKIE CHIPS

MAKES 12 TO 16 "CHIPS"

4 tablespoons unsalted butter, at room temperature

⅓ cup sugar

1 large egg white

½ teaspoon vanilla extract

⅓ cup plus 1½ tablespoons flour

Preheat the oven to 350°F. Lightly butter a baking sheet and dust with flour.

In a medium bowl, beat the butter and sugar with an electric mixer set on medium until creamy and light in color. Beat in the egg white and the vanilla. Beat in the flour.

Drop the batter by teaspoonfuls onto the prepared baking sheet about 2 inches apart. Flatten with a spoon into ovals.

Bake for 5 to 6 minutes, until golden brown. While they are still warm, lift the chips one at a time off the baking sheet and drape over a small rolling pin to curve them. Let cool slightly.

Gently lift the cookies from the rolling pin and transfer to a wire rack to cool completely. When the chips are cool, store them in an airtight container.

HOT FUDGE SAUCE

MAKES ABOUT 1½ CUPS

¾ cup cocoa powder

¼ cup hot water

½ cup heavy cream

½ cup granulated sugar

½ cup packed brown sugar

5 tablespoons unsalted butter, at room temperature

1½ teaspoons vanilla extract

Pinch of salt

Put the cocoa in a small bowl and whisk in the hot water until smooth.

Combine the cream and both sugars in a large saucepan and heat over medium heat, stirring occasionally, until the sugar has dissolved. Add the cocoa mixture and bring to a boil. Remove from the heat and whisk in the softened butter, vanilla, and salt until smooth.

Serve the sauce warm over ice cream. It will thicken slightly as it cools. The sauce may be kept for 1 to 2 weeks in a covered container in the refrigerator. Reheat in a double boiler over hot water.

BUTTERSCOTCH SAUCE

MAKES ABOUT 1½ CUPS

1 cup packed brown sugar

⅓ cup corn syrup

3 tablespoons water

⅓ cup heavy cream

3 tablespoons unsalted butter, at room temperature

½ teaspoon vanilla extract

Pinch of salt

Combine the brown sugar, corn syrup, and water in a heavy medium saucepan and bring to a boil over medium heat, stirring until the sugar has dissolved. Brush down the sides of the pan with a wet pastry brush. Increase the heat and boil, without stirring, until the syrup registers 234°F on a candy thermometer (a little bit of the syrup dropped into a cup of cold water and then rolled between your thumb and forefinger will form a soft ball).

Remove from the heat and stir with a wooden spoon for 1 minute, to cool slightly. Stir in the cream, butter, vanilla, and salt and beat until smooth.

Serve the sauce warm over ice cream. It will keep for 1 to 2 weeks in a covered container in the refrigerator. Reheat in a double boiler over hot water.

CARAMEL SAUCE

MAKES ABOUT 1 CUP

¾ cup sugar

¼ cup water

¼ cup plus 2 tablespoons heavy cream, warmed

2 tablespoons unsalted butter, at room temperature

1 to 2 tablespoons dark rum, Calvados, or applejack (optional)

Put the sugar in a heavy medium saucepan and shake the pan so that it covers the bottom evenly. Carefully pour the water around the edges of the sugar to moisten it. Let the sugar and water sit for a few moments so that the moisture spreads.

Cook over low heat until the sugar dissolves; do not let the syrup come to a boil until all the sugar has dissolved. Brush down the sides of the pan with a wet pastry brush. Raise the heat, bring to a boil, and cook, swirling the pan occasionally, until the caramel turns an amber color. Remove the pan from the heat.

Carefully add the warm cream to the caramel; the caramel will froth and steam. Return the pan to low heat and heat, stirring gently to dissolve any solidified caramel, until the sauce is smooth. Remove from the heat and stir in the butter and rum.

Serve the sauce warm over ice cream. It can be stored for 1 to 2 weeks in a covered container in the refrigerator. Reheat in a double boiler over hot water.

Mail-Order Sources

American Spoon Foods (catalog available)
1688 Clarion Avenue
Petroskey, Michigan 49770
1-800-222-5886

Wild hickory nuts; dried cranberries, blueberries, and cherries; honey; fruit catsup; wild rice, dried wild mushrooms; barbecue sauce; much more.

Burger's Ozark Country Hams (catalog available)
Highway 87 South
California, Missouri 65018
1-800-624-5426

Country hams; bacon; sausages; much more.

Crowley Cheese and Gift Shop
Healdsville Road
Healdsville, Vermont 05758
1-802-259-2210

Vermont cheese.

D'Artagnan (catalog available)
399 St. Paul Avenue
Jersey City, New Jersey 07306
1-800-327-8246

Buffalo; fresh game birds; game, free-range chickens; spring chickens; foie gras; sausages; much more.

MMA/Earthly Delights (catalog available)
4180 Keller Road, Suite B
Holt, Michigan 48842
1-800-367-4706

Wild mushrooms; domestic exotic mushrooms; American chestnuts; truffles, baby white asparagus; dried beans and rices; much more.

San Francisco (catalog available)
250 Fourteenth Street
San Francisco, California 94103
1-800-227-4330

Herbs and spices.

Index

dressing:
Appalachian, 174
bacon–sour cream, 69
blue cheese, 150
ginger, 183
mustard, 66
see also salad dressing
dried sour cherry scones, 240
duck:
adobo-style, with salad, 164–165
cakes with toasted pumpkin seeds, roast, 160
chile pilaf, 172
crisp breast of, Julie Anne, 168–169
crisp roast, with wildflower honey glaze, 170–171
grilled breast of, glazed with molasses and black pepper, 166–167
grilled breast of, with cracklin' sauce, 163
sausage, grilled, pasta with wild mushrooms and, 162
sausage, homemade, 158
sausage with lentil salad and cottage-fried sweet potatoes, 161
soup with wild rice, hearty, 31
duff, old-fashioned apple and quince, 247

Escarole chicken soup, Grandma's, 27
étouffée-style shrimp, 90–91
Evan Jones's American Food, 18

Field salad, American, 41
fish:
boil, Wisconsin-style, 131
chowder, smoked, 19
stew, Albemarle Sound pine bark, 18
stock, 34
see also specific fish
fish cakes:
deviled crab, 65–66
New England cod, 58
foamy sauce, 257
foie gras, nutted, 53
forest mushrooms, *see* mushrooms, forest
"franks," barbecued, in a soft pretzel, 194
fresh corn spoonbread, 239
fried:
catfish, Southern-, 97–98
green tomatoes, 149
Ipswich clams, 62
oysters, 69
fritters:
deviled crab and oyster, 64
lobster and rice, 67
Rhode Island clam, 60

fruits, maple-stewed summer, 260
fudge brownies, 272

General Robert E. Lee's favorite soup, 17
ginger:
crisp, sesame rockfish with soy and, 110
dressing, 183
ice cream, spiced, 280
and oyster bisque, 24
scalloped, sunchokes, 182
spiced ice cream, 280
goat cheese, baked, in country ham with ramps and morels, 205
goose, roast, with plum glaze, 173–174
grain mustard sauce, 111
Grandma's chicken escarole soup, 27
Granny's:
chocolate cake, 261–262
Irish soda bread, 242
greens salad, wilted winter, 42
grilled:
bass with radishes and orange, 95
breast of chicken with sticky rice cakes, 137–138
breast of duck with cracklin' sauce, 163
cèpes, asparagus, and sweet peas, salad of, 45
chicken with summer vegetable compote, 139
duck breast glazed with molasses and black pepper, 166–167
halibut with shrimp and forest mushroom compote, 102
halibut with stewed fresh tomatoes, 101
lamb chops, new potatoes, and asparagus, 218
lobster with herb salad, 82–83
loin of lamb with creamed hash browns, 219
mahimahi with lime and avocado, 104
mahimahi with pineapple-chile barbecue sauce, 103
marinated quail with chestnuts and wild huckleberries, 184–185
quail with grilled forest mushrooms, 183
salmon with pumpkin seed vinaigrette and braised kale, 114–115
sea scallops with orange, red onion, and cilantro, 84
soft-shell crabs with sweet potatoes, 76
spring lamb with rhubarb and dandelion, 221–222
sturgeon and oysters in barbecue, 120–121
swordfish, 122–123
T-bone steak, 192–193

veal chops, 214
veal chops with grilled beefsteak tomatoes and red onions, 213
grits cakes, 87
grouper, spicy honey-glazed, with figs, 100

Halibut, grilled:
with shrimp and forest mushroom compote, 102
with stewed fresh tomatoes, 101
ham:
baked country, with red-eye gravy, 206–207
baked goat cheese in country, with ramps and morels, 205
cheese, and scallion biscuits, country, 237
country, and sweet potato salad with honey vinaigrette, 52
Smithfield, sautéed soft-shell crabs with spinach and, 75
hash browns:
creamed, grilled loin of lamb with, 219
parsnip, 197
spicy sweet potato, 167
heartland chowder, 29
hearty:
duck soup with wild rice, 31
white bean soup, 11
herb salad, grilled lobster with, 82–83
hickory nut vinaigrette, wild, 43
hollandaise, chile, 127
homemade duck sausage, 158–159
honey:
-glazed grouper with figs, spicy, 100
ice cream, baked banana and, 279
vinaigrette, 52
hot fudge sauce, 282
Hudson Valley Camembert crisp, 50

Ice cream:
baked banana and honey, 279
chocolate, 277–278
chocolate chocolate chip, 278
coconut, 278–279
mint chocolate, 278
sandwiches, peanut butter, 281–282
spiced ginger, 280
strawberry, 280
toasted almond, walnut, or pecan, 278
vanilla, 277
Ipswich clams, fried, 62
Irish soda bread, Granny's, 242

Joy of Cooking, The, 128

tropical fruit:
  ambrosia, 259
  sauce, 265
tropical relish, 107
trout, lake, panfried, 126–127
trout with pumpkin seed brown butter,
    seared, 124–125
tuna:
  charred, 129
  wrapped in bacon with clams casino
    sauce, 128
turkey:
  pemmican, leftover-, 157–158
  roast, and pan gravy, 156–157
  roast, with maple corn sauce,
    154–155

Vanilla ice cream, 277
veal:
  chops, grilled, 214
  chops, grilled, with grilled beefsteak
    tomatoes and red onions, 213
  steak with roasted corn and black pepper
    sauce, 216–217
vegetables:
  chicken noodle soup with, 28

compote, grilled chicken with summer,
    139
roasted root, sautéed beef fillets heaped
    with, 204
sauté of spring, double loin lamb chops
    with, 220
soup, cream of any, 12
soup, puree of any, 12
venison:
  and barley soup, 33
  pan-roasted, with dried cranberry sauce,
    188–189
  pan-roasted, with wild mushrooms
    and Brussels sprouts, 187
vinaigrette:
  berry, 41
  fresh cranberry, 100
  honey, 52
  lemon, 83
  mint and black pepper, 218
  olive oil, 51
  red pepper, 123
  sage-mint, 46
  spicy charred tomato, 129
  warm sherry, 42
  wild hickory nut, 43
Virginia-style sherry sauce, 109

Waldorf salad, 39
warm:
  baby green asparagus salad, 44
  sherry vinaigrette, 42
watercress, sautéed shrimp with, 86–87
white beans, lobster with braised
    chanterelles and, 80
whitefish:
  in tortillas, Southwest-style,
    130–131
  Wisconsin-style fish boil, 131
wild:
  hickory nut vinaigrette, 43
  mushrooms, see mushrooms, forest
wild rice:
  bread, 230
  harvest cakes, 185
  hearty duck soup with, 31
  roast pheasant with glazed pearl onions
    and, 179–180
  vegetable salad with marinated
    mushrooms, 47
winter greens salad, wilted, 42
Wisconsin-style fish boil, 131

Yeast-raised corn bread, 231